MY HORSES, MY TEACHERS

Also by Alois Podhajsky

THE COMPLETE TRAINING OF HORSE AND RIDER
MY DANCING WHITE HORSES
THE WHITE STALLIONS OF VIENNA

MY HORSES,
MY TEACHERS

by Alois Podhajsky

translated by Eva Podhajsky

Trafalgar Square Publishing

First paperback edition published in
the United States of America in 1997 by
Trafalgar Square Publishing, North Pomfret, Vermont 05053

Hardcover edition published in the United States
of America in 1968 by Doubleday & Company, Inc.

Published originally under the title *Meine Lehrmeister
Die Pferde* by Nymphenburger Verlagshandlung, München

Photographs by

Robert A.E. Bauer (1), *Daily Graphic* (1), Foto Grauer (2), Albert
Hilscher (1), *Irish Times* (1), Bruno Kerschner (2), A. Menzendorf
(4), Werner Menzendorf (1), John Nestle (2), Alois Podhajsky
(23), Lothar Rübelt (2), Schmidt Luchs (1), Franz Votava (1)

Library of Congress Cataloging-in-Publication Data

Podhajsky, Alois.
   [Meine Lehrmeister die Pferde. English]
   My horses, my teachers / by Alois Podhajsky ; translated by Eva Podha
     p.   cm.
   Originally published: Garden City, N.Y. : Doubleday, 1968.
   ISBN 1-57076-091-8 (pbk.)
   1. Spanische Reitschule (Vienna, Austria) 2. Podhajsky, Alois.
   3. Horsemen and horsewomen--Austria--Correspondence.   I. Title.
   SF309.5 .S63P6413   1997
   798.2'3--dc21   96-50410
                                             CIP

ISBN: 1-57076-091-8

Cover design by Sally Sherman

Printed in the United States of America

10 9 8 7 6 5 4 3 2 1

Contents

Preface

Following the suggestion of many friends and horsemen I have decided to compile riding instructions of a very special kind, easy to understand and, with good will, easy to practise. They are not meant to be academic or strictly systematic, for those who would teach them if they could talk are not much impressed by such approaches. In short, I would like to speak for my horses. Out of my lifelong experience I want to tell what they taught me and introduce them to you as my most loyal riding instructors.

With great pleasure I have noticed on numerous occasions that instead of blunting the feelings of man for the beauty of nature and her creatures, the enormous technical progress in our life has made our appreciation even keener. Nothing underlined this fact better than what took place at the performances that the Spanish Riding School gave in New York. In this gigantic city where everything including the daily rush seems larger than life, people sat quietly as they admired the movements of the dancing white horses and tried to understand what they were seeing. An old habitué of Madison Square Garden told me: "I come every year but for the first time I have seen happy horses at the horse show—your horses."

In spite of today's materialism, the love for animals has also steadily increased. It is especially evident in the big cities and is proved by the spreading interest in the sport of riding. This development makes it easier for me to try to bring horse and man nearer to each other, to further insight into the mentality of the horse, and above all to promote the attitude of ease and unprejudice that we should adopt with animals.

Consequently this book does not relate the story of my life, which has already been told in my autobiography, *My Dancing White Horses,* nor is it meant to be a book of riding instructions. These have been set forth in *The Complete Training of Horse and Rider.* The present book will deal with the relationship between horse and rider as seen through a biography of my horses. These observations, made from an unusual angle, and the advice resulting from personal experience may be of help to the reader who wants to make his horse not only his mount but also his friend.

MY HORSES, MY TEACHERS

Man and the Horse

In the life of each of us, teachers play an important role. How important a role it is I am, I believe, quite well qualified to judge, for as the son of an army officer I spent my childhood in the Austro-Hungarian monarchy, which encompassed a vast territory and many different nationalities speaking many different languages. Whenever my father was transferred to another post I was confronted not only with new teachers but also with teachers who taught in a different language. There are good teachers who set examples which we may strive to emulate all our lives, and there are the bad ones of whom we do not like to be reminded. But we may learn from both. From the bad ones we learn how not to proceed if we want to gain the confidence of our pupils, and from the good teachers we learn that with dedication and kindness we may pass on our knowledge and experience to be preserved for future generations.

I do not want to talk about those schoolmasters in the eastern provinces of the empire who taught me incorrect German for which I was rebuked by professors and ridiculed by classmates when I later came to the high school in Vienna, the first German-speaking post to which my father was assigned. It is of the four-legged teachers that I want to speak, those who my interest in and devotion to the sport of riding made me learn to appreciate, to understand, and to respect from my earliest childhood.

This should not mean that all horses belong in the group of good teachers. Not at all. For instance, I remember the horses of the Furioso-line half-breds which were raised in the first republic of Austria after the First World War. At the beginning of the lesson they were full of temper and high spirits, snatching every little opportunity to try to rid themselves of their riders so that all one could do was hang on and hope not to be thrown. After the first fifteen minutes the horses calmed down, but they had spent themselves completely and went through their paces with tired and dull movements. The utmost you could learn from them was how best to avoid being thrown, which is really not sufficient to bestow on them the title of instructor.

I have often met two-legged instructors, too, who did not rank among the good ones because they asked of their pupils more than they were able to perform themselves. A good instructor should first of all set an example through his own knowledge and ability; then the pupil will follow his orders willingly. Only the teacher who has himself mastered what he is teaching will know better and never ask more of his pupil than he is able to do. It is human nature for the student to try to seek an excuse or an explanation for his lack of knowledge. If, on the other hand, the teacher is not able to demonstrate what he demands, all his corrections and reprimands will not impress the pupil, who will only think: "You cannot do it yourself!" One of the worst cases is a teacher who is himself inclined to treat his horse roughly but who rebukes or, worse, shouts at his pupil for the same offence. Would the latter not think of the proverb about preaching water and drinking wine and have no respect for his teacher?

In discussions about the intelligence of our domestic animals, horse and dog especially, opposing views are expressed as to which animal is more closely related to man. It is often maintained that the dog is superior to the horse in intelligence and understanding. In my opinion this comparison is not just, because the dog shares our lives to a much greater extent than the horse. He is always with us and we spend much more time with him and give him much more attention without, however, constantly making demands on him. The horse cannot take part in our daily life in this way. We bring him out of the stables for a few brief hours in order to go through a determined programme of work and then put him back into his solitary box for the rest of the day. If, however, the rider tries to see in his horse more than some sort of equipment for sport, if he tries to understand his nature and study his character, then the animal will reward his master with willing cooperation and an absolute devotion. Like the dog or the child to whom we devote much of our time, the horse in close association with man will develop his mental abilities and grow—if this expression may be permitted for an animal—in personality.

This conviction is founded on years of experience I have had with both animals as my companions: with the horses who have been partners in my career as a rider and with the dogs—those irresistible and cunning dachshunds—who have been my loyal friends in good and bad days and have made me sad only when they have left me forever.

But how do we learn to understand our companions? When riding and training my horses I was forever trying to put myself in the place of the animal and to think from his point of view, especially in order not to demand more than he could perform. Retrospectively I realise that the constant endeavour to understand the creatures entrusted to my care became the reason why, though I was their trainer, I feel as their pupil today. Although they had no faculty of speech, they taught me more than many humans did. Therefore I feel that I should relate my experiences with my horses for the sake and benefit of future generations of horses and riders.

From my earliest childhood it was my most ardent desire to ride, and I dreamed about it night and day. I wanted to ride and believed I would experience the greatest happiness of this world on the back of a horse. I wanted to ride and develop the horse's movements into dance and music . . . to ride and feel and learn from the smallest signs of the mute creature how to communicate with him, how to understand him and to create a language between horse and rider which would always remain simple, distinct, and constant. This attitude means thinking from the point of view of the horse, knowing what the horse feels, what he likes, what difficulties he has to overcome, and how he, too, is influenced by moods or the surrounding atmosphere.

It is the long way of learning, and looking back, I understand now that the process never really comes to an end. The apprenticeship may be roughly divided into three phases. In the first, the rider must learn to maintain his balance in all movements of the horse and to remain "on top." Some are content with this modest result and may feel they are already great riders at this stage. But soon the student must realise that he has not reached the summit with these simple achievements. The aim from now on is to set the programme of work for the horse, to strengthen him by physical training, and to develop his mental abilities. This is the beginning of the second phase, and in the course of it the rider often despairs of ever learning this art. If the rider has succeeded in penetrating into the sphere of the art of riding and has trained a horse up to the standards of high school, he has overcome the second phase and progressed to the third, but he has not gone all the way to the ultimate of learning. For a single horse trained to this degree does not yet make a perfect rider. There are quite a number of horsemen, however, who have to content themselves with this sole achievement. There is many a "rider" in full paraphernalia who has his horses trained by somebody else, who mounts them for horse shows only, who has never trained a horse himself, and who therefore will never understand that it is he himself who has to learn from the horse if he strives to reach the highest level of equitation.

As the son of an Austro-Hungarian officer I grew up in the busy life of the barracks. Even before I had learned to speak correctly I knew the names of all the regiments, and my favorite pastime was to watch the drill of the dragoons. Whitey, my dappled rocking horse, was my dearest pet. I tended and groomed him as I had seen the grooms in the courtyard do with their charges, and when I mounted him for a gallant ride through the nursery I felt that the world was at my feet. Unfortunately he became a victim of my younger brother's passion for medicine: he ripped him apart "to see what was inside." Whitey was the first of the long series of horses in my life.

Many names—simple and elaborate—are stored in my memory and, closing my eyes, I may conjure up the horses I have met through the years. Out of the distant past there appears Olga, a good-natured and somewhat stout chestnut mare who was my father's charger in Neu-Zuczka, a garrison in the easternmost part of the Austrian monarchy. Years before, the grooms had clandestinely lifted me up on the horses before taking them back to the stables. But now I was allowed to do a few rounds in the courtyard of the barracks—at the walk, of course, which made the seven-year-old boy thoroughly happy. This secret, carefully kept from my father, became the highlight of the day, for which I waited with excitement. Olga became my first teacher in these repeated riding experiments. Her patience and good-naturedness taught me to settle and feel at ease on her back, to get confidence and even forget the possibility of falling off. I grew accustomed to seeing the world from an elevated position and learned—unconsciously but once and forever—how much confidence in the horse and in one's own abilities depends on those first impressions and consequently how important it is that the young rider should not be thrown in the beginning of his training.

When Olga's career as a charger had come to an end and she was used in a carriage, she was replaced by my father's second horse. Salome was an elegant liver chestnut full of temperament, as capricious as her name. Immediately she made it unmistakably clear to me that it is by no means the privilege of the rider to part with his horse solely by his own will. She got rid of me quickly and without fuss. This occurred repeatedly and led to a new understanding: soon I realised that it was not at all terrible to fall and that it was least harmful if it happened unexpectedly. These first experiences were later enriched when I found out that the rider can get hurt much more when falling at the walk than at the canter. At the canter it happens so quickly that he has no time to stiffen his muscles in defence, which may lead to broken bones or sprained muscles.

There was yet another experience I gained in these very modest lessons: I learned to guess from the smallest signs at what moment Salome's lively temper was nearing the point of explosion and to find means and ways to remain on her back in spite of her violent movements. When she held her head high and pricked her ears I knew that something had aroused her attention and suspicion, which might easily result in a sudden jump. I grabbed the saddle in time and held on. If she stopped unexpectedly and refused to go forward in spite of the commands of the groom, I knew that she would get up on her hind legs, thus offering me an elevated viewpoint but also a very slippery seat. I tried to overcome this uncomfortable situation by leaning forward and throwing my arms around her neck until another four-legged teacher convinced me, much later, of the treacherous effect of this defensive reaction. Things became most critical, however, when Salome began to move with very short steps and a swinging back so that the groom had difficulty holding her and finally, she leaped into the air with an angry snort, demonstrating the force with which she could send me to the ground. The first few times I was completely dazed but then I realised that when I bent forward and pulled my tummy in I made it much easier for her. If, on the contrary, I leaned back I gained a much firmer seat. This was one of the basic discoveries which was confirmed many times in my life as a rider.

Salome even conveyed psychological insight to me although I did not grasp the essence until much later. Besides her lively temper she possessed a virtuosity in kicking with her hind legs when somebody came near her, and the grooms were often forced to jump aside when grooming and saddling her. But one day when she was in the paddock I saw my youngest brother, then two years old, approach her from behind, grasp both her hind legs with his tiny hands, and crawl between them. Under her belly he halted, turned round, and crawled back through her hind legs, holding on to them. He repeated this pleasant little game several times while my mother, who was also witness to the gymnastics of her youngest son, held her breath and did not dare to move or call for fear that Salome might awaken from her uncommon placidity. At last, much to our relief, my brother discontinued his exercises and toddled towards us, while Salome looked after him in motherly understanding and went on grazing quietly. This episode remained forever engraved in my memory, because it demonstrated so clearly that horses are very good-natured as a rule and that most behaviour that we thoughtlessly call viciousness originates from fear or from bad experiences. Horses are easily frightened and have a tendency to flee. If there is no possibility of flight they defend themselves as best they can according to their intelligence and physical dexterity and so gain a reputation for viciousness. This reputation may induce the rider or the groom to approach these horses with special attention and by this attitude even further arouse their suspicion.

It was years later that I found confirmation of this probability with my jumper Karwip, who was assigned to me in my first year at the Austrian Cavalry School. In this institute the officers of the mounted troops received instruction in more advanced riding. In the first year the officers were trained to be riding instructors for the cavalry regiments and in the second and third years to instruct at the Cavalry School and also to enter competitions. When the horses were first allotted there was great excitement, for each of the horses had his reputation, good or bad, which the grooms had a habit of spreading under their breaths when they brought the mounts into the arena. We stood in rank and file and watched with apprehension as our riding instructor, Colonel Paumen, rolled his eyes from the lined-up horses to us who awaited execution. At last he made his decisions and Karwip was to be my horse. When I fixed the length of my stirrups the groom whispered into my ear: "Careful, the horses are full of nonsense today!" No wonder, for they had not had much work during the holidays of the past two months.

This first riding class had much in common with an American rodeo—which I had an opportunity to see twenty-five years later —and in many cases it ended with the rider being thrown while everybody else ran to try to catch his horse. Karwip, too, took part in the general bucking and kicking, but I was lucky enough to remain on top. I was so pleased about this that I decided to pay a visit to my horse in the stables in the afternoon. When I stood in her stall patting her neck the groom rushed into the stables and motioned frantically that Karwip was a notorious kicker and had laid many a person low who had tried to enter her stall. But I, not aware of her bad reputation, had approached her so innocently and directly that the idea of defending herself had not entered her mind. Of course, I had talked to her before and caressed her hindquarters in order not to frighten her. A direct and calm approach is the best attitude to adopt with very shy horses.

Difficult Beginning

When I was twelve years old my father consented at last to regular riding lessons, which I was to be given by a sergeant of the Fourth Dragoon Regiment, stationed in Wels in Upper Austria. Gabriel was of medium height and stout; he wore a beard and whiskers like the Emperor Franz Joseph, and possessed a tremendous voice which would have been sufficient to drill an entire squadron. He was dead serious about his new job.

After a short introduction a horse with a saddle but without reins or stirrups was brought into the open arena in front of the barracks. There were side reins which led from the rings in the snaffle to the front girth of the saddle. I was given a leg up and was allowed to hold on to the saddle while the horse moved on a circle around Gabriel, who stood in the center and held a long rein of hemp. First used in France in the seventeenth century, it is called a longe rein. By his rhythmic movements the horse was to teach me to find the proper balance on his back, which is easiest at the walk and most difficult at the canter.

It is not absolutely necessary that riding be first taught on the longe, especially if there are no suitable longe horses or experienced riding instructors. My own experience in many years of activity as a teacher, however, has confirmed that although it seems to be a long way and a waste of time to train a young rider on the longe, it is the best means of teaching him perfect control over his body, with harmony and suppleness, so that he does not disturb the balance of his partner and both finally will fuse into one. This was the goal that lay in a very distant future in those days, because my first problem was to remain in the saddle during the different movements of the horse.

My first longe horse was an honest trooper who had taught many a dragoon to serve his country and who now opened for me the doors to a world of which I had dreamed since my earliest childhood. Sigi was a peaceful-looking bay gelding without markings and of medium height. Today when everybody prefers big horses he would have been called a small horse. He turned his head with his calm and somewhat sad eyes towards me when I was lifted into the saddle, and had he had the gift of speech he would have said: "Don't worry, there will be no trouble." Right away I felt confident and endeavoured to live up to his friendly sympathy. Sitting without stirrups in the hard army saddle, I religiously followed the commands of my instructor and tried to hold on to the saddle with less tenseness when so requested and later to do such gymnastic exercises as swinging my arms or turning my body. I saw that Sigi reacted stoically to the commands of the sergeant, and his obedience set an example I tried to follow. I was so impressed by his willing submission that I did not flinch even when I felt an unmistakable burning on my knees, thighs, and seat. The tender skin did not stand the hardships of riding, let alone of the army saddle, and later I discovered large areas of a truly classical "rub." Of course I kept this painful secret from my mother in order not to interrupt my beloved riding lessons. This was my first but certainly not my last sacrifice on the altar of my passion.

Soon my dogged determination to hang on gave me the opportunity to sacrifice for the second time. Evidently Gabriel was of the opinion that I was a prodigious child. Furthermore he was encouraged by the balance I was able to maintain on the horse's back at the trot and canter, which, however, was only due to Sigi's good temper and smooth movements. Already on the third day the sergeant asked me whether I would like to jump over a fence which had been put up in the arena. With misgivings I eyed the solitary fence; it was very narrow and about three feet high. Truthfully I said "No." But my severe teacher would not hear of it. "A real rider is never afraid of an obstacle; he throws his heart over the fence and jumps after it!" He led the horse with the longe towards the fence, cracked his whip, and Sigi cleared the obstacle.

I cannot tell whether I threw my heart over the fence or whether I had it in my mouth. The fact is that I landed with a crash in the sand where I sat dazed, trying to recover from the shock. When I lifted my head I met the compassionate eyes of my Sigi, who seemed to say, "I am sorry, this was not my fault, I tried my best." There was not much time, however, for silent conversations with my partner, for Gabriel shouted: "Get up into the saddle and repeat the jump!" No sooner done than I found myself once more on the ground covered with sand and dust. But even this second unsuccessful attempt did not soften my ardent archangel, and he repeated the excruciating experience until, after the fifth or sixth time, I succeeded in remaining on top, desperately clinging to the saddle and the mane of my brave Sigi. Gabriel was extremely proud of this achievement, I was black and blue all over, and the horse was quite obviously relieved that there was no more jumping with this greenhorn. I did not, however, share the opinion of my instructor about the "success," and I am sure that Sigi would have agreed. My confidence was seriously shaken, and for years to come, even as a successful show jumper, I approached each fence with a sinking heart.

I have explained the goal of training on the longe. It took many years to get nearer to it, though, and I reached it only with the help of countless longe horses. I do not remember all the names of those patient creatures who carried me during my first military training, during my attendance at the Cavalry School, and later on when I was stationed as a student at the Spanish Riding School. What they taught me, however, I have tried to keep in mind and to improve by constantly correcting myself. They were my most tolerant teachers, those longe horses that allowed the boy to sit on their backs, that laboured under the young soldier and made the student of the Spanish Riding School realise the importance of the correct seat. They taught me to see the world with their eyes and to try to penetrate their minds and to understand the reasons for their behaviour. The knowledge and experience I gathered on their backs were of precious help when, years later, I held the longe myself for the training of young riders and horses.

The most important thing is the mutual confidence which is the basis on which the horse may grow into a cooperative friend. As a brutally subjected creature the longe horse would never give the feeling of security so necessary to a young rider. Work on the longe is of eminent importance for all training. By riding without stirrups the young rider gains a firm seat and learns the correct position. Later on I learned that the work on the longe is also valuable when training a young horse. The regular movement on the longe strengthens the horse and teaches him suppleness and obedience, thus preparing him for the work under the rider. Horse, rider, and instructor are governed by the same rule: the horse should carry the rider in regular, controlled movements; the rider should try to control himself when exercising his body in order to achieve the correct seat; and the instructor should excel in self-control even when his commands are not executed on the spot. Much patience is necessary in order to reach the goal, and temperance should guide all demands. The rider should know that the path to success is long and often difficult and must not ask too much of his horse out of ambition and vanity. The teacher should know the exact measure of work for both horse and rider in order not to tire and discourage them.

The self-control that the rider should practise when being longed was taught to me in a very special way by a stallion of the Furioso line, which was used at the Spanish Riding School along with the Lipizzaners for the training of the students. I had to ride him often during the years 1933 and 1934 when I was assigned as a student to the school. He was very sensitive and not willing to put up with any faults. If the slightest incorrectness of the rider's seat disturbed his balance, he showed his annoyance with a tremendous kick and threw many a hopeful rider into the sand of the most beautiful riding hall in the world. Such a mishap was not only embarrassing but also cost a fine of ten pounds of sugar. Consequently whenever the stock of sugar threatened to run low, one of the weaker riders was commanded to ride this stallion, who was nicknamed "sugar supplier." He was quite a terror, and there were riders who preferred to pay for the sugar voluntarily rather than ride this uncomfortable longe horse.

When longeing a young horse—and it is the best preparation for every type of riding horse—much can be learned from watching and observing the animal. During a recent stay in the United States I was asked by a very keen young rider to help with the longeing of her young stallion. He had injured himself when gambolling in the pasture and had to be worked with great care. He had not been longed before, and the six weeks of rest in the stables had made him explosive with strength and friskiness. The young lady had not dared to longe him for fear he would hurt himself again. At first he tried to rush off on the longe, so I led him again at a walk on the circle on which he was to go while I talked to him soothingly. After a while I withdrew slowly and, standing in the center of the circle, I maintained the movement gently with the whip. Since all this was unfamiliar to him and there was a brisk wind blowing his mane and tail and the other horses were playing in the field nearby, he took off now and again and raced around on the longe, bucking and kicking. When this happened I took him calmly into the circle with the longe, led him on again at a walk, and repeated the procedure until he had understood what I wanted. In a relatively short time he calmed down and went quietly on the circle at a walk and later even at a trot without ever thinking of running away. He learned to distinguish the commands by the tone of my voice and lengthened his strides when I said "trot" in a sharper tone and fell into a walk when I called out "waaaaalk" in a soothing sound. With the same patience and calmness I was able to overcome the difficulties that arose when I changed the rein.

In general a horse is accustomed to being led by the right hand of a person who walks at his left ("near") side. Therefore on the longe, too, he prefers to go on the left rein, that is, with his left side turned towards the center of the circle. If he is asked to go on the right rein it is strange to him that his trainer is now on the other side. It is good preparation to lead the young horse in the stables or in the arena with the left hand sometimes, that is, walking at his right ("off") side. In England, where the horses must always gallop to the left on race tracks, I noticed that the Thoroughbreds have especially great difficulties growing used to going to the other side. In the beginning they will constantly try to turn and go on the left rein, which may be very uncomfortable for the rider. Such was the experience of my wife, whose own lifelong dream came true at last. From her earliest childhood she had wanted to learn to ride, but, strangely enough, her first opportunity was during a fairly recent stay with friends in England. Unfortunately there was no ideal longe horse but instead a retired Thoroughbred, which in true race track manner did not see the reason he should remain on the right rein. To the left side there was no problem, but after half a round on the right rein he turned sharply and shot through the circle onto the left rein which was familiar to him, while my poor wife held on to the saddle for dear life. In this case again, patience and constant calm repetition helped Black Thunder to get used to going on the right rein at last.

The longeing horses have also taught me how important it is to give our partners time to understand the correct aids and to grow accustomed to them. When as a consequence of a serious heart disease I was not allowed to ride for two full years—the hardest blow that could possibly hit me—I did not want to miss my horses altogether and was happy to be able sometimes to work my dressage horses Nero and Teja on the longe. These two loyal friends sharpened the eyes of their master to a much greater extent than all the longe horses before. They taught me, for instance, the correct use of the longe whip, because their high degree of training made them react immediately to the slightest mistake. It is essential when working on the longe to make the horse understand and accept the whip as an aid. Under no circumstances should he be made suspicious or frightened by it. He should respect it and not be afraid. One day I saw the horse of a well-known and successful dressage rider flee into the remotest corner of the riding hall when his master lifted the longe whip. There is no sadder testimonial for a rider.

One of the most important aids is the voice. According to the tone and modulation it may be soothing or exhorting. It is important, however, that word and sound remain the same for the same commands. Horses have extremely keen hearing and remember the words for the different exercises. This is of great help when working the horse on the longe but may be a disadvantage in the training of the rider. When I commanded a class of my pupils at the Cavalry School and later when I trained the young riders at the Spanish Riding School, the horses knew my voice so well that in a short time they changed the pace (or gait) upon my command "trot" or "canter" without waiting for the aids of their riders, which of course was not at all the idea of the lesson. We decided on different commands. I said "walk" when it should be trot and "trot" for canter, and yet in a few days we again had to invent new commands in order to make the horses concentrate on the aids of their riders.

When longeing, the whip replaces the aids of the legs and the longe prepares the horse for the aids of the reins which the rider will use later. Therefore this valuable means of education should not degenerate into a tug-of-war in which the horse would be the victor because of his greater weight. With repeated short actions of the longe, giving and taking as with the reins, the trainer establishes an elastic contact with the horse which holds him "on the bit" instead of holding him "with the rein." I learned this from experience when I had to longe the stallion Gidran, who had come from the stud farm to the Cavalry School for four weeks. He was not at all pleased with this work, did not like going round on a circle, and every now and again tried to run away. He was incomparably more powerful than I, and besides I never had much strength in my arms. The only way was to counter his force with my skill. I slackened the longe for a short moment in order to take it up again and make him understand my will. Gidran was astonished at first but by and by he decided to follow my commands and go in the direction I prescribed. The success achieved in little over one week reminded me of the importance of the "giving rein" which Xenophon described twenty-five hundred years ago.

Furthermore, I learned to be twice as careful if the horse stopped suddenly and threw his head up. This lesson was again demonstrated to me by a horse during a recent stay in Canada. Friends offered me a small grey Thoroughbred mare called Blue Bird as a longe horse for my wife. Before beginning to work with any strange horse and even more so in this case I wanted to get to know the four-legged teacher and took the mare on the longe, without the rider at first. There was immediate proof that my tactics were correct. Blue Bird was very reluctant to go forward and when I began carefully to push her she kicked against the longe whip with her hind legs. This attitude of defence might be of much trouble for the trainer and his pupil if it is not nipped in the bud. The idea of the work on the longe is not only to achieve a firm seat but also to establish the young rider's confidence. In this case the horse also threw her head up, which is a very serious warning.

After adjusting the bridle and lengthening the side reins I once more led Blue Bird on the circle and used the whip again with much precaution. This time Blue Bird got straight up on her hind legs, demonstrating a resistance which was the result of tenseness and restraint. A spectator who knew the mare shrugged her shoulders: "Nothing doing, she always rears on the longe!"

But I do not believe in standardised ideas, and it is my conviction that there are no vicious horses but only spoiled ones. Blue Bird was quite obviously afraid of the whip. I showed it to her, patting her and talking to her in order to make her realise that she need not be afraid. I led her again on the circle and made her go forward briskly—forward is always the best remedy—while I kept talking to her in a calm voice. When she had moved quietly on the longe for a few rounds I called her to me, rewarded her, and repeated the whole procedure. Soon Blue Bird found out that there was no reason to be frightened and she also understood what was demanded of her. She never offered resistance again and became an excellent longe horse. The regular and systematic work strengthened her muscles and improved her paces beyond expectation. From a hasty running gait the trot emerged with long and regular strides. Her movements, which had been stiff and hard in the beginning, became soft and smooth so that my wife, riding without stirrups, was able to sit even through an extended trot.

On this same trip I encountered a rather unruly Thoroughbred in California. Kahili had come from the race track and was certainly the wildest horse I had seen for a long time. Riding him was out of the question, although there was a German girl who managed to sit through his incredible bucks and kicks, holding on to the saddle and hanging on the reins with iron fists. But this could not have been called any schooling and would not lead anywhere. When I took Kahili on the longe for the first time I had to put all my weight against the line to hold him. He stormed away, rearing, standing on his front legs, kicking, and bucking with his mouth wide open and a wild expression in his eyes. Although he was a good-looking creature there was no trace of gaits to be detected in his wild and uncontrolled movements. As my arms are not strong at all this experiment was exhausting to me.

On the second day he began to go forward for a few steps before beginning to kick again. I was not too hopeful about being able to cure this horse of his bad habits because I knew that I could not stay long enough. There was one thing, however, that made me wonder. This savage creature was the sweetest horse when in the stables—he allowed anybody to come near him and never tried to nip or to kick. So the reason for his behaviour was to be sought in the fact that he was reluctant to go forward, which is very often to be found with Thoroughbreds taken onto the racecourse and worked when they are too young and not strong enough. Besides Kahili was probably not getting sufficient exercise now. After all, he was a strong and healthy five-year-old. It took a few days to come to know him sufficiently so that I could anticipate his bucking and prepare for it. In the second week I succeeded in cutting it short by shouting "No!" at him at the top of my voice, and his attempt to rush off faded away into a limp little hop. Although he still managed to rush off and race around wildly, there were periods now when he went calmly on the circle and his paces gradually developed. Of course I practised walk and trot only, because a canter would have excited him too much and the imminent goal was to make him calm and obedient. He had lost the worried look in his eyes and kept his mouth closed at moments.

On the very day when I thought that I had overcome the worst difficulties an unexpected incident happened. As Kahili was being prepared for his work he nibbled at the rope of the halter, caught it in his teeth, and in fear jerked his head up and tore out his tush (the tooth that stands by itself in the lower jaw) so that it pierced his lip. The vet came and removed it and treated the wound in the jaw. Again I was amazed at how calmly and patiently Kahili tolerated these manipulations.

Fortunately there was no infection, and on the third day the vet consented to my suggestion that I exercise Kahili on the longe. Of course we did not put a bit into his mouth but fastened the side reins into the cavesson as I had done many years ago with my dressage horse Otto, who had torn his tongue in rough play with his neighbour in the stables. That day Kahili acted in an exemplary manner, obeying the commands of my voice and not trying once to run away or buck. We all laughed and joked that he had to have his tooth out in order to behave himself.

From that day on, progress was constant. Kahili's paces improved steadily and he developed a very beautiful extended trot.

When he was going calmly for long periods I tried the canter, which did not excite him any more but which in true Thoroughbred fashion came in smooth and long bounds. His neck, which had been somewhat skinny, began to fill out and to shape beautifully. He kept his mouth closed even when, after two weeks, his jaw had healed and we put a very thick rubber bit into his mouth. With the exception of slight attempts to gambol there were no more fits of bucking, and when I decided that the time had come to put a rider into the saddle my wife bravely volunteered. Kahili behaved very well and went calmly on the circle even when she did some exercises such as swinging her arms above his head or leaning back or forward in the saddle. At last Kahili had grown up.

No discussion of work on the longe, which is so often minimized, neglected, or misused, should fail to point out an error made more and more often in recent years. Instead of the longe rein being clasped into the cavesson, it is fastened to the ring of the snaffle, which is not only incorrect but also absolutely harmful. The tender mouth of the horse will become hard and irresponsive through the effect of the longe, which is so much stronger when it is exercised directly on the bit. Thus the essence of longeing is lost, which is to educate the horse to take a light and constant contact on the bit. Longeing like this is nonsense and brutality, placing laziness and the desire for quick work above consideration for the animal. The only correct method is that which our forefathers have conscientiously studied and applied with success.

In the Austro-Hungarian Cavalry and also in the Austrian Federal Army after the First World War, every young horse was worked on the longe at the beginning of his training before being mounted. This made the work less strenuous than going immediately under the rider and increased their stamina and their life span. Besides, work on the longe improved their balance and their paces and made them more comfortable riding horses.

Also all soldiers of the cavalry regiments were trained on the longe for about four weeks before being turned loose on the world. They learned much more quickly to find the balance in the saddle and to adapt themselves to the rhythm of the horse's movements. Of course this training was sometimes somewhat harsh, as the language of barracks is not meant for tender ears anyway—and Sergeant Gabriel was no exception. He did not always choose the

most elegant expressions and was truly ingenious in inventing
all sorts of names to apply to horse and rider. The corrections
were limited to the most primitive details and conveyed to me at
the top of his voice. Sigi, the longe horse, was used to all that
and stoically obeyed the commands. I followed his example and
saw in this rather rough training a toll that I had to pay for the
fulfilment of my passion.

After several weeks of training on the longe with many loosening
gymnastic exercises I felt quite at home on horseback, and Sergeant
Gabriel decided that this was the moment to turn me loose. I said
good-bye to Sigi, for now I would get another horse. I was going
to use the stirrups and take up the reins and lead the dark gelding
Maxl on his way around the arena. I had not expected that this
would confront me with so many new experiences.

Apparently my new comrade did not feel at ease either, for he
was terribly excited. When a soldier brought him into the open
arena, ready for the lesson with saddle and bridle, he was scared
out of his wits when a sparrow flew up or some other unknown
object aroused his suspicion. The situation became quite comical
when he began kicking with both hind legs as if he wanted to do a
capriole. The soldier had great trouble holding him and rolled his
frightened eyes back and forth between the sergeant and the wild
horse. The horse bucked some more until the soldier lost the ground
underneath his feet and let go of the reins. The gelding raced around
the arena enjoying his liberty. Of course he immediately headed
towards the exit. However, the way home to the stables was blocked
by a gate and he lacked the courage to jump or was too clever to
jump on the hard paved road that led to the stables. When the
wrath of our teacher had ceased to pour on the contrite soldier, the
three of us began to encircle the fugitive in a corner of the arena
that was fenced in with thick beams and finally succeeded in catch-
ing him. We were all exhausted when we were ready at last to
begin to work. For a while the sergeant muttered under his breath
about the "blasted idiot" while the dragoon busied himself with his
dust-covered uniform. And I, with a sinking heart, prepared myself
to face what was yet to come. Maxl shook his head; he could not
understand why he of all horses had to come out and work in the
afternoon and all by himself without the moral support of his
"buddies," with whom he would have been able to converse in

his own language so that the tedious work in the arena would be a little gayer. Poor fellow, he had to work at a time when the others peacefully dreamed in the stables!

When I mounted at last I was confronted with a new situation. Previously the horse I was on had been led by the longe rein, but now I alone was responsible for guiding him. The longe whip, too, which had held him in motion, did not operate, and I had to push Maxl forward all the time. Now that he had spent himself in his escapades he decided to make work as easy as possible for himself and dragged himself across the arena. We were both startled by the cracking of the whip and the yelling of our teacher. These tactics led to a more lively movement of my horse; consequently I lost the stirrups to which I had not yet become accustomed and, trying to fish for them, I lost my balance and my seat slipped into a precarious position. It was the very end of my poise and confidence when Gabriel hurled the longe whip in the sand and with unmistakable meaning shook his hands above his head.

Years later, when I myself was standing in the arena in the place of the instructor, I knew from my own experience about these things and waited until the pupil had settled in a new situation without making him all the more nervous by my impatience. I had learned the hard way that for a young rider a new horse means an entirely new situation and that he cannot be expected to cope with it like an experienced horseman. It takes some time until the rider has got used to the different movements of a different horse and also to his particularities. Both have to take in each other's scent, as it were. Later, too, I recognized that there is a great difference between the horse going on a circle under the immediate control of the instructor and his going independently at large.

After a while it dawned upon my Sergeant Gabriel that it is far more difficult to ride a trooper all by oneself when he is used to working in a group and even more so in an open arena with all sorts of diversions. Also it was in the afternoon, while the riding instruction usually took place in the morning. It was decided that during the holidays I was to join the riding lessons of his Dragoons. For Gabriel, too, this solution was much more convenient, and I was thrilled to be allowed to ride in a group under military command and to execute the various paces and figures. I was filled with pride when I found that I was able to keep pace with the soldiers, and when I was even praised in their presence on several occasions, I began to think of myself as a perfect rider. But my hard-boiled trooper soon made me revise my arrogant ideas.

In the first lesson after the Christmas holidays Maxl suddenly left the formation of the soldiers and ran away with me at top speed. Luckily for me this happened in the indoor riding school and not on one of the vast open arenas. On the other hand, in there I had to pass through one corner after another and Maxl slipped precariously in the soft sawdust each time he whisked round a corner. Gabriel yelled after me, "Hold your horse!" but the more I pulled at the reins the more Maxl increased his speed. At last I crashed to the ground, disappearing in a cloud of dust, and the savage creature became again the most peaceful horse, walking willingly up to the groom. Maxl seemed thoroughly satisfied with his success. Having clearly demonstrated that I was not yet much of a rider, he had crushed my budding conceit and provided a very welcome diversion to the soldiers in their grey everyday routine. They roared with laughter over the funny sight and were obviously pleased that Gabriel's thunder exploded on somebody else's head for a change. This experience took me down a peg or two and I realised that riding is much more than sitting on a quietly walking horse.

Maxl was the first of a series of runaways in my life, and only after a number of excruciating experiences did I understand that a bolting horse cannot be slowed down or brought to a halt by simply pulling at the reins. According to physical laws, when both horse and rider pull at the same rein, the stronger and heavier one will be successful, which means the horse, of course. The orders of the instructor such as "Apply the reins!" or "Don't let him go!" are of no value to the fledgling horseman in need; neither does it help to yell at him or to call him all sorts of inelegant names. If the rider, however, gives only a short action of the reins, relaxing them immediately and repeating the action, he may compensate for his inadequate power and control the most unreasonable animal. In order to apply these short actions of the reins effectively, the rider must have an independent seat, which he should have learned in the correct work on the longe.

When I was seventeen the dream of my childhood came true at last. In May of 1916 I joined as an officer candidate the Dragoon

Regiment No. 4, "Emperor Ferdinand," in Wels, with my mind full
of the romantic tales of the old proud cavalry. For a little while
I was allowed to preserve my ardent enthusiasm. As it was the
tradition in the Austro-Hungarian Army, I was given regular riding lessons, at first in the preparatory group in Wels and later in
the officers' school. It was a strange sensation to ride as a soldier
in the same arena following the same commands as when a boy,
with the exception that now I enjoyed the lessons much more because I had learned a number of things in these past years. Besides,
for the first time, in accordance with the rule for each young officer,
I rode a horse of my own. My coal black Neger was a decent chap
even if he tried to run away with me sometimes or to buck me off.

After a few preparatory weeks in Wels we went to the officers'
school in Stockerau for six months, where some hundred officer
candidates were assembled. Three squadrons of officers belonging
to Dragoon, Ulan, and Hussar regiments made a very colourful
picture, like one of those huge paintings of a cavalry battle come
to life. It was for the last time perhaps in the dying Austro-Hungarian monarchy. Ardent young warriors that we were we did not
notice anything alarming but were full of ambition and fervour.
We were prepared to give ourselves, soul and all, to our Emperor.
We wanted to learn as much as possible, and riding, for me, was of
course in the foreground.

The first thing we were to learn was that those two weeks of
preliminary training in Wels had been but a mild introduction to
serious army life. Arriving with two comrades at the Stockerau
station, which is not far from Vienna, we took a *fiaker*, a carriage with two horses, and drove through this small provincial town
to the barracks. We felt very grown up in the smart uniform of
the Dragoons—red breeches, a red cap, light blue coat with silver
buttons, and the distinctive regimental colours on the high collars,
which were green for the Dragoons. We laughed and joked and
thought that all pretty girls who went for walks on this Sunday
afternoon were turning round to look at us. As soon as we arrived
in the barracks we reported to our superior. The reception that
Captain Schildenfeld reserved for us was like a cold shower on
our holiday mood. "Here they are, these three laughing heroes
driving in a *fiaker* into the barracks in bright daylight. Where do
they think they are? Did you come from the *Heurigen* (small

wine taverns in and around Vienna)? I'll teach you to be soldiers. And which of you had the bright idea of sticking a feather into his cap?" And so on, and so on. . . . He was right as far as our gayety was concerned, although he ought to have been pleased that we came with so much enthusiasm into the officers' school. The idea of the feather, however, was certainly a mistake, but the captain did not believe our explanation that one of us had held his riding whip upright in such a way that the leather flap at its end might easily have looked like a feather from a distance. Captain Schildenfeld had very little sense of humour and an extremely severe conception of duty with which we should soon become better acquainted.

Next day when the newcomers waited in formation to be assigned to the different squadrons, he asked which of us knew how to ride. I was one of the few who came forward while the majority preferred to remain in the rank. They were wise because the answer was: "Aha, you do know how to ride! Well, let's have a look!" We had to go into the arena, wait for the horses that were ordered, and mount. The horses were fresh and frisky. They easily got rid of their riders, and our little group soon had shrunk to three trembling horsemen. A fence was brought in which we had to jump, and there were only two of us left to be chased over the obstacle. The captain drove the horses on with the longe whip and shouted: "Fall off, fall off, you don't know how to ride. You have to fall off. . . ." We entrusted our souls to God, for it is not at all easy to fall on command, but at last, mercifully, the horses kicked us off and this strange test came to an end.

I was ordered to the third squadron under Captain Count Teleki and had every reason to be happy about it. This wonderful teacher soon became the idol of all of us, and we would have gone through fire and water for him. Our days were filled to the brim. In the morning riding lessons, drill and military training on horseback. In the afternoon military training on foot, tactics, and theoretical instruction. We were kept busy with a relentless timetable. The bolting horse was again my special nightmare in the riding lessons. Repeatedly Neger proved to me how much of a greenhorn I was and how much there was yet to be learned. Although I was able to master him quite well in the indoor school he ran off with me ever so often in the vast training field. Downcast, I had to suffer many a rebuke from my captain because of his behaviour. But since everything negative in our lives has a positive side, Neger made it clearer to me than any riding instructor could that my seat was not yet sufficiently independent. Whenever I was in serious trouble I did not use the reins exclusively to guide my horse but hung on to them to restore my lost balance and consequently was incapable of the giving and taking action that alone would have been my salvation.

By these escapades Neger aroused the attention of Captain Teleki—not always in a positive manner, though, as for instance when he threw me at a jump and dragged me across the arena because my foot got caught in the stirrup. But because of these difficulties Neger taught me much more than I could have learned from a demurely obedient horse. One of the most important lessons was that the rider should not try to stop a runaway horse by pulling at the reins but by that giving and taking action, which, as I've suggested, makes the horse obey at last. A few months later in a battle Neger saved my life by his huge bounds at the canter. He had been wounded by shrapnel and yet did his duty until his last breath. I am not ashamed to admit that tears came into my eyes when I bid farewell to this brave and loyal creature. I had lost a teacher and a friend.

This first military training with much drill on horseback, which was to underline the role of the horse as a comrade in war, was of comparatively short duration and was to be my last in the old Austrian Empire. When I was sent to the Russian front I had to face the facts of life. Horses were used for short patrols and messenger rides only, and most of the cavalry had to fight on foot. The situation became even more depressing when in 1917 we had to give up the horses altogether because they were desperately needed for the artillery. What a difference from the dreams of my youth and how I suffered under the stress of the hard reality!

In October 1917 I was severely wounded by a bullet in the throat and was sent home by way of various field hospitals. Life at home, too, had much changed and the endless war was weighing on the people. In July 1918 after my recovery I was ordered as a lieutenant to the alarm squadron in Vienna. This squadron was to maintain order in the city and protect the Emperor and was formed of a platoon of each of the Dragoon regiments Nos. 3, 4, and 11, and of the Ulan regiment No. 5. I commanded the platoon of the Dragoons No. 4. Although I was glad to be with a cavalry group, my youthful enthusiasm did not come to life again. Too deep were the shadows that the oncoming end of the war and imminent defeat cast over our whole life. Only when I worked with my platoon in the Riding School and saw with what interest and zeal the soldiers, who were many years my superiors and who had all had several years of experience on the front, followed my orders was I happy and able to forget the bleak future. In these months full of uneasy forebodings, the exemplary attitude of the sergeants and soldiers underlined once again the educational value of riding and proved again that, as in the past centuries, the horse was still teaching chivalrous behaviour.

When the war had come to an end at last, it meant more than a defeat. It was the death of the Austro-Hungarian monarchy. The vast Empire, which through centuries had united millions of people of different nationalities, collapsed and with it our whole world. The places of my childhood became foreign countries. The Empire had ceased to exist; each of the nations founded its own government; and the small remainder of German-speaking people proclaimed the First Republic of Austria. This upheaval entailed a social revolution and inverted standards and values.

The first political meeting of soldiers of the revolution took place on the vast training field where we had worked with our horses. The squadron was lined up in formation on foot and I stood in front of my platoon as I had so often before during military drill. With misgivings I observed the disorderly soldiers who shared the barracks with my squadron. Some politician talked to us and my uneasiness grew when soon after his first words vituperations towards the officers rose from the ranks of the soldiers and violent shouts and threats filled the air.

At this moment the man behind me called out softly as he had done so often during the drill to correct my position: "Don't worry, Lieutenant, we stand behind you as always, whatever will be. . . ." To me this is the most beautiful proof of the spirit that unites horsemen even across gulfs and borders and that I was fortunate to encounter often again in my life.

This political meeting was the beginning of a series of sad and incomprehensible events which culminated in the saddest of all, when the Imperial Army was dissolved and we had to part with our horses. In spite of the small ration of food and other difficulties, the horses were in excellent condition because we all were attached to them, officers as well as soldiers. But now when they were to be given away, doubtful figures sneaked into the stables and peered into the boxes, calculating their price. Every free moment I spent with Medea, my black and temperamental mare, patted her neck and offered her small pieces of corn bread that I had saved from my frugal meals. Luckily she did not know how her life would change! I was relieved when we were ordered to give fifty horses over to the mounted police and I recommended Medea to the police officer. Although this was some comfort in those days of darkness, my throat was clogged when I watched the group of horses clatter out of the barracks, Medea leading under her new rider. In the following years I was to see her often when the police officer was on duty in the streets of Vienna and, nostalgically, I would pat her neck.

This separation from the horses was the beginning of the saddest period of my life and set a temporary end to equestrian ambitions.

My Hunters and Jumpers

When life eventually became more or less normal, I was very fortunate to be admitted into the newly established Federal Army. Out of fifteen thousand officers of the Imperial Army, only fifteen hundred were accepted. For four years I did my duty in various offices in the Department of Defence and when I was transferred to the Infantry Regiment No. 5 I came at last in touch with horses again. I had to train the mounted messengers and supervise the training of horses for the officers and the carriages. When I saw horses again after so long a time my love for riding blazed anew and my imagination soared to realise my dreams. I took a big strong chestnut out of the field kitchen and began to ride him regularly. His temperament and impulsion had struck me. His name was Napoleon; his papers had been lost in the revolution, which had made all creatures equal, but his career was to be worthy of his great namesake. In spite of my modest abilities we soon understood each other. I discovered his talent as a jumper and together we competed in the few horse shows that took place in the twenties.

Napoleon transmitted his impetuosity and eagerness to me, and the fusion of horse and rider in the desire to go forward, encouraged by the applause of the enthusiastic public, led to success. My knowledge and experience grew, and so did my reputation in the regiment because the commander was an enthusiastic rider himself and very proud that an officer of his regiment—and of an

infantry regiment at that—counted among the most successful
show jumpers of those years. My outlook on life changed completely; there was a sense and a meaning again, and the successes
with Napoleon stimulated me to do my duty with doubled eagerness. Until one day the colonel asked me why I did not participate
in the dressage competitions, too. Truthfully I answered that I
thought this kind of riding too difficult and far above my abilities.
But he would not hear of my objections and there was nothing else
to do but obey. The colonel's wish was an order for the first lieutenant.

And this first lieutenant was now confronted with a problem for
which he was not prepared and for the solution of which he had
no other assistance than Napoleon. But Napoleon's lively temperament, which had been so important for jumping, was more of
an impediment now and at first he was not willing to accept the
strict rules of dressage. He could not understand why all of a sudden
it should be the rider who decided on which leg he was to canter,
why he should strike off not only from the trot or walk but also
from the standstill and even from the rein-back. But because we
were friends we found a basis of understanding in a few days and
began regular teamwork.

My first concern was to cultivate Napoleon's paces and thanks to
his sensibility he became an excellent teacher. He reacted immediately when I made a mistake, when my seat was not balanced
enough, or when I did not give the aids in the correct manner.
This sensibility helped me to discover my faults in time and nip
them in the bud. For weeks we concentrated on the simple exercises that are the foundation of dressage: changes of tempo, strike-
off into the canter, breaking into a trot, large circles and voltes,
last but not least going straight, one of the most insignificant and
at the same time one of the most difficult exercises. Napoleon began
to move in rhythm and balance: he submitted his lively temperament and became attentive and obedient.

With the exception of a few indispensable exercises I did not
dare to jump him during this time for fear of disturbing his
physical and mental balance, which I had built up in these weeks of
patient work. And strangely enough, although I had begun this
work rather reluctantly, gradually it gained in interest and captivated me more with every day. Instead of getting tired and bored

with the painstaking and not very spectacular details of dressage, I became so absorbed that the time was always too short. With eagerness I waited for the next day to set forth where I had left off to eradicate faults and to find new ways of understanding with Napoleon. When training for jumping I had never felt that way.

When at last the dressage test of the preliminary class was over and we were placed among the first, the colonel's wish had been carried out to his satisfaction and I participated with pleasure and relief in the jumping competitions of the various horse shows. That year I had my greatest success as a show jumper, for I left all the cavalry officers and students of the Cavalry School behind me even though they had much better horses. I was declared the most successful jumping rider of the year 1926.

What had been my first contact with dressage made me realise its enormous value in the training of jumpers and hunters—as a matter of fact, of every type of riding horse, beginning with the hack. How much greater is the pleasure of sitting on a well-trained horse who follows the rider's slightest command than of fighting one's way across a course of obstacles. The advantage of a show jumper with a basic training in dressage was especially apparent on occasions when the other competitors had clear rounds and when the time factor was to decide the victory. By the basic training in dressage Napoleon had become stronger, more supple, and easier to turn. He had learned to maintain his balance and to control his lively temperament. Instead of rushing wildly towards the fence, he allowed me to lead him up to it. His suppleness permitted us to make sharp turns and shorten the distance between the obstacles. Because he cantered so calmly the spectators very often thought that our ride was slower than that of the others, and yet by our shortcuts we had gained precious seconds.

Besides these obvious advantages, my short appearance in the dressage arena had yet another result, and of far greater consequence to the course of my life. My success had aroused the interest of the cavalry inspector and upon his orders I was transferred back to the cavalry. This decision was of great importance for my career because it meant a course of three years and the possibility of advanced training at the Austrian Cavalry School in Schlosshof near Vienna. There would be qualified riding instructors and better horses than in the infantry regiments. As a rule the best horses in the Army were to be found at this institute, although their quality was still far below that of private horses because the Army could not afford to pay better prices. The next best came to the cavalry and artillery troops and the rest to the infantry. Horses that the cavalry discarded were also passed on to the infantry, as had been the case with Erna, the second jumper in the infantry regiment with whom I had also been successful in competitions.

Now I was to receive systematic and extensive instruction; there were lessons on the longe, training of remounts (young horses in the first year of their training were called remounts in the Austrian Army), hunting, and dressage. Every day I had to work five to six horses. For many of my comrades, however, who were not as fanatic about riding as I was, it was a less pleasant experience to be stationed at the Cavalry School. The reason in most cases was that the instructors did not attempt to build up the necessary confidence beween pupil and teacher and between horse and rider. Especially some of the weaker riders were in great trouble with the remounts. These young horses came from the stud farms for a few months of training at the Cavalry School. They were well fed and not sufficiently worked and full of nonsense. Some of them were experts in bucking and even the more experienced riders were not spared a fall. One of these terrors whose reputation was well established was Juro, a bay gelding of the Furioso line. Thanks to him the beginning of my time at Schlosshof is vivid in my mind up to the present day.

In the first minutes of the riding lesson with the remounts, the slightest noise immediately caused hectic confusion. Several riders found themselves more or less comfortably on the ground while their horses raced up and down in the arena, enjoying their freedom and inspiring their colleagues to do the same. Juro used to do a particularly thorough job: he threw his rider with such vehemence that the poor man left the place of his defeat on a stretcher. Victorious, Juro was led into the stables. On the following day the instructor had to name a new rider for him because his own was still in the infirmary. Within a few minutes Juro had repeated his feat and was again led into the stables, visibly satisfied to be thus rewarded for his deed, which saved him from working for the rest of the day.

Since horses have a very good memory they will keep on trying to get rid of their riders if they find their naughtiness rewarded by being given a rest. The children of Canadian friends had to discover this the hard way when, recently, they were expected to learn how to ride on a completely untrained pony. During the week Bobby stood peacefully in the paddock, eating much and moving as little as possible. Of course he did not like being disturbed on the weekends and soon found out that all he had to do was to perform a few clever bucks and kicks to get it over with and return to the pasture while the little girls, in tears, were removed by their disgusted mother. By regular and correct work on the longe, however, I soon taught Bobby reason and with the increasing confidence and feeling of security the girls took pleasure in their riding lessons again.

But back to Schlosshof! After a few days the riding instructor looked about for another victim for Juro and his choice fell upon me. Casualties had diminished the number of riders, and our class was not more than half of what it had been in the beginning. In the meantime I had had the opportunity to study Juro's technique. After a sharp turn he used to put his head between his forelegs and buck and kick until he had got rid of his rider. In the first lesson I succeeded in riding out his bucks by taking the upper part of my body back. This was my first practical experience of how much the rider can influence his horse with the aid of his weight. When taking the upper part of his body behind the vertical he increases the pushing aids of legs and seat and puts more weight on the hindquarters of the horse. This makes bucking difficult for him; besides, a horse that is pushed ahead energetically has to employ his strength for going forward and has no time left for bucking.

There was yet another lesson: I learned how important it is to have confidence in one's own abilities. In those days I was certain that I was the man to master Juro. And even when he proved to me, too, that he was the stronger, I achieved a modest success. Although I had landed in the sand with a crash I was not carried out of the arena on a stretcher but was able to remount immediately. This was a new experience for Juro. So far, he had been taken back into the stables after his misdeeds, which was equal to a re-

ward. But now I made him work hard in order to drive silly ideas
out of his mind.

The cause of his bucking was evident: he was not going forward
and he was bored. It was certainly much more fun to buck and
kick instead of working and then to enjoy having everybody run
after him and try to catch him by offering oats and all kinds of
titbits. My tactics were therefore to ride him briskly forward and
keep his mind busy by riding turns and circles and many other
figures so that he found little time and opportunity for his escapades. Although he succeeded several times in throwing me, my
skill in maintaining my seat during his bucks increased in the
same measure as he failed to take me by surprise, until at last he
gave up his naughtiness. As the weeks passed he became quite
obedient and so well mannered that I could ride him in the lesson
without stirrups and even took him out hunting.

When transferred to the cavalry I had had to leave Erna and
Napoleon behind with the infantry regiment, because the officers of
the newly established Austrian Federal Army were not allowed to
have horses of their own. In the first ten years of its existence
there were no chargers either. A charger was a horse belonging to
the cavalry that became the property of the officer who had ridden
him for six years without interruption. It had been sad to part with
Napoleon but our last competition was worthy of our work together. In the year 1927 at the great horse show in Vienna we
won the "Farewell Jumping" against the best international riders.

The Cavalry School had a number of well-trained school horses
who were to teach me the basics of dressage. And there were also
jumpers whom I could not only ride to hounds but also enter in
competitions. It was very much appreciated by the superior officers
when the young students of this institute participated in horse
shows. I am unable to name all the uncountable horses who carried
me successfully through courses of obstacles. They have all contributed to the development of my equestrian education, but only
a few grew to a level where I may call them my teachers.

After Juro it was a good-looking stallion of the Gidran line,
Harry, who became my taskmaster and made me work by the sweat
of my brow. At first I was thrilled to get this attractive chestnut, a
good mover with an enormous ability to jump. But when I rode him

in the Riding School for the first time my enthusiasm was somewhat chilled. His contact with the bit was far too firm—he leaned on the rein with all his weight and made it impossible for me to guide him correctly. He was difficult enough to ride in the arena but cross-country he was a serious problem. As soon as the hunt took off there was no holding him. With all his weight he lay on the rein; he was completely on his forehand and became lower and lower in front and faster and faster in his speed. Like a tank he ploughed through the group of riders cantering in front of him, apparently intent on overtaking the Master, who rebuked me for leaving my place in the field. I would have loved to carry out his orders if I had succeeded in making it clear to Harry. But he reacted not at all to the action of the reins because he pulled at them with all his strength. It was impossible to turn him to one side either; all he seemed to have in mind was to overtake the hounds as well, a very severe infraction of protocol. Exhortations about my behaviour did not help me in my plight, neither did contrition about my own helplessness—although it is said to be the first step towards improvement. Any remedy I could think of failed pitifully. When I rode at the very rear or at the side of the hunt he tried to be in front just as much as when I succeeded in riding a very large circle. As long as we rode in the opposite direction he slowed down some-what in order to increase his speed with full power when he saw the other horses in front of him again. It was a constant fight to ride this horse as he stormed over the fences and ditches with his head so low that it almost touched the ground. It was certainly no pleas-ure and wore me out physically and mentally.

Soon I realised that there was no possibility of bringing Harry to his senses while riding cross-country, because he was carried away and made deaf and blind by excitement and hunting fever. As a remedy I used every opportunity in the indoor arena to make him more supple and obedient by riding turns and changes of speed and paces, by half-halts and halts, and to make him accept the rein as a guidance and not abuse it constantly as a support. To my surprise he made good progress in the indoor school but in the hunting field it was lost immediately again. For a long time hunting fever remained stronger than education. However, gradually the work in the arena began to bear fruit and Harry's behaviour in the country improved so that at last I began to enjoy the hunts across the fields and woods in the lovely colours of autumn.

Karwip was the horse whom I rode in the greatest number of hunts and with whom I also participated successfully in many horse shows as a show jumper. She was a very sensitive lady—I have told the story about our first encounter—but soon we became good friends. Sometimes, though, she became absolutely hysterical. When I took her on a hunt and she saw the hounds for the first time she trembled and snorted, she leaped and reared. Her whole body was covered with lather in a short time and she would not stand still for a moment. She presented a pitiful sight. It was hopeless to try to calm her, and when the hunt took off with the hounds crying and the horn sounding, she shot after it madly. Again I was rebuked by the Master and regarded with misgivings by the other members of the hunt whose horses began to be nervous too. Luckily, I was able to turn Karwip and perform large circles, which saved me from overshooting the Master. The behaviour of the mare was by no means viciousness but simply fear. She was not at all prepared for hunting, was hardly used to carrying a rider, and was now expected to canter up- and downhill with an unaccustomed weight on her back. In addition there was the excitement of the other horses, the hounds, the cracking of the whip, and the sound of the horn. This experience taught me how to win my horse's confidence. As often as possible I took Karwip out into the fields alone or with a few other riders and practised quiet transitions from trot into canter and vice versa. I taught her to keep a certain distance from the other horses and finally to remain at a standstill while the others cantered on. Above all I took care not to make her nervous and if she became excited I calmed her by patting and talking. By rewarding her for the smallest progress I built up the confidence that is so necessary between horse and rider.

When cantering quietly in a group across fields and obstacles horses will educate each other. They take each other's fear of unknown objects away—everybody is more courageous when in a group—and by the herding instinct they stimulate each other to go briskly forward. I made good use of this advantage and completed her training by giving Karwip a sound foundation of dressage. For several years Karwip remained my favourite hunter and jumper and together we had much success in competitions. She taught me many things which were of invaluable help in my later career as a riding instructor. From her I learned about the close relationship between hunting and jumping and the advantages of hunting as a preparation for jumping competitions. But it is absolutely worthless and even criminal to go hunting if a horse has not already learned to carry his rider calmly and to obey. Hunting on a "green" horse, that is, a horse who has just begun to learn to carry his rider, will lead to the result that Karwip demonstrated so vividly in our first hunts.

A good teacher's endeavour should be to make learning as easy as possible for his pupils by taking advantage of their talents and abilities. Therefore he will first try to get a good knowledge of his pupils and find out about their weak and strong points. This is even more important with four-legged students for they have no gift of language and are unable to tell for what reason they fail to carry out the master's commands. How often did my own instructors fail to follow these fundamental pedagogical principles!

Once we rode cross-country with four-year-old stallions that had come from the stud farm to the Cavalry School for a short period of training and were to be tried out before they were to participate in some easier hunts. The instructor rode in front on his old charger and we tried to follow with those green horses, which had been ridden for a few days only after a short period of training on the longe. When he cleared a small brook a wild confusion broke out behind him. Each rider had a violent fight until one after the other succeeded in driving his horse across the water. At last three riders remained on the other side and the instructor continued with the remark that they would follow in a while. But the herding instinct can be relied on only as long as the "decoy" horses are in sight. Moreover, my stallion had a tendency to run away from any obstacle and carried me off a few yards. When I had succeeded in turning him back the two other horses had decided to jump the brook and had caught up with the group. I remained alone in front of the obstacle. My stallion's fear increased when he found himself deserted and he stood as though rivetted to the ground. And here the instructor committed a grave mistake. He dismissed the report of my comrades that I had not yet cleared the brook with the remark: "He will follow eventually," and rode on with the entire group.

There was no doubt that my young stallion was afraid. This fear cannot be overcome with the aids of legs, reins, or weight alone, especially not with a practically green horse. The correct method would have been to clear the brook several times with a calm horse just in front of the frightened one. The stallion would have seen that there was nothing dreadful about it since the other horse jumped without fussing. He would have followed and, having gained confidence, he would have given no more trouble the next time. But there I was left alone in a field which my stallion's hooves cut up as he pounded back and forth in front of the water. After a full hour's fight I succeeded in forcing him across but, green as he was, it was an uneven fight. Besides he was not at all cured of his fear and distrust and certainly gave much trouble to those who rode him later on.

When I was an instructor at the Cavalry School in later years I made a point of preparing my pupils physically and mentally for the hunting season. In four weeks of training the degree of difficulties was gradually increased with the result that they enjoyed hunting right from the beginning. When I say pupils I mean not only the officers but also their horses. Both needed the physical training to increase their suppleness and abilities and both needed time to gain their mental balance. Above all, the mutual understanding between horse and rider was to be established. The appreciation that the young officers expressed to me was, in fact, due to the horses who had taught me this understanding.

The famous French riding master de la Guérinière, who had such beneficial influence on the art of riding in Europe in the beginning of the eighteenth century, put it so pertinently when he wrote: "Be it a school horse, a hunter or a charger, the aim of training should be to make him quiet, supple and obedient, agreeable in his movements and comfortable for his rider who should be able to experience the greatest pleasure on his back." Is it not the wish of every rider, and especially of one who wants to go hunting and hacking, to enjoy his ride in the beautiful countryside as much as possible? Therefore he needs a horse that is comfortable, which is only the case if he is agreeable in his movements as a result of suppleness, calmness, and obedience. This underlines so clearly the fact that the various kinds of riding cannot be separated from each other and are all founded on the same basis. Only recently in England this was brought to my mind when there were complaints that the interest in hunting was slackening and that the number of riders participating in hunts was diminishing. Many beginners lacked the necessary basic knowledge and their horses were not sufficiently schooled. Since they could not cope with them in a hunting field they lost interest and gave up hunting altogether.

Having explained how beneficial hunting or riding cross-country is for show jumpers I want to mention that according to my own experience it is a very good preparation for dressage horses as well. Riding cross-country makes the horse go forward and this is more important for a dressage horse than it seems to be at first sight. Taking him out across the fields is the best stimulus and relaxation during concentrated training. It is an excellent remedy when the rider's demands have been too high and the horse has become stale. It offers the best opportunity to loosen the horse's mind and muscles and to brush up mutual understanding and confidence. No serious dressage rider should forego this advantage and he should use it as much as possible rather than employing some forcible means. He will be surprised by the effect. Just as a student in the midst of intensive work for exams is airing his mind in a long walk, so will a horse relax during a ride cross-country; he will gain new impulsion and return with fresh energy to the concentrated work in the arena. And all of a sudden exercises will succeed that before had presented unsurmountable difficulties.

On the other hand a well-trained dressage horse will be a good cross-country horse, too, provided his rider has an independent seat and does not make use of the reins to restore balance he may lose on uneven ground. This was demonstrated by my dressage horse Otto when I came home from the Olympic Games in 1936 and Chancellor Schuschnigg invited me to the St. Hubert's hunt in recognition of my success in Berlin. I had participated in several horse shows and had had no time or opportunity to train Otto out of doors and went to the hunt, as it were, straight from the dressage test. Otto remained wonderfully light in contact, he cantered in front of the hunting field as willingly as in the rear or at its side, and in spite of the long duration of the canter, to which he was not accustomed, he did not get out of breath. What better proof could he furnish of how much the training in dressage strengthens the horse and improves his condition?

The importance of an independent seat was demonstrated during an unforgettable hunt in Fuerstenwalde near Berlin in 1938. In order to spare my dressage horses, the commander of the Cavalry Regiment No. 9, Colonel Angern, offered me an Army horse for a hunt that was to lead over a particularly difficult course with many large ditches and wide walls and high fences. My horse was a Trakehner, the breed that came from Eastern Prussia, and was an excellent jumper but one with a very strong contact with the bit. In other words, he was a notorious puller. But I made him give up pulling in a short time because by giving the reins I prevented him from lying on them. On the other hand this enabled me to repeat the action of the rein and make him carry himself, instead of going on his forehand. This aid is possible only when the rider's seat is so independent that he may use the reins to guide his horse instead of holding on to them. After a while the Trakehner cantered calmly with a steady contact with the bit, much to the surprise of many officers who had had their troubles with him on previous hunts.

One of my most successful dressage horses, Nora, also helped to prove the theory that a well-trained dressage horse may be an excellent hunter at any time. With great pleasure I rode her in hunts at Laxenburg, which had formerly been an imperial summer residence outside of Vienna. Unfortunately I had to pay dearly for this experiment. Nora stepped into a rabbit hole and tore a ligament in her right foreleg. She was injured so badly that she never again showed the level and pure paces that are expected from a dressage horse. Within a short moment the work of years was annihilated. This is the reason a dressage rider should be more careful when his horse has reached an advanced stage of training and why today I seriously advise not taking a highly trained dressage horse on a hunt.

During the three years' course at the Cavalry School I participated in many horse shows with my own horses as well as with others that I was assigned to ride. It was good training to ride so many different horses and to have the opportunity to learn about their characters and temperaments as well as about their physical and mental abilities. An especially interesting case was a big horse named Broomhill that a wealthy gentleman had bought in Ireland. He did not get along with the horse, though, and in 1930 sent him to the Cavalry School to be retrained. All we young officers ardently wished to ride this superb chestnut whose qualities were so superior to those of our ordinary horses. To the great disappointment of the rest of us he was allotted to one of the favourite pupils of the instructor. But soon our disappointment was appeased when we witnessed the daily fight of rider and instructor with this gorgeous creature. Broomhill was an excellent jumper—if he chose to be. If he was in a bad humour, which was often the case, he knew how to make his own will prevail. His rider had so much trouble with him that three days before a show the instructor had to find another rider for Broomhill. I was chosen and when I rode him for the first time he jumped the course beautifully and without the slightest trouble. Quite obviously he wanted to demonstrate how well he was able to jump if he pleased. Consequently it was decided that I should participate with him at the International Horse Show in Salzburg.

I was not at all happy because I knew that most horses are somewhat careful with a new rider and try to know more about him before they begin to play their tricks on him. Moreover, I had but one day before the horses were to be put on the train to Salzburg. I decided to use my time in trying to get better acquainted with Broomhill. I took him out in the fields in order to give him as much opportunity as possible to look around and see unfamiliar things. When leaving the barracks we had our first disagreement. In a way I was not too much annoyed because it offered a chance to study his methods right away and not just when entering the ring. His method of resistance was to stiffen against the pushing aids and become slower and slower. At last he rose on his hind legs, whisked round, and rushed off in the opposite direction.

The experience of many years and with a number of horses had taught me that in this case it is absolutely wrong to lean forward and throw one's arms around the horse's neck as I had done when I was a boy. The important thing is to remain firmly in the saddle. I had learned also that a horse will rear when he is tense and reluctant to go forward. Giving the reins almost completely, I administered an energetic blow of the whip behind the girth, driving him forward both with legs and weight. Startled by this quick reaction he forgot to turn round and rush off but leaped forward and behaved like an angel for the rest of the day while we rode briskly through fields and woods. This single lesson seemed to have impressed him to such an extent that he did not try to give me any trouble on the only day of training we had before the show, much to the amazement of the other riders who knew him only too well.

On the next day, however, when my turn came, he tried to play his trick on me. In front of hundreds of spectators I felt my heart sink. In a single action I gave the reins, leaned back, and hit him with the whip behind the girth. He leaped forward, cleared all the obstacles without a single fault, and won the class. For the rest of the two months our cooperation was untarnished by any difficulties. We won another competition and became good friends until, well behaved, he returned to his owner, who received him with open arms.

The correct application of the aids of weight may be greatly supported by the appropriate attitude of the upper part of the rider's body and will allow him a much stronger influence on his horse. Such was the experience I gained in a Combined Training event in St. Poelten. In the midst of the horse show I had to replace a rider who had suddenly fallen ill and ride Conrad of the Dragoon Squadron No. 3. The Combined Training event may also be called Military and consists of three competitions: a dressage test, a cross-country course, and stadium jumping. All three must be ridden with the same horse either on one day or on three consecutive days, according to the degree of difficulty. Therefore it may be a One Day Event or a Three Day Event.

With this unknown horse I succeeded in the dressage test rather well and took off for the cross-country quite confidently. It led along the banks of a small river which was to be crossed at a determined point later on. All along the way I noticed that Conrad eyed the water with great distrust. He tried to edge away from it and ended up by moving sideways, bending his hindquarters away from the bank. His behaviour was not very reassuring for the prospective ride through the water! There, of course, it had to happen. Having taken every obstacle willingly and in good style so far he refused absolutely and determinedly to slide down the steep bank into the river. First he tried to run away, which I succeeded in preventing, and then he remained rivetted to the ground, his legs wide apart, his neck stretched out, staring as though mesmerized into the glittering water.

In the midst of these difficulties I had to leave the obstacle to make way for the following rider who was not to be hindered. When I rode a second time against the obstacle I managed to bring Conrad near enough so that his front legs stood on the upper end of the slide. Frightened by his own courage he wanted to run away to the left or to the right, which I was able, however, to prevent in time by the aids of legs and reins. Desperately he tried to rear in order to evade my influence. This was the crisis. Would I be able to take the obstacle or would I be defeated? I pressed my legs against his body, gave the reins completely, and leaned back as far as possible. Conrad's attempt to step back or to rear was nipped in the bud. Because of the pushing action of my upper body he was unable to lift his forelegs off the ground for more than six inches and remained in this uncomfortable position for a few seconds. Finally he followed the invitation of my whip and slid into the water. The points we had lost at this obstacle were retrieved in the stadium jumping on the following day. Conrad and I won the Three Day Event and received a beautiful trophy.

Among the experiences with my numerous jumpers I want to tell about my charger Cosmos. He was a strong bay with great jumping abilities but he had no courage. If there was a new obstacle he wanted to have a good look at it, sniff at it, and take in its height and width and degree of difficulty before jumping it. Having at last decided to jump he did it in very good style. There was no progress after cantering briskly forward cross-country or in the indoor school. Every new obstacle had to be inspected and Cosmos continued to stop in the midst of the greatest speed to eye it from all sides. Once familiar with the fence at last, height or width was no problem. On the other hand, Cosmos was too young to be jumped too much and I did not want to ruin his legs. At last I decided to build a number of miniature fences in varied forms and colours, none higher than three feet. I cantered Cosmos over these, changing continuously the sequence and the combination of the course, and changing also the time and the place of our exercises, so that everything should seem new to him. The low height of the fences allowed me to jump them often without harming Cosmos' legs until he cleared them fluently and without hesitation. When taken over the real course after this preparation, Cosmos was no longer worried about the different fences. There were no more difficulties even with the most unexpected combinations. Steadily he improved his form and together we earned many a beautiful trophy. Later I learned that at the famous Cavalry School of Hannover the jumping team was trained in much the same way. The success of its riders between the two wars certainly corroborated the psychological value of this method.

While Cosmos lacked courage in the beginning, the somewhat puny brown gelding Elk jumped with great impulsion and boldness but rather inexactly. He was fast and agile and never refused an obstacle, but his carelessness very often cost us a victory. In those days there was a new method for correcting these troubles. At the moment when the horse was above the jump, iron bars were brought up to knock against his hind legs or against his cannon bones or hooves to force him to lift his legs higher. This is called poling. A rider who poles his horse during training will easily be found out because the horse pulls up his hind legs in an unnatural manner at the moment of the jump. In some shows I have even seen horses that perform a sort of capriole when they are above the fence. Since I have always been opposed to forceful methods I wanted to overcome Elk's bad habit by more traditional means. Again work in dressage was intensified; by changes of speed especially and frequent halts and half-halts I tried to make him accept the tempo that I had decided on and prevent him from rushing up to the fence. By practising jumps over immovable obstacles I began to induce him to lift his legs, destroying his illusion that all he had to do was to touch the upper part of the fence in order to make it lower. By this method his style was gradually improved until he, too, won several competitions.

The most impressive proof of the importance of dressage for the training of a show jumper was given by Goetz, one of the best horses of the Austrian Cavalry School. He was a beautiful bay stallion of the Furioso line and the pride and joy of the federal stud farm. Although he would jump anything during training, he regularly let his rider down in the ring and his record showed little success. Very often he began to jump the course beautifully and in an impressive style and then all of a sudden he stopped at a fence and was not to be persuaded to jump before the rider was disqualified. Since the administration of the Cavalry School wanted to avoid disappointing the director of the stud farm, who had to decide which horses were given to the Army, every time Goetz proved a failure he was given to another rider in hopes that he might behave better with the new man. It was my turn in the autumn of 1930 when, at the International Horse Show in Salzburg, I was placed second and Goetz was mine for the next few months. Meanwhile I had reached the third stage at the Cavalry School, in which the officers worked mostly on their own, and so I began an intensive dressage training with Goetz because when jumping him I had noticed many gaps to be filled in this respect.

Soon Goetz began to show improvement. He was willing and eager to learn and in a short time his progress not only in the simple exercises but also in lateral work and work at the canter was such that the onlookers took him for a dressage horse and not for a jumper. Twice a week there was a jumping lesson under the command of the instructor. Goetz behaved beautifully and never failed at a fence although the demands were increased to obstacles of the "difficult" class. So I hopefully expected to be well prepared for the shows. Meanwhile spring 1931 had come and the season of the horse shows was drawing near.

Working intently with his horse and constantly observing his reactions quite naturally makes the rider more sensitive and alert. Thus I had the unmistakable feeling that the instructor was waiting for the slightest mistake in order to take Goetz, who had grown to be my favourite horse, away from me. We were always ordered to be the first to jump a course and very often were the only pair to make it. Once we even had to take a course of twelve obstacles from both sides, with the triple bar from the wrong side being as dangerous as the whole procedure was unsportsmanlike. A triple bar is a high, wide jump consisting of three bars, the first of which is the lowest and the third the highest. But Goetz mastered even this unfair test and did not refuse a single fence. The next day, though, the instructor approached me with an overly friendly smile.

"All these months you rode Geotz extremely well," he said. "I am going to report it to the commander of the school. We must all try to be sure now that Goetz will win in the coming horse shows. Therefore I will give him to Lieutenant W., who is smaller and lighter than you. Because of the enormous progress you will, however, continue to train him in dressage and Lieutenant W. will just jump him. . . ."

Bewildered I replied: "Lieutenant Colonel, will you please take this order back? I am a captain and not a trainer for Lieutenant W. . . ."

This was the end of my promising work with Goetz. The favoured Lieutenant W. rode him in the show without obtaining the expected success, though, and the annoyed instructor wrote into my report of the third stage at the Cavalry School: ". . . has attained the limits of his abilities. Cannot be considered for further advanced training. . . ."

What a difference between the two teachers! The memory of Goetz is still vivid in my mind. I think of him with pleasure and gratitude. But I could not forgive the instructor his unfair decision. Oddly, after my success at the Olympic Games in 1936, it did not prevent him from throwing his arms around me with the exclamation: "I am so proud of you. You were my best pupil!"

School Horses, the Most Important Assistants of the Instructor

During my period at the Cavalry School I had to ride the horses I have mentioned and also remounts, that is, young horses that had to be broken in. Besides, there were the school horses on which I was given one or two lessons daily and which helped me to understand even better how important the training of dressage is for every type of riding horse. In general a horse may be called a school horse if his training in dressage has reached such a degree that he is able to convey to the pupil the correct feeling for movement and balance and the subtlety of the aids. No instructor is capable of teaching this delicate language between rider and horse without the willing assistance of the horse. The young rider, eager to learn, may rely on his four-legged teacher whose importance sometimes even rises above that of the two-legged one. The privilege of learning on a school horse is an invaluable help for the rest of the rider's life. I will be forever grateful to my school horses, for I continued to learn from them when I was given no more lessons and was working on my own and also when I was instructing other riders.

A teacher will be successful with his teaching when he is understood and respected by his pupils. In much the same way a horseman will be able to learn from his horse only when he respects him as a creature and has affection for him. Since the horse cannot speak the rider must endeavor to guess his thoughts and to interpret his reactions and draw conclusions from his behaviour. Mutual understanding will also depend on how two creatures take to each other, which may be even more important between horse and rider than between human beings. Therefore the selection of a horse is a vital point in the future relationship. This knowledge, which I gained at the Cavalry School, was further extended at the Spanish Riding School.

There are horses who appeal to the rider immediately, whom he understands easily and likes in a short time. In such a case it is easy to adjust to each other; work becomes a pleasure; and success is certain to follow. But now and then a rider comes across a horse who is alien to him and whose reactions he cannot understand. He is quickly annoyed by repeated faults and naughtiness and often an aversion develops which compromises progress and success. Such an inexplicable aversion does not appear only in the rider but certainly also in the horse. This is why some horses who give nothing but trouble to one rider change completely with a new master and work with him in full harmony. The reason does not lie in the better abilities of the new rider and, therefore, must not be taken as a gauge of standards. It is the magnetism between two creatures, which cannot be explained by the intellect.

Matching horse and rider is an art founded on a profound knowledge first of all of the physical conformation, of the habits, and last but not least, of the characters of both partners. The stable masters at the royal courts of bygone days had to possess this knowledge to a high degree, for they had to choose and prepare the horses for their "highnesses." A prince had to be superior also in mastering his horse and it was unthinkable that he fight with him or lose his dignity and reputation by falling off in public. Therefore the books that the reputable riding and stable masters of old have left to us—there are only very few because not every good rider is a good writer and vice versa—are still of great value for us today. The horse still moves in the same way as always; he thinks and feels in the same fashion; and the conformation of his body is unaltered. He is the wonderful creature of nature as extolled in the Koran. The riding masters who attained such high and responsible positions had the duty and the leisure to study this product of nature profoundly. In every book on riding of those days there are detailed instructions about the horse's body and its functions, about stable management and saddles and bridles.

Today, however, few riders know their horses and the causes of their behaviour. Everything has become superficial nowadays, except technology. With machines the physical laws may not be disregarded as we often disregard the laws of nature with our animals. The well-founded doctrines of the old riding masters are frequently rejected today with the remark that these methods are old-fashioned and not applicable in our present times, which demand quick success. And what is the result of this fast training? The standard has declined until the once so beautiful movements have become caricatures of what they were. And yet a performance of the highest standard must be built up step by step and on a well-founded basis. I have learned by experience that today's riders may indeed rely upon the teachings of our predecessors, for they are of invaluable help in the reasonable development of this sport. If a rider thinks that he has found a new method he may be sure that if it is any good he has come upon it by instinct or by chance and that it was practised long ago by the old masters.

Speed at the cost of quality is always wrong, not only in riding. When the famous New York City Ballet performed in Vienna I asked the ballet master George Balanchine whether he would take the so-called modern conception into consideration when training his dancers and shorten the time of their education. Excitedly Balanchine jumped off his seat and exclaimed: "How could I? The human body is still the same as always. The old schools of ballet demanded a certain amount of time and they were right. Did they not achieve perfection and have they not been our ideals for hundreds of years? Why should we change?" It is exactly the same with equitation if it pretends to be an art.

But let us go back to a small part of this art, to the choice of the right horse for the right rider, which is a sort of matchmaking between the two creatures, and should be one of the most important concerns of any good riding instructor. Unfortunately only a few of my instructors possessed this tact. In most cases the horses were allotted in a rather superficial way. Very frequently the horses were exchanged in accordance with the obvious principle of giving the difficult horse to the more accomplished rider, which would have been the correct method had it not been for the fact that as

soon as the difficult horse had been somewhat retrained by the
good rider, he was returned to a weaker one. In a short time there
were new difficulties and the vicious circle began again. This method
made the riders lose interest and pleasure in their work and did not
allow a friendship to grow between horse and rider. The horse as a
teacher did not come into action.

Because of these frequent changes I remember only a few school
horses from my time at the Cavalry School. My first experience
was a negative one and rather discouraging. From the chestnut
mare Fanny I learned how vital it is for successful cooperation that
the two partners be sympathetic to each other and how dismal may
be the daily lesson if horse and rider do not meet in friendship.
As with every school horse, I had to ride her without stirrups for
several months. I did not succeed, however, in finding contact
with her and my vexation grew when, every day, she gave me
trouble, unseating me by sudden leaps and starts at the most
unexpected moment and at the slightest provocation. I could not
discover the reason for her behaviour or bring about a change by
calming her or administering punishment. With every new day it
became harder to remain patient. Eventually I took such a dislike
to her that I began to be annoyed the very moment she was brought
into the arena. Very probably she disliked me as much as I did her;
there was just no getting along with each other. And Fanny of all
horses I had to keep for such a long time! But even those nerve-
wracking fights had a positive result. I learned that the willing cooperation of our horses is not to be taken for granted and began
to pay greater attention to the psychological relationship between
horse and rider. This approach has been of great help to me in my
later career as a rider as well as an instructor.

Even though I was not able to get along with Fanny I grew
conscious of the fact that horses cannot all be trained after the
same set pattern. The phlegmatic horse should be taken with a
firmer hand and the willing horse, inclined to nervousness, should
be treated more leniently. Between the two there are a number of
nuances, of course, and I realised these contrasts especially when
changing from a lazy horse to a temperamental one and vice versa.
Clinging to habits as every human being does, I applied the aids
in the same manner and was surprised by the results. While the
first horse's nervousness grew into excitement, the same degree of

aids did not get the other going. As it is vital for correct and successful work to know one's partner intimately I adopted the habit, later, of eliminating difficult exercises when first riding a new horse. We are indulging our human vanity if we produce difficult airs and figures with an unknown horse. So I have also taught my pupils to take time to get to know their partners and also to give the horse time to grow accustomed to a new rider. I learned how to study the horse's movements, his suppleness and sensitiveness to the aids. I took time to understand his temperament, his character, and his capacity to learn. The horse should have the opportunity to grow accustomed to the difference in weight of a new rider, which might even be distributed in a different way, and also to the different nuances in the application of the aids so that they are understood completely. Horse and rider *must* first of all understand each other in the language of the aids before they can find understanding in the balance, rhythm, and tempo that are necessary for the harmony they should strive to achieve.

Rarely, and never in later years, did I allow the spectators to infringe upon this necessary period of getting to know each other, even if the onlookers were waiting eagerly to see how the horse—sometimes it was even their own—would go under the new rider. Nothing can prevent me now from riding an indifferent horse briskly forward in order to awaken him by changes of speed and make him take pleasure in his own movement. An excitable horse I calm by steady and almost sleepy work and coax him into finding his mental balance, which is as important to animals as it is to humans. By this careful investigation rather than with some spectacular exercises I am able to decide on the appropriate intensity of the aids, learn about the strong and weak points of the new partner, and can build up the training progressively. It enables me to reach my goal more successfully and more quickly than by rushing ahead. Having laid the foundation of confidence and friendship in this preparatory period, I have my horse "there" when I begin with the real work.

One should also consider the differing attitudes of different horses towards rewards and punishments. The tender little soul blissfully accepts the smallest caress, as was the case with Neapolitano Africa, who would have purred like a kitten had he not been a Lipizzaner stallion. The slightest rebuke, however, was a tragedy for him and he became nervous and anxious. The more materialistic horse obviously prefers sugar or other titbits to patting and stroking as if he would say: "Don't make all that fuss, go ahead and give me the sugar!" In most cases such a horse is much less impressed by a reprimand and easily digests a much stronger one. This knowledge of character is an important part in the education of a horse and a sound foundation for successful cooperation.

As I have mentioned, not every school horse is necessarily suitable for dressage competitions, but at the Cavalry School each dressage horse had to be used as a school horse outside the season of horse shows. In the second year of my appointment there I was lucky to have as my riding instructor Major Jaich, who was a successful dressage rider himself. He limited to a minimum the unpleasant changes of horses and riders and had great ability as a teacher. He was an excellent instructor who directed with tact and whose knowledge and method had sprung from practical experience. His best assistant was my school horse Greif. The two of them enriched and consolidated my equestrian knowledge to a great extent.

Greif was a big strong chestnut gelding with great intelligence and docility. Although his paces were not too brilliant, he ranked among the best school horses and was chosen to participate in the dressage competitions at the forthcoming horse shows in the spring of 1930. Thus a definite goal was given to my training and I accumulated valuable experiences in these lessons. Under the expert instruction of Major Jaich, Greif grew into an excellent teacher who took me through the dressage training up to the standard of a difficult class. On his back I learned lateral work in all paces, flying changes at every second stride, and pirouettes. The rider can learn these exercises only in this practical way and not from explanations of even the best instructor.

First of all I learned from this well-trained school horse that with riding the regularity of the movements has the same importance as the rhythm in music. To begin with I had to learn to feel this regularity and then to realise the difference whenever it changed and apply the correct means to regain this most beautiful feeling a horse can convey to his rider. Whenever his steps became irregular I could clearly feel it in the movement of his back and would then ride him briskly forward at a rising trot until he had regained his balance. When he made hasty steps I had to reduce his speed until tempo and rhythm were again regular. The most important thing was to take care not to disturb his balance with my seat. In this way I was able to maintain the same rhythm on the straight line as in lateral work. In lateral work the horse moves forward and sideways and his legs cross each other. It is a frequent fault in this movement that the horse either increases or decreases his speed. When I succeeded at last in maintaining the same rhythm whether increasing or decreasing the tempo and was able to bring about this difference by lengthening or shortening the horse's strides instead of making them faster or slower, I began to feel the full harmony of all movements. This difference of length in the horse's stride in the different speeds while the same rhythm is maintained gives brilliance to riding just as *fortissimo* and *pianissimo* give brilliance to music.

It was Greif who made me understand the flying change, that is, the flying change of lead in which the horse changes from, say, the canter right to the canter left without intermediate steps. The term right or left canter refers to the leading foreleg. For example, if the left foreleg is the one that reaches out, we speak about a canter left. Greif taught me that the rider should not attempt to indicate this change of lead to the horse by twisting his body or throwing it from one side to the other but by quietly changing the aids of leg and reins, on the condition—and this was the most important thing—that the horse moves in a lively collected canter. Thus Greif made me consider more seriously the basic gymnastic schooling of the horse, which is the foundation for more advanced training. If it is neglected, numerous difficulties will arise that will eventually hinder progress.

After a while I was able to induce Greif to execute a flying change without my aids being noticeable to the onlooker and to increase the difficulty of the exercise by repeating it after a given number of strides until Greif made a flying change after every other stride. If with all my other dressage horses later on I seemed to achieve flying changes without an apparent effort, I am indebted to Greif and the experience I gained in my work with him, which taught me never to neglect the basic schooling, i.e., the correct development of the paces.

Greif taught me also how easy it is to achieve pirouettes if the horse is in full balance. A well-balanced horse should maintain the regularity of his steps even in the smallest turns and in the pirouette should not change the rhythm of the canter but turn in regular bounds around the inside hind leg. If he loses his balance and consequently his rhythm, we have proof that the horse was not ready for this difficult exercise. The rider should concentrate again on cultivating the basic paces and ride briskly forward, executing changes of speed and small and large circles. He should practise extension and collection until the horse maintains the rhythm and the regularity of his stride even in small and smaller turns and voltes. Thanks to Greif again, there were never difficulties with my own dressage horses in the following years. After the conscientious preparation of the foundation, these difficult exercises seemed to drop into my lap like ripe fruit. And the success of my cooperation with Greif became apparent not only in my enriched experiences but also in the numerous trophies we won in various horse shows.

The second horse that I rode under the direction of Major Jaich was Jodo, a very good-looking chestnut gelding from the federal stud farm. He was the first horse that I had trained all by myself, beginning with the young remount and proceeding up to the standard of a school and dressage horse. Jodo was full of temperament and good will and he learned quickly and easily, but he had to be given enough time to understand what was required of him. Above all I had to be careful not to make him nervous. As a young rider I was full of zeal and ambition to achieve noticeable progress and so it happened repeatedly that I overlooked this point and made excessive demands on him. Fortunately I had Major Jaich at my side to interfere at the right moment and prevent me from making grave mistakes. I had to take Jodo into a walk, pat him and talk to him until he had calmed down. When he was quiet I was allowed to begin again very carefully with the exercises. The right advice at the right moment is of invaluable help but can be given only by an instructor who has learned by practical experience to adjust work appropriately to the degree of training.

However quickly I succeeded in calming Jodo when I conscientiously followed Major Jaich's advice, I had great difficulties in regulating his paces. At the trot he had a tendency to take hasty steps. In the beginning it was impossible to ride an extended trot, which is an increase in speed by taking longer steps and by no means faster ones. My instructor employed a method that led to success in this case but that was not suitable for every horse, as I found out later. He ordered me to push Jodo forward at the rising trot until he finally took longer steps and then to reward him by a period of rest at the walk. Gradually this method proved effective with Jodo and at the end of his training he was able to perform a very brilliant extended trot. But I did not obtain the same result with other horses, especially not with those with a high knee action, such as the Lipizzaners. When pushed forward energetically, they went faster but also were more and more hasty in their steps. They became nervous and excited and lost the regularity of their paces altogether. When talking about the Lipizzaners I will explain this phenomenon.

Having worked through the winter, Jodo and I entered several competitions and right from the beginning were first or at least among the first, which was rather remarkable inasmuch as these were my first dressage tests on a horse that, apart from my short episode with Napoleon five years ago, I had trained entirely on my own. During that year of 1930 I was successful in all the horse shows in dressage tests as well as in jumping competitions—until a fall laid me up for many months.

I had to take a young Thoroughbred mare over a course for the first time and she was so excited about this new experience that she rushed like mad up to a fence that had a bar across the top. She did not jump high enough and the bar got caught between her front legs and we both rolled on the ground. The fall itself would have been nothing serious but when we both had scrambled back on our feet she kicked out with both hind legs—out of fear or anger, I never knew—and hit me in the back. I went down as though struck by a lightning, was unable to get up, and was carried out of the arena with a crack in my spine. It was a very painful injury and took a long time to heal, but there was also a positive side to it. When at last, after having been partly paralysed, I was able to ride again, I had to give up jumping altogether because I could not lean forward. So I concentrated on dressage riding with all my zeal and ambition, although in the beginning I had to be lifted into the saddle.

Three years later I rode school horses again when I was posted as a student to the Spanish Riding School. And there for two years I had the privilege of learning from the Lipizzaner stallions. The

Spanish Riding School is the oldest riding academy in the world. Its existence may be traced back as far as 1565. Formerly a property of the imperial court it was taken under the control of the Department of Agriculture after the fall of the Austro-Hungarian monarchy in 1918 and continued its work of cultivating the classical art of riding. Every year the best officer of the Cavalry School was sent to the Spanish Riding School for about six or twelve months of more advanced training.

In these Lipizzaners I encountered extremely intelligent and powerful teachers who registered the smallest fault in seat or guidance and were forever ready to take advantage of their students. This "dangerous" intelligence was compensated for by the immediate advice of the riding instructors. In the daily lessons each of the three head riders dealt with a single pupil at a time, who rode a stallion that the instructor himself had trained and ridden, and with whose character and strong and weak points he was thoroughly familiar. Consequently he was able to give the appropriate order the very moment it was needed. This is certainly the most ideal method of instruction for a rider.

Up to my appointment to the Spanish Riding School my lessons had taken place in groups—one might call them classes. The instructor had to teach eight to twelve riders at a session. There were several possibilities for organising these lessons. The instructor could take all pupils at the same time, which more or less restricted the lesson to commanding the paces and exercises and allowed only very brief corrections of the single rider. In most such cases the lesson was hardly more than a shouting of "Trot!" or "Walk!" and the possibility of learning was also very limited because each student had to pay attention to the other riders. The horse as a teacher hardly came into the picture even if he possessed the capacity. An alternative was that the instructor took on one pupil after another, correcting the worst faults of the rest who worked on their own in the meantime. If he was fair and just and wanted to give each rider the privilege of this private instruction, there were not more than five to seven minutes to give to each, a span of time far too short for even the best teacher. This was in theory. In actual practice most of the instructors concentrated on a few favourite students and did not pay too much attention to the rest.

What a difference there was in the detailed and thorough instruction at the Spanish Riding School! Each of the school stallions had a personality of his own, which was marked by the personality of his rider, who had formed his individual character. The basis of the training was the same for all of them and yet the personal touch was unmistakable. Every four weeks I had a new school horse and a new instructor and I had to adapt myself to this change. The slightest difference in the training also had a repercussion on the training of the other dressage horses which I rode in the afternoon in the Prater, a large natural park on the outskirts of Vienna. Usually they took a few days to adjust themselves to the different nuances of the aids.

Riding master Polak was a great pedagogical talent, as just in giving reprimands as in giving praise. He expressed his commands in precise form and knew how to encourage the rider and give him confidence. His horses, too, went in much the same way. They were light and steady in contact and followed the slightest command. Temperamentally they were as easy and cheerful as their trainer, who was a great music lover and played the violin excellently.

Head rider Zrust had great instinctive knowledge about his horses. He was very calm with his students and followed the rule that what cannot be obtained now will succeed without effort some other day. Instead of criticising he preferred to say something agreeable, and when a pupil could not cope at all with a stallion, he mounted him himself and by the influence of his seat and legs solved the hardest problems without difficulty. His horses, however, were not as easy to ride as those of Polak and were also more difficult in temperament. They demanded an extremely quiet seat and a well-balanced application of the aids of reins and legs. But when they went well they conveyed a wonderful feeling to the rider.

Head rider Lindenbauer was an industrious man and very serious about life in general and riding in particular. He was not satisfied with himself very often and therefore did not believe in expressing any approval. The student heard hardly anything but criticisms until he succeeded with his exercises, which usually took several lessons and sometimes made him feel quite discouraged. Lindenbauer's horses went in a similarly severe manner: they demanded a correct seat, strong aids of the legs, and a firm contact with the bit. They were more work to ride inasmuch as they gave nothing without being obliged to do so, which corresponded exactly to the outlook on life of their master.

It is to the credit of the three great head riders that they preserved the standard of classical riding at the Spanish Riding School even after the breakdown of the Austro-Hungarian Empire. They continued the tradition that had been handed down through generations and they did not merely talk about it but lived it. They proved it true that the character of the rider forms his horse both physically and mentally. Under their wonderful tuition the stallions themselves grew into great teachers who helped to spread the fame of the time-honoured Riding School. From all over—from Sweden, Hungary, Germany, Switzerland, Denmark, and even Mexico—officers came to the School to learn the classical art of riding.

My first instructor was riding master Polak, who in my eyes was the best rider and unsurpassed as a teacher. My first school horse was Pluto Kerka, who reminded me immediately and unmistakably that the reins were for the horse to be guided and not for the rider to hold on to. When my contact grew too strong he leaned on the rein with all his weight or he rushed off. He could not have demonstrated more clearly how important it is to have an independent seat. But when I was able to accomplish the giving and taking action of the reins, sitting upright and bracing my back, Pluto Kerka would move with enormous impulsion and give his rider the completely new feeling of controlled power. This wonderful feeling was lost the moment the legs did not remind Pluto Kerka that the horse will move in full balance only when the hind legs carry a sufficient proportion of the weight of both horse and rider. In this respect there was much to be learned from Pluto Kerka that, as I have mentioned before, was of great help also when hunting.

Speaking about the feeling that Pluto Kerka gave me, it was by no means as I described it right from the beginning. When I rode him for the first time he surprised me by his smooth but at the same time extremely powerful movements, which I had not yet experienced with any horse. Riding without stirrups, my seat, I admit, ran into trouble, especially because the stallion was rather small and my legs are very long. When I shifted my weight about trying to regain my seat, I irritated Pluto Kerka and immediately received the message in the change of his movements. When I tried to reestablish my balance, he struck off into the canter instead of continuing his regular trot, or worse, he moved in a passage-like hovering trot that disconcerted me even more. I almost had the impression that I was on a horse for the first time in my life. I felt completely at the mercy of this ardent Lipizzaner stallion and I would never have thought that this could happen to me after all those years of riding experience. The wise old truth that with riding there is never an end of learning did not help much in this situation.

Riding master Polak, however, knew how to comfort his pupil: "Don't worry, Captain. This has happened to every new rider here!" and began to correct my seat. I had to lower my heels and sit deeper and heavier into the saddle until my weight was distributed equally on both seat bones with my spine vertical to the center of the saddle. This is how he helped me to find my balance and with Pluto Kerka calming down at once I regained my mental balance, too. Now the stallion knew what I expected from him and was no longer disturbed by my uneasy seat.

The most important thing I learned in these first lessons at the Spanish Riding School was that it does not count so much "what" is done as "how" it is done. As in any other sport, in riding it does not matter what kind of exercise the horse is executing but in what manner he performs it. But soon it dawned upon me that the correct "how" is the most difficult thing on earth. On Pluto Kerka I had to learn all over again how to break into a trot or strike off into the canter. But this time with the correct aids of seat and legs, which means that the onlooker has the impression that the rider is thinking and that the horse is executing his thought after an imperceptible communication. How difficult it is to fulfill this simple demand was proved in those first lessons with my two new masters.

Polak severely controlled my seat in all transitions and Pluto Kerka did not strike off into a canter, for instance, before he had approved of my aids and found them correct. And so it happened that in spite of years of experience on horseback I was sometimes incapable of striking off into a canter! Either I allowed the stallion to become too fast at the trot which preceded the canter, or I applied the reins too firmly and he happily offered a passage. I admit that I often felt completely ignorant and like a beginner but then on some other occasion I heard Polak's "Very good!" and picked up courage again. Maybe I was not as incapable as I sometimes felt. Gradually Polak's words of praise came more and more frequently and my despair decreased in the same measure. I was proud and pleased when after a few weeks I was able to take Pluto Kerka correctly through the corners, to execute well-rounded voltes and other exercises, and to achieve smooth transitions of paces and speed.

Perhaps it sounds strange to speak about a round volte since a volte is a small circle of six yards diameter and every circle is supposed to be round. Although a circle is supposed to be round, a volte is not always that way, as is often proved in dressage tests. In a correct volte the horse is bent in his whole body according to the circle and the inside hind leg should step under the center of gravity and therefore be bent more than the other legs, which demands a greater effort. If I did not apply Pluto Kerka's outside rein sufficiently, he turned his head too much to the inside, and if in addition, my outside leg did not hold him on the track, his hind legs would not step into the hoof prints of the forelegs. Consequently his hindquarters swung to the outside and soon there was no longer a round volte but a many-sided figure. These voltes caused more headaches to us pupils than the later execution of the most difficult exercises, which we were to learn comparatively quickly on the foundation of this minutely detailed basic training.

When I was able to perform these simple exercises according to the demands of classical riding and to the satisfaction of my instructor, Polak gradually increased the degree of difficulty. Finally, as a reward at the end of the lesson I was allowed to ride a passage on Pluto Kerka. Passage is a solemn and impressive movement which may be compared to a trot in slow motion. In the beginning, Polak with his whip supported my leg aids, which are particularly important in this pace, for the passage is dependent on the lively activity of the horse's hindquarters. Later I had to rely solely on my own aids when I wanted to enjoy having my stallion float weightlessly above the ground. The Lipizzaner has a special talent for the passage. If he is correctly trained he cannot be equalled by any other horse in this brilliant and expressive pace. Maybe this is the reason why at the Spanish Riding School the passage is called the "Spanish step"!

Lipizzaners may be very cunning, too, if they find out how to make life easier for themselves. There was the stallion named Maestoso Borina, who reached the unheard-of age of thirty-three years and whom I kept in retirement in the stables when I had become Director of the School. Under his master, the head rider Zrust, he was able to show a very brilliant passage, but one day when he was being ridden by an elderly civilian student, I saw him perform a rather strange movement which with some imagination might have been taken for a passage. Lifting his front legs high and slowly as for a passage, he followed with his hind legs at a comfortable walk, swinging his back in such a way that his rider bobbed up and down in the saddle. When I pointed out this extraordinary sight to head rider Zrust he winked at me and smiled: "Just leave him alone! Why shouldn't he? The old gentleman is happy because he thinks he is riding a perfect passage—and the stallion does not tire himself out!"

Polak's favourite was Favory Montenegra, to whom I owe a great deal. He was a gorgeous stallion, very graceful and remarkably intelligent. Under his master he was capable of performing piaffe and passage with a perfection I was absolutely unable to achieve. Either my seat disturbed his balance, to which he reacted immediately with less elevated steps, or I applied the reins too strongly so that his hind legs were pushing more than carrying the weight and the movement was no longer floating. Often I was in despair of ever reaching perfection, but then for the fraction of a second I felt how the stallion became higher in front and as light as a feather before this extraordinary sensation was lost again. When I succeeded in controlling my seat and guiding the stallion with ever lighter contact, these moments were more and more frequent until Favory Montenegra effortlessly floated above the ground in a piaffe and passage of such brilliance that the spectators at the morning training broke into spontaneous applause although this was not at all "done" in those days. When Polak nodded "beautiful" in my direction I felt royally rewarded. Forever will I be grateful to these two great masters.

Most of my lessons with head rider Zrust were on Conversano Nobila. I was allowed to ride him even though he went under his master in the Sunday performance. As he gave me quite a bit of trouble I learned from him how to ride the more difficult horses.

But when I succeeded in making him understand what I wanted, he gave me the wonderful feeling of a passage full of impulsion. Presently I found out that there was a difference between his passage and that of Pluto Kerka. Pluto Kerka bent his forelegs in the front knee and lifted his forearm until it was horizontal to the ground before putting it down in a beautifully round motion which gained little ground to the front. Conversano Nobila lifted his legs in the same way but stretched them out more before putting them down in a longer and more forward action. I was told that the first kind is called the "round" passage and the second kind the "long" one. Later I found out that horses with a high knee action have greater ability for the "round" passage but that in the extended trot their legs do not reach forward to a very great extent. Those that are capable of a brilliant extension in the trot tend to perform a "long" passage, which is what we see with most dressage horses since they are generally half- and Thoroughbreds and very seldom Lipizzaners.

This description should not, however, give the impression that I was riding the paces of the high school, among which we count the passage, right from the beginning of my lessons with head rider Zrust. On the contrary, it took a long time to obtain this privilege because at first I had great difficulties with Conversano Nobila. I was unable to collect him because he was inclined to go above the bit. Lifting his head and losing contact with the bit, he dropped his back and by this attitude made it impossible to execute any exercise correctly. Zrust had infinite patience with me and I was intent on following his example. I pushed Conversano Nobila carefully forward with both legs and tried to absorb the impulsion with my braced back and the reins well applied. He was supposed not to increase his speed but with a beautifully shaped neck become short in his whole body—collected is the technical term.

Finally I succeeded in achieving this form when riding on the large circle, and was able to begin work on the track in the whole arena, trying to maintain this collection when performing various exercises. If I lost it again I had to return to the large circle, where it is easier to obtain collection because of the increased bend of the horse's inside hind leg. Thus I realised the meaning of collection, which might be compared to the mental concentration of a human being. If the collection was assured, if Conversano Nobila accepted the bit in the correct attitude and position of head and neck and his hind legs stepped sufficiently under his body, then even the most difficult exercises succeeded without apparent effort. If I did not obtain the correct collection, horse and rider were covered with sweat without obtaining a satisfactory result. This proves how important it is to prepare the horse correctly and how much of the daily work should be devoted to this preparation. It consists of the correct execution of the simple exercises such as straightening, loosening, and relaxing the horse, physically and mentally, until he is concentrating completely on his rider. At this point the rider may collect his horse and then even the most difficult airs of the high school seem easy as play. Conversano Nobila was the first Lipizzaner I rode after being appointed Director of the Spanish Riding School in 1939, thus renewing an old friendship.

It was a special mark of distinction when head rider Zrust entrusted his favourite horse, Conversano Savona, to my care. In the performances he presented this beautiful stallion in the levade in the pillars and in hand and sometimes in the most superb manner under the rider. For many years Conversano Savona had been the best in levades. In the lesson he had to be led with very delicate aids and not disturbed by any awkwardness for he was full of temperament, which he preserved until his old age. If Conversano Savona worked especially well with me, I felt very happy and his master also beamed. As a reward I was allowed to perform a levade with this wonderful Lipizzaner.

In the levade the horse rises on his lowered hocks with his forelegs tucked under him and remains motionless for a few seconds in this position. Many equestrian monuments depict horse and rider in this attitude—for instance, that of Prince Eugene of Savoy which stands on the Heldenplatz in Vienna. In bygone days the airs above the ground, that is, exercises in which the horse lifts his forelegs or both fore- and hind legs off the ground, belonged to the training of every school horse and every rider. They may be seen on many old etchings and paintings. Today they are preserved in their living form only at the Spanish Riding School.

The correct levade is developed from a lively piaffe in which the hind legs will step more and more under the body until the weight is finally shifted onto the hindquarters and the forehand is lifted off the ground. I had a strange feeling when Conversano Savona did his first levade with me. He lowered his hindquarters as if he was going to sit down and lifted his forelegs until his body formed an angle of forty-five degrees to the ground. I sat on an oblique basis and had to maintain unaltered the position of my body vertical to the ground. If I leaned forward ever so little Conversano Savona ended his levade. The same happened if I took my body behind the vertical line. To me he seemed like a juggler who will try to step under the center of gravity of the object he is balancing. It was yet another proof of the eminent importance of balance in any kind of equitation.

When head rider Zrust died in 1940 I took Conversano Savona under my special protection and tried to make his retirement the pleasant one he certainly deserved. In hand he showed the levade for many more years and gave pleasure to thousands of spectators from all over the world. When he died this great stallion from whom I had learned so much was twenty-nine years of age, which was the best proof of the correct training by his master. For like any other gymnastics, riding should strengthen the horse and prolong his life.

With head rider Lindenbauer it was chiefly Pluto Austria that I had to ride in the lessons. This stallion demanded that the aids be given in a particularly strong manner. Besides he had an inclination to go above the rein. He carried his head high and payed more attention to what was going on around him than he did to his rider. Because he raised his head and neck too high he dropped his back and consequently could not step sufficiently under his body with his hind legs. If this was the case his movements became very uncomfortable, so rough and difficult to sit that I bumped clumsily on his back. The more heavily his rider hit the saddle the higher he raised his head and neck and the more he dropped his back. It was by no means a pleasure to ride him, especially not with the criticisms of the instructor as a musical background. Once dismounting after such a lesson without any tangible result and having saluted head rider Lindenbauer according to the tradition of the School, I sighed in complete dejection. "I think I better give up riding altogether," I said. "I am never going to learn it!"

Lindenbauer was all the more vexed by this remark. "Nonsense, Captain, you should have more confidence in yourself!"

This put the lid on my discouragement and I replied: "Even if I had had confidence in myself this lesson today would have shattered it completely. But it's my nature that I am hardly ever content with myself!" Smiling at last, Lindenbauer shook my hand and said that he could understand me so well because he, too, was always so strict with himself.

At long last I succeeded in riding Pluto Austria energetically forward and by repeated short actions of the reins made him accept the bit with a lowered head and a long neck until he arched his back and his hind legs were able to step sufficiently under the body. This made the correct collection possible and I could sit comfortably and with a good feeling at last.

There was another school horse who gave me some trouble. His name was Maestoso Africa and not Maestoso Austria. The reason I mention this is because a book was published with the title *Maestoso Austria* when I was Director of the School and many visitors came to see this famous stallion. They were very disappointed when all I could show them was either Maestoso Africa or Pluto Austria. A stallion with the name of Maestoso Austria has never existed at the Spanish Riding School.

Maestoso Africa was a problem for me to ride because he was very small and I had great trouble placing my long legs and putting my knees in the correct spot. Since the aids of my legs could not be fully employed I was reduced to giving the aids mainly with the weight of my body. This was quite difficult in the beginning but helped to establish an independent seat. After a while Maestoso Africa and I got well on together and I was very pleased when head rider Zrust asked me one day teasingly whether I would not want to be transferred to the Spanish Riding School and employed as a rider since I rode Maestoso Africa better and especially in a more brilliant passage than his own rider. Although said as a joke this remark was a sign of esteem which any instructor should express to his pupil at the right moment. When I was an instructor myself I followed this example whenever appropriate praise was justified.

During the two years in which I was stationed at the Spanish Riding School as a student I had the opportunity of studying the characters of both horses and riders and, in the twenty-six years during which I was responsible for the School as director, I enlarged my knowledge considerably. Just as human professors de-

velop into real characters in the course of their long lives, so did
the four-legged teachers who all year round had to submit in obedience to their trainers and also to endure the awkwardness and
clumsiness of the students. It was certainly no pleasure to have to
begin all over again with each new pupil, forever feeling the
wrong kinds of aids and suffering an incorrect seat that irritated
the balance. But because they were personalities they found out how
to take it easy or to play tricks on their riders, as did Generale
Malaga, a school stallion who had been trained by head rider Zrust.

Generale Malaga's specialty was pirouettes. With great skill and
perfection he performed this exercise, which is the smallest turn at
the canter. Once there was a dressage rider, a lieutenant colonel
who had encountered difficulties when he wanted to teach these
pirouettes to his dressage horse. He came to head rider Zrust
for a few lessons in order to learn the correct feeling of this exercise. He was a very good-looking officer and quite arrogant. He
brought his wife to the School so that she would be able to see how
well he would execute the pirouettes right at the first attempt. He
mounted Generale Malaga and began to limber him up, disregard-
ing Zrust's corrective remark that he should not take his upper body
so much forward. He replied simply that he was used to riding like
this and that the position of the upper part was a matter of taste and
varied according to the individual. Zrust shook his head and pointed
out that the stallion was accustomed to the rider sitting in the manner traditional with the classical art of riding, and that he was
unable to feel the aids of the seat if the rider leaned forward. The
lieutenant colonel shrugged and retorted: "He will have to get accustomed to it. After all, I am the boss!" Zrust lifted his shoulders as
was his habit and said that Generale Malaga was sufficiently
warmed up and the officer might begin the pirouettes now.

Full of enthusiasm the lieutenant colonel followed the suggestion. He paid hardly any attention to the commands of Zrust and
rode as near as possible to where his wife sat so that she would
be able to admire his beautiful pirouette at close range. Generale
Malaga, however, obviously thought that it was too much to insist
on pirouettes without exercising the appropriate influence with the
correct seat. In the middle of the turn he performed a tremendous
leap and the rider sailed through the air. Zrust winked an eye
towards me: "A hair's breadth and Mandi [this was what he

called the stallion] would have landed him in his wife's lap. Why didn't he believe me when I told him that he should sit more upright?"

By the way, the stallions were not at all impressed by any kind of uniform. They unseated the lieutenant colonel in mufti just as readily as the major in uniform even if he came from across the ocean. The Mexican Major Rodriguez was stationed at the Spanish Riding School for two years and later was for many years the teacher of the famous and successful Mexican jumping rider General Mariles. He, too, was deposited in the sand, by Maestoso Sardinia, after a short altercation, but got on his legs with the agility of a cat, bent down, and said to his instructor with a smile that he had wanted to pick up his whip which he had dropped. Thus he saved his face and avoided paying the usual fine of ten pounds of sugar. The instructor did not dare to contradict the foreign officer.

We have already talked about the cunning Maestoso Borina. He did not limit his tricks to the arena but expressed his personality at every occasion. When he was advanced in age he was included among the happy few who appeared in the floodlights of the Vienna State Opera. In the opera *The Girl of the Golden West*, to the melodies of Puccini, he had to carry the famous singer Maria Jeritza onto the stage. She was an accomplished rider, and he made an excellent appearance as he entered with graceful steps and stood like a monument while the artist sang her aria. It was a most impressive scene, and Maestoso Borina seemed thoroughly to enjoy the special applause he received. Soon he knew his part so well that he was not to be held backstage and pushed ahead when the music for his scene began. One day there was a rolled-up carpet in his way. Madame Jeritza, very excited, demanded that this obstacle be removed, and in that moment the music set in. There was no holding Maestoso Borina. With determination he cleared the obstacle, much to the dismay of the lady on his back, and precisely on time, he appeared before the public, which greeted him with applause while his rider tried to recover breath for her song.

Having grown old and wise, Neapolitano Montenuova ranked among those conscientious creatures who take their work very seriously and know exactly what they want. This stallion had been trained by head rider Lindenbauer, who tenderly called him Peppi, which in Vienna is short for Joseph. He had enhanced the school performances by his great abilities and the beauty of his movements for more than twenty years. In his old days—he reached the age of thirty-one years—his task was to examine the candidates for careers as riders at the Spanish Riding School who, until 1944, came from the Army. While willingly following the commands of good riders and executing all exercises with his habitual submission, he found out the weak ones with incredible instinct and embarrassed many a rider who took himself for a great artist.

There was another of these characters who helped him as a co-judge. Pluto Siglavy had formerly performed caprioles and his trainer Polak had called him Schatzl, which means "little treasure." Having reached the age of twenty-two years, he no longer appeared in the performances but continued to serve as a school horse. He was more severe than Neapolitano Montenuova and when he encountered a clumsy rider he wasted little patience on him. With a tremendous capriole he set an end to this unpleasant experience and landed the all-too-hopeful candidate in the sand.

On one occasion I was confronted with a difficult situation. I had to choose one candidate from two young riders of approximately equal qualifications. Together Neapolitano Montenuova and Pluto Siglavy were brought into the arena. Both riders mounted at the same time and rode in accordance with my commands, which gave me the opportunity to compare their abilities. Again they seemed quite equal and the decision was really hard to make. All of a sudden Pluto Siglavy came to my rescue and spilled his rider. I was glad to have support for my decision, but in order to be absolutely just, I had the riders change horses. What followed now was totally unexpected. Maybe Pluto Siglavy was annoyed by this additional work and, remembering the pleasure and relief of a capriole, after a few minutes landed the second candidate in the sand, too. Thus he evaded his responsibility and left the difficult decision entirely to me.

Oh, those school stallions—there is no end to stories and anecdotes about them. I have certainly learned to respect their personalities and to acknowledge them as teachers. On the other hand they become teachers only when the rider endeavours to understand their reactions and their behaviour. Since they cannot speak they are limited to signals. Perhaps many a rider may even be called lucky that they are unable to speak because they would often have occasion to put in complaints about incomprehension, ignorance, impatience, injustice, and ingratitude. Instead they serve man in silent and irrevocable loyalty.

My Dressage Horses

Although I have already pointed out the difference between a school horse and a dressage horse, it seems necessary to say a few words about dressage in general. In my opinion the expression "dressage" for the systematical physical training of the horse is not at all well chosen and may even lead to confusion. The word may induce the non-expert to think of the dressage of a poodle or of teaching the horse a number of tricks such as may be seen in the circus.

In the Austro-Hungarian monarchy with its many different nationalities and languages, terms and expressions had to be kept as clear and simple as possible. For instance, what is called a dressage test today had the name of "prize riding" in those days. It may remind us of what we call a "Grand Prix de Dressage" now. When I was a boy I remember that among cavalry officers of the Army prize riding was generally called "riding for style" or "beautiful riding," which, perhaps subconsciously, best expressed the deeper meaning of this kind of riding.

The rider should sit in beautiful style and his horse should move beautifully and in harmony. The noblest of all sports was in former times an essential means of education and today should not be restricted to seeking ribbons and trophies, for then it is no longer an education but the mechanical exhibition of tricks showing a few spectacular exercises only. Since the word dressage, however, has come into official use nowadays, it seems vital to stress that it never means anything else than a performance which has been built up through systematic physical training and in which the two creatures have blended into one. It is a performance in which the rider thinks and the horse executes the rider's thought. The horse should be guided by his rider in such a way that the onlooker is unable to detect any aids nor should the horse realise that he is being guided. Both horse and rider should present the image of two happy creatures.

When my time at the Cavalry School had come to an end, I was posted to the Dragoon Squadron No. 2, which was stationed in Vienna. My jumpers and dressage horses, with whom I had been successful in the past years, had to remain in the institute as the officers of the Federal Army were not allowed to have horses of their own. It was not easy to find a suitable charger among the horses of the squadron for I am tall and they were mostly rather small Thoroughbreds. The most suitable I could find was a four-year-old bay mare from the Burgenland, the Austrian province on the Hungarian border. Her name was Nora and she was by no means a beauty, being big and rather coarse, but she had lovely, expressive paces. Her walk was like a tiger's and her trot was smooth and of great impulsion. During the winter I worked her in the indoor arena and introduced her to the basic dressage training. She was willing and understood quickly and there were no difficulties worth mentioning. There was no trouble with the turn on the haunches in which the hind legs are expected to move on the spot in the unchanged rhythm of the walk. Trot and canter were regular and full of impulsion; the transitions and changes of speed were fluent; and transitions into the walk and later into the halt became smooth and supple. Nora conveyed to me the wonderful sensation of absolute control when upon the aids of my braced back alone she came to complete immobility out of a brisk canter or trot.

Since her collected trot had become very supple by the frequent transitions from the halt or the walk and changes of tempo there was no trouble with shoulder-in. In the beginning I demanded a few steps only and rode forward in an animated trot to take new impulsion. Gradually I was able to ride longer periods of shoulder-in and having mastered this exercise it was no problem to execute half-passes correctly. Because of her elastic canter there was no difficulty in teaching her the simple change of lead. Exactly as my school horse Greif had taught me, I tried to render the collected canter more elastic and impulsive by frequent changes of speed both on the large circle and the straight line. By transitions into the walk and into the trot and striking off again alternating the leading leg, Nora was taught to concentrate completely upon her rider and to react at once to the aids. The technical term for this immediate reaction is instantaneous obedience. After a while I began to reduce the number of these steps at the trot until Nora performed the change of lead smoothly after a single step at the trot and struck off correctly into the canter left or right. Of course I rewarded her for even the smallest progress—patted her neck and allowed her a rest in a period of walk. As she was a very sensitive lady and eager to please me, these recompenses and my gentle words of praise stimulated her much more than the sugar she received after work every day.

By now, Nora had reached the standard of a dressage test of the medium class and I planned to participate with her in the horse shows in the spring. As was the custom in the Army, I needed official permission to enter in any test. This was given by a military commission and was to prevent officers from appearing in public with horses not sufficiently prepared or not up to the standard of the competition. When I had presented Nora in a test before this commission the cavalry inspector informed me: "This horse is very well trained indeed but her looks are so poor that she is not eligible to be shown in public. I cannot give you the permission to enter in this competition. This is not a suitable charger for a captain. In fact, this horse should be discarded from the Army!"

Crushed by this verdict I passed a sleepless night and by the next morning I had decided to remain loyal to Nora, whose willing cooperation had grown into a friendship and to continue my work with her.

While I had started my work with Nora, I was instructor at the squadron for the remounts. I had found out that their training improved very quickly by rides cross-country and even in the beginning I often took them out every day. The Vienna Woods with their wide fields and hills were not far away from the barracks and we all enjoyed these rides. The success was remarkable and became especially obvious on the occasion of the first visit of the cavalry inspector. The group of older remounts, who were mostly worked in the indoor arena, quickly failed when the inspector made unexpected demands for which they were not prepared. My young horses, on the contrary, felt immediately at home in the arena although they were hardly used to it, and they took every obstacle put before them without hesitation and full of impulsion. It was a pleasure to see how calmly and especially in what balance they moved about in the ring. On principle I rode a remount myself on these cross-country rides because I knew from my own experience at the Cavalry School that it is unfair if the instructor is on a better horse than his pupils and that he can give an example only if he rides under the same conditions. My remount was a delicate little mare by the name of Swallow, who had to be the first to canter up and down hill and jump over ditches and fallen trees.

In order to prepare these rides and reconnoitre the various courses, I used to take Nora out into the country and used the opportunity to make her familiar with uneven ground and to increase her impulsion and balance. Back in the indoor school I found the same improvement with her as I had with the group of remounts. I was surprised by her progress and the pleasure she took in her work. She was relaxed in mind and body.

General Arthur von Pongràcz—he had been adjutant of the Emperor Franz Joseph for many years and was well known as a dressage rider—once came with us on one of these rides on his Turidu, with whom he had participated in the Olympic Games in Amsterdam in 1928 and with whom he also took part in jumping competitions. Incidentally, the general had held the record in 1902 for the highest jump. After the ride he said with appreciation: "Well, I'll be d . . . d! For many years I have not cantered up and down such steep hills! Surprising how calmly these young horses are following the commands of their dragoons. I am most impressed!" Many years later the general was still talking about this cross-country ride.

The basic training is much improved with young horses on these cross-country rides if the rider is not content simply to be carried through the landscape but rides his horse with intelligence. Many incidents occurred during these rides which have enriched my experience with horses much more than any theoretical lesson. Once we rode through a shallow groove the bottom of which was filled with water. We took our time and gave the horses a chance to have a good look at the situation. Most of them remained calm and looked at the water with long necks as if they wanted to drink. Another began to throw up the water with his front leg, much to the amusement of his rider who suddenly found himself in the mud because after this overture his horse lay down and began to roll in the water. My shout of warning had come too late. If a horse begins to scrape the ground with his foreleg it is a signal that he is going to lie down. This is very important for every rider to know when he rides through water.

The basis which I gave Nora by riding her cross-country alternating with work in the arena was built up in the further course of her training to the standard of high school. In the meantime I had been assigned to the Spanish Riding School and had considerably enlarged my knowledge. I had been taught to do work in hand by riding master Polak, who was a genius in this field. It was a great help with my training of Nora and made it possible for me to teach her piaffe. Piaffe is a trot on the spot, an elastic and dancing movement that is supposed to look easy and effortless and yet is a great strain on the horse. This difficult exercise should not be begun before the horse has gained sufficient strength by systematic training and is smooth and relaxed in all his movements. At first the horse should be given an opportunity to become familiar with this new demand without the weight of the rider. The trainer leads him on the short leading rein alongside the wall in a lively trot which he collects more and more, shortening the steps until the horse puts his feet forward at a hoof's breadth only and finally trots on the spot. In between the horse is taken forward at a brisk trot in order not to lose the impulsion without which it is impossible to obtain a correct piaffe. The horse would just step about on the spot. The description of the piaffe sounds so simple but it is difficult to teach and takes a long time and above all demands infinite patience and tact on the part of the rider. In the beginning he must content himself with the smallest progress, be forever patient and ready to accept a setback in his work. Again the doctrine "I have time" is the best counsellor.

In the autumn of 1933, one and a half years after Nora had been refused permission to enter in competitions, she had mastered all exercises that are demanded in the Grand Prix, the test ridden at the Olympic Games—all, that is, except the flying change of lead at every stride. This flying change at the canter was disapproved of by the Director of the Spanish Riding School in those days because he proclaimed that it did not count among the exercises of classical equitation. Consequently I had not learned it during my attendance at the School. I hesitated to ask General von Pongràcz to teach these one-time changes to Nora because so far I had trained my horse all by myself and did not want to depart from this principle. I remembered, however, that the general had told me some time ago that on the occasion of the Olympic Games in 1928 the riders of the Hungarian team had come to Amsterdam without being able to perform changes from stride to stride, which were on the programme for the first time, because they assumed that the riders of the other nations would not be capable of executing this "unnatural" movement either. Much to their surprise they discovered that almost all the other participants performed this disputable flying change. In this plight the captain of the Hungarian team, who was a comrade of General von Pongràcz from the days of the Austro-Hungarian Imperial Army, turned to him for advice and asked him how to teach this air to a horse. "Oh, this is very simple," was the answer. "You strike off into the canter right and into the canter left and you go on repeating this until the horse performs a change from stride to stride." This advice was not much help to the Hungarians, though, because the time was too short and, as General von Pongràcz remembered it, they withdrew their entry and did not participate in the Grand Prix in Amsterdam.

This story came to my mind when I found myself in a similar plight and had no one to turn to for advice. For some time I practised a great deal of canter, striking off frequently and alternating the canter right and left. I shortened the intervals between the strike-offs gradually more and more until one day Nora performed two successive changes. Overjoyed, I dismounted on the spot, rewarded her lavishly with sugar and caresses, and sent her back into the stables. On the following day I repeated the exercise with the same result and the same reward. On the third day, when I struck off into the canter Nora performed immediately two perfect changes from stride to stride. Now I knew that she had understood but this time I did not send her back into the stables because

she had to become used to executing these changes at every stride
upon my command and then continue her work. When the flying
changes were quite established and succeeded every time I demanded them and in different places of the arena, I was able to
repeat them as often as the dressage test demanded and even as
often as I desired.

The recompense of this serious and steady work with Nora did
not fail me, and she matured into a great horse. Having become
wise by experience I avoided presenting her at a standstill where
she still was no beauty. But once in motion, the play of her
muscles, her balance and impulsion, and her absolute relaxation
were of such striking quality that the spectators completely forgot her somewhat coarse looks. A year later, at the horse shows
in Vienna, I was the first Austrian to win international dressage
competitions for my country after the First World War. One day
after another of these victories the cavalry inspector approached
me with the question: "What is this exquisite horse with which
you won again today?" It was with some satisfaction that I answered, standing to attention: "It is the horse that you wanted discarded from the Army, General!"

With this "discarded" horse I was sent, together with General
von Pongràcz, to the 1934 Concours de Dressage in Thun (Switzerland) by the Equestrian Federation of Austria in order to defend
the colours of my country in the Grand Prix against the best
riders of Europe, which included the highly favoured German
dressage riders. It was the first time that I had entered in a competition in a foreign country and I was more than excited. I
was also more than pleased for I was third with Nora in spite of the
extremely well-ridden and also very beautiful horses of the other
competitors, who had already had opportunities to make reputa-
tions for themselves in previous horse shows.

The Zurich paper *Sport* wrote on July 2, 1934: "With Nora,
a horse was placed third whose qualities become apparent only
when you look at her at close range. Her conformation is nothing
extraordinary and not at all brilliant. But in motion she displays
correctness, impulsion, and balance. Her best moments were in the
half pass on the center line at the canter. Captain Podhajsky impressed by the sensitiveness of his aids."

I mention this episode for a special reason. It underlines better than all explications to what degree constant and serious work may improve the outward appearance of a horse and how the performance wins over beauty. This should be engraved in the minds of young riders especially. Beauty alone does not guarantee the success of a dressage horse; above all it is his rhythm and balance in all movements. There is no appeal in beauty if the creature is not capable of moving correctly and gracefully. Correct training renders the horse more beautiful, the great Greek riding master and philosopher Xenophon said four hundred years before Christ. The improvement of the physical form is the result of any intelligent and well-developed gymnastics. Although it cannot turn an ugly duckling into a gorgeous swan it can make it into an attractive personality. Nora's successes were convincing and nobody ever thought of calling her ugly any more. To me she had never been ugly because I knew her wonderfully straight and decent character, her tenderness and her loyalty, and because I loved her.

With Nora, whom I had trained from a green horse to the standard of high school, as I did all my dressage horses later on, I had entered a new phase of my equestrian career. The human instructors who had helped me during my stay at the Cavalry School and again one and a half years later at the Spanish Riding School were no longer at my side. From now on I was alone with my four-legged partner, with no one to give advice. I was on my own to overcome difficulties and, what is more, to recognise them in time. Although I possessed a well-founded knowledge, the question was whether I would be able to employ it effectively. In this new phase of my work I lacked a vital element, which is the control or check by an expert on the ground. Every rider needs this control of his seat, of the movements of his horse, and, above all, of his feeling. It is well known that faults are far easier to combat at the moment when they first appear than when they have become established habits. First this control is exercised by the instructor and later, with advanced riders, among each other. The more I advanced in my performance, however, the less I could rely on the control of other riders. It is an old truth that methods applicable to one case fail in another. To teach me the correct way to find the right remedy for each individual case was from now on the task of my dressage horses.

It was General von Pongràcz again from whom I learned how to counteract the lack of control. The general had his horses stabled in the barracks of my squadron and participated in many horse shows and, at the age of seventy-two, represented Austria in the Grand Prix de Dressage at the 1936 Olympic Games in Berlin. Often he rode in the arena at the same time as my groups and I had the opportunity to observe him at work. He, too, was conscious of the necessary control of his work and relied upon his groom to whom he had given minute instructions what to watch out for in the various exercises. I still have the scene before my mind's eye. Pongràcz tried to execute pirouettes with his Georgina, whom he rode later in Berlin, but he did not obtain a satisfactory result. At least this is what the groom thought for he demanded that the general repeat the exercise. This went on for some time until the general brought the horse to a halt and asked with his deep voice: "Nowotny, have I a pleased expression on my face, at least?" I listened, intrigued, and inquired at a later occasion about the meaning of this question and the general declared: "Listen, you are young, I will give you a valuable piece of advice! You must keep in mind that the worse your horse is going, the more pleased with yourself you must look. Then the judges will think that you are very satisfied with your horse and will give you better marks. You will have the look on your face controlled just as your seat!"

Inspired by the general I have accepted the control by my groom from then on and with success. Of course I had him control not only the "pleased" look on my face but above all my seat and the movements of my horse. When I was made Director of the Spanish Riding School I did not want to disturb my former teachers, the three head riders, Polak, Zrust, and Lindenbauer, or the other riders whom I trained myself in their work, and so I consulted my grooms, especially Flasar, who had been at the Spanish Riding School since 1924, and who for me was an excellent and sincere critic. His remarks always hit the point and he knew my horses and me so well that very often before a horse show or an important performance he would whisper into my ear: "Don't be nervous! The horse is all right, if he does not go well now it is because you have made him nervous!"

Of this active interest in my work there grew a trifold friendship among horse and rider and groom that was based on sincerity and which became a blessing for all of us. Flasar spent many hours in the stables with the horse and was able to study his character much better than I could in the daily work of one hour's duration. He could best judge from his behaviour whether I had made too great demands on our four-legged friend and call my attention to this fact. Every experienced rider knows how a good groom will make the horse calm and confident and how much of the successful work in the arena may be annihilated by rough and unreasonable treatment in the stables.

To what extent Flasar felt part of my work was revealed to me on the occasion of the Olympic Games in London in 1948. After the dressage test in which we were not successful I came to see my horse Teja in the stables and gave him his usual ration of sugar. Flasar looked on and nodded his approval. He said that I was right because Teja had deserved his sugar for he had given his best. Turning to the horse he sobbed: "How lucky that you don't realise how unjustly you have been treated today!" In the end, although I was downhearted myself, I had to cheer up my tearful groom.

With my honest Nora I learned how to build up the work progressively from the simplest exercises to the demands of high school, and it was she who paid for the mistakes I committed out of ignorance and that my later dressage horses have been spared. She taught me the great importance of impulsion and relaxation for every dressage horse and how these two qualities have to be in true relation to each other so that all movements remain smooth and supple in spite of brilliant extensions. General von Pongràcz was the only one whom I allowed to ride Nora before she terminated her career after her accident at the hunt and served as a school horse. When he dismounted he said enthusiastically that he had never ridden a horse with smoother and more pleasant movements. "At the extended trot she gives the feeling as if she would go on rails!"

When I was later instructor at the Cavalry School, Nora's important role was that of an assistant. She helped me to explain the correct application of the aids. She simply did not take any notice of wrong or inexact aids and by her constant behaviour and precise reactions she soon gained the reputation among my pupils of the best school horse of the institute. When I was transferred to the regiment after several years I had to leave Nora behind at the

Cavalry School. She was needed as a school horse and my offer to buy her was turned down. It was a sad occasion when I heard that a year later she was sold to the owner of a larger butcher shop in Vienna. It hurt me to see her under her new master in the Prater Park. He weighed well over two hundred pounds and took every opportunity to show off with her high school movements and rode piaffe and passage with growing enthusiasm. All my efforts to buy Nora from him were in vain. He refused obstinately for he had never had such a good horse. And Nora? She was not asked. . . .

In the years during which Nora rose to the top, another trooper accompanied our way, the dark brown Thoroughbred Kunz. In contrast to Nora he was pretty and dainty but could not equal her in the least as far as impulsion and movements were concerned. I realised that impulsion is not necessarily innate in Thoroughbreds, which years later was confirmed by another Thoroughbred by the name of Bengali. Kunz had reached approximately the standard of a dressage test of the preliminary class and by his intelligence and willingness made work easy and pleasant for me. Easily and quickly he learned the flying change as the canter was his strong point. When he was able to perform a single flying change of leg correctly there was no problem in repeating it after a given number of strides so that we could enter in a dressage test of the difficult class after a few months of training.

The trot, however, remained his weak point because he lacked impulsion and besides his stride did not cover sufficient ground to the front. By riding briskly forward at the rising trot and the appropriate gymnastics of changes of speed and transitions from trot into the canter and vice versa I achieved an increase in impulsion. In spite of this improvement, however, I was unable to fill the gap in the natural abilities that had been denied to him. With Kunz I learned that the flying change is developed from a correct canter, that is, from a lively canter in which the hind legs jump well under the body of the horse and I used this experience in my training with Nora. If the rider insists on beginning with flying changes before this condition is met, his work will be far more difficult and besides many faults will appear which later will be hard to correct or eliminate. In most cases the horse will become crooked or not jump a full stride with his hind legs or not in the same rhythm with his forelegs. Instead of performing the change in a smooth forward bound he will execute it nearly on the spot; this gives the impression of hopping clumsily and is also most uncomfortable for the rider. When with Nora I noticed such unpleasant varieties I discontinued the training immediately and for a while practised changes of speed at the canter and paid special attention to her hind legs, which were to jump briskly and energetically under her body. The result of these gymnastics was striking when after a while I tried again to execute flying changes and they succeeded immediately and without further effort.

With Kunz I was able to enter in dressage tests and jumping competitions in a relatively short time but decided after a while to exchange him for a younger charger because I had always been of the opinion that impulsion and going forward were the conditions of successful work. But impulsion and good paces must be given to a horse by nature. With one of the sergeants of my squadron, Kunz continued to appear in horse shows and I was pleased with their success. By the way, because of Kunz I had to swallow a rebuke by the commander of my squadron one day. We marched out for a parade in the center of Vienna and since it had just rained, the cobbled streets were very slippery. As it was winter, our horses had sharp studs screwed into their shoes but nevertheless they went with uncertain steps. I commanded the first platoon and rode behind the commander of the squadron. Kaerntner Street was thronged with curious spectators for the Viennese loved parades and especially the cavalry. As we rode along feeling like heroes at the acclamations, I suddenly heard a terrific noise behind me. It was the sound of sabre and helmet clattering on the pavement. Turning round I saw my sergeant together with Kunz flat on the ground. Both jumped to their feet in a moment; nothing serious had happened. The commander turned round also and hissed: "There, you see how carelessly your men ride, with the reins not sufficiently applied. What a mess!" No sooner said than a few steps further on his horse slipped and he, too, found himself on the ground with his horse beside him.

In place of Kunz I chose Otto, a four-year-old gelding of the Furioso line. He was a big horse, almost black with beautiful far-reaching paces, and had not yet had any training. I was pleased about this because it is so much easier to train a young horse from scratch than to try and retrain an older one who has had time to acquire bad habits. If Nora's training had not presented any serious problems, Otto's education made up for it.

When I began to ride him I made use of all my experiences and followed the principle of riding him forward briskly and allowing him to seek contact with the bit with a long neck and lowered head. The initial progress was quite promising so that I thought he would be a worthy successor for Nora, who was well advanced in her training at that time. Subconsciously I allowed Otto a lower position of his head and neck than my other horses had adopted and heard a good amount of criticism and advice from the older rider-comrades. Finally I gave in and tried to raise Otto's head and neck and give him a more elevated position. With the result that he who had been so willing began to be resistant. In spite of his good paces he lost all impulsion, his reluctance grew, and at last he refused to go forward altogether. In excitement he raised his head too high and came above the bit. If I tried to ride him forward energetically he pressed himself against my pushing aids and finally rose straight up on his hind legs. The difficulties increased in the same measure that he became conscious of the means with which he could give me trouble. Once when I tried to give his head a lower position, he pushed me with all his weight against the shaky rails of a bridge in the Prater Park and increased his effort at each action of my rein so that, looking down at the water rushing under me, I was forced to dismount. I felt utterly defeated and the disgrace was not to be obliterated by the weak consolation that he who is cleverer will give in.

When I was assigned to the Spanish Riding School I complained to riding master Polak about my trouble with Otto and he was immediately willing to help me. He mounted Otto in the Prater Park and when he did not get along with him on good terms he took him on more severely. There was a short but violent fight. Otto reared up straight and when this did not impress Polak, he carried his rider under a tree and squeezed him against the branches. Helpless Polak was at the mercy of the big strong horse. His attempts to bring Otto away from this spot remained without result and at last even this great riding master had to give in and dismount, bleeding from the nose. Exhausted and out of breath he stammered: "He is a suicide! Rather than yield he kills himself—and his rider!"

On my own again I decided to choose the long way and begin the training all over again from the very start. In life, sometimes, one has to return to the crossroads when one discovers a mistake before being able to continue on the right path. The time it takes to make such a correction effective is twice as long as that of the training that has been correct from the beginning and it may never suffice to eradicate the faults. Therefore, it is vital for the rider in the course of his training to check again and again whether he has not digressed from the correct method.

At first I tried to make Otto forget his habit of rearing. The only effective means was to give the reins completely, to lean back with the upper body and administer a sharp blow with the whip near the girth. Otto leaped forward, which was the first success because his rearing was the result of not going forward. After a while he understood that his bad habit did not lead anywhere and gave it up. With infinite patience I continued on the way his training had begun but it took a long time until I was able to calm him so that he gave up trying to come above the bit and I had to ride him carefully forward with a very long neck and low head. This gave him the chance to use his hind legs with more energy and carry my weight better. He forgot his reluctance to go forward and gradually there was more impulsion in his stride. I was satisfied with infinitesimal progress and rewarded him amply with sugar and kind words. His confidence was reestablished slowly and as before he neighed softly when I entered the stables. Although hardly noticeable, there were favourable results, and on the basis of these I continued his training with the utmost care. Above all I tried to avoid anything that might irritate him so that he himself did not seem conscious of the difference in his behaviour.

This bitter experience with Otto taught me that the rider must never give more elevation to his horse than is allowed by his conformation and the stage of his training and by no means by taking his head and neck up. Otto was young and in spite of the fact that he looked to be a strong horse, he had a weak back like most young horses. When I raised his head and neck his back began to ache and induced him to defend himself with what, given his intelligence and personality, were rather vehement means. After this disaster I allowed him time for his development and tried to obtain the elevation in the natural way and make him raise his head and neck by an increased action of his hindquarters. Now his back was well arched and able to carry the rider. He felt no discomfort or pain and there was no reason for resistance. As time went on he forgot his bad habits completely and was willing and cheerful at work. In a way, these battles had consolidated our companionship.

In fact, half a year after his fight with riding master Polak in the Prater Park, we won a dressage test in a horse show in Vienna. It was only a competition of the preliminary class but Otto pleased by his impulsion and the correctness of his movements and, to my relief, by his happy submission. In the following year he appeared in medium tests and won them: another year was sufficient to bring his training further along and allow him to participate in the competitions of the difficult class, which he won also against famous riders and accomplished horses. Otto had become worthy of his stablemates, my dressage horses Nora and Nero. At last he reached the highest standard of a dressage horse. He mastered the Grand Prix de Dressage and was taken to Berlin in 1936 as a reserve horse for the Olympic Games. Even though it was not necessary to replace Nero at the games, Otto was first at the great horse show in Aachen a few weeks later. This was a remarkable accomplishment because most of the riders had come directly from Berlin and he had to measure himself against Olympic participants. In 1937, however, we had to part from each other. The cavalry inspector offered me Teja, the Hungarian half-bred, and I could not afford to decline this mark of distinction.

In Otto's training I had to put up with much disappointment, sweat, and vexation before reaping the reward of success. Nevertheless, the experience I gained for the training of difficult horses was of such value that I count Otto, too, among my great teachers. The work with him and the failure I suffered in its beginning taught me to turn away once and forever from forced training and to give true measure to the factor of time!

This reminds me of the cavalry inspector of the Austrian Federal Army. When inspecting any cavalry groups, General Hoeberth used to ask the dragoons what they had to do when the command "Strike off into the canter" was given. The answer the general expected was: "First of all I think that I have time!" When I was a young officer I was inclined to smile about my superior officer and take this stereotype answer as his peculiar whim. In the course of years, however, I realised the deep meaning of this ready-made sentence. I understood its wisdom and learned to apply it to many other things besides the strike-off. The phrase "I have time" should prevent the novice with his limited equestrian knowledge from giving sudden and violent aids and help to avoid having horses run away as often happens when the command "Strike off" is given. Looking back on my personal experiences I would like to impress this "I have time" upon all riders who have run into trouble with their horses and have come to a standstill in their training. "I have time" should be the guiding word especially of every dressage rider during the entire course of training and remind him of the fact that the goal of the classical art of riding is to be attained only by the gradual increase of demands.

During the first year of my attendance at the Spanish Riding School the cavalry inspector offered me another horse in addition to my two chargers Nora and Otto. It was Nero, a German Thoroughbred whom Count Seilern had bought as a race horse for ten thousand marks but, disappointed, had sold to the Austrian Federal Army for two thousand schillings because he was no good for the fast work on the racecourse. Nero first came to the Cavalry School but the commander did not want to keep him because Nero manifested no ambition and courage for jumping and seemed to lack completely the impulsion necessary for a dressage horse. I accepted the offer eagerly because the horses were allotted in a very modest measure as the Federal Army could not afford to pay high prices or buy too many horses. The reaction of the public was brought to my knowledge a few days later when head rider Lindenbauer received me with the following words: "What is this new horse of yours? Everybody in Vienna is laughing about this poor little sausage you have acquired."

I knew that Nero was by no means a striking beauty. But he had good paces which, however, became visible only when after much coaxing he decided to go forward. As he was very reluctant to do so, strong aids were necessary to make him move. It was quite clear to me that only due to these deficiencies had I been given Nero and that public opinion did not give me much chance. I clenched my teeth and began to work.

In the very first week there occurred an incident that did not

First encounter.

Olga, my first teacher.

Lumpi's levade is being admired

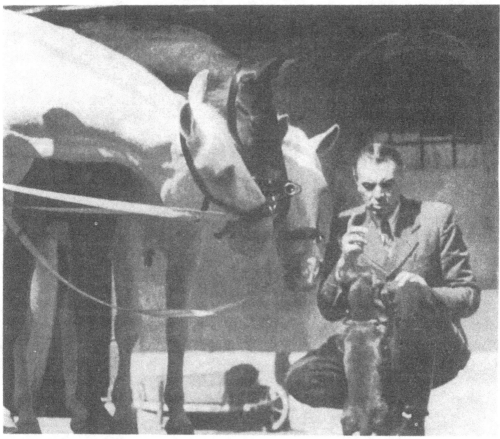

Work on the longe

With Neger into battle

Parade on Elk at the head of my platoon

Karwip at a jumping competition

Hunt at Schlosshof

Riding master Polak on Neapolitano Adriana in a levade

Head rider Zrust on Conversano Brezovica in a courbette

Head rider Lindenbauer on Conversano Bonavista in a passage

School stallion Conversano Savona in a levade

First success in dressage with Greif

"Poor little sausage": Nero at the beginning of work

Nero after one year's training

Nero wins the bronze medal at the Olympic Games in 1936

Twenty-year-old Nero in a brilliant passage

Nora, who was to be discarded, wins over international horses

Strong-minded Otto

Rokoko, a young lady without problems

Faithful little Judith

The ardent Teja in an extended trot

Teja conquers Ireland

A graceful little Englishman, Forty Winks

Valentine, a promising English Thoroughbred

help to encourage me. Nero had been brought into the stables of the Wilhelms barracks near the Prater Park in which both my other horses were stabled for the two years during which I was assigned to the Spanish Riding School. One night for no explicable reason Nero took a great fancy to the tail of his neighbour, Nora, and instead of sleeping spent his time chewing it until in the morning the groom found Nora in her stall with her tail almost bald. Our dismay was even greater because it was a few days before a horse show and Nora was no beauty anyway. My anger about Nora's disfiguration was overshadowed by the worry about Nero, who stood in his box exhausted and indifferent to his surroundings and refusing any kind of food. We tried to make Nora presentable by attaching an artificial tail to her dock, which succeeded surprisingly well and made it possible to participate successfully at the horse show. For Nero we had to call the vet, who diagnosed a beginning jaundice after having observed him for two days. Nora's tail had certainly not agreed with him and he was laid up for more than four weeks as a consequence of his strange appetite.

Such was the discouraging overture for our work together, but nevertheless Nero soon became a good-natured and willing friend who tried to do his best to follow my demands. He was very intelligent but easily frightened and, as I have mentioned, very reluctant to go forward. This was the first thing to cure because in the beginning he manifested a desire to go forward only when he came on green grass. In this moment he began to tremble in all his limbs and tried to rush off. There was no doubt that this behaviour was due to the memory of the racecourse, which evidently he did not cherish. But after a while he understood that he was not going to race and relapsed into an indolence that was sheer laziness and drove me to despair. The point was to wake him up, to make him move out of his own impulsion without making him nervous and excited. For this work I preferred to ride into the Prater Park where I could take long straight lines, for at this stage any turn has the effect of slowing down. Within a few weeks progress became visible. Nero began to take pleasure in these rides cross-country and no longer trembled at the sight of the green meadows. Neither was it necessary to push him all the time. When alternating these rides with short periods of work in the arena I endeavoured to preserve the impulsion I had so painstakingly obtained and did not think of shortening the tempo for the moment. With great care I made Nero familiar with the sitting trot but switched to a lively rising trot as soon as he seemed to lose impulsion. To my great surprise and pleasure Nero began to reveal that he was capable of extraordinarily beautiful movements. Intensely cultivating his impulsion made it no longer necessary a few months later to push him. Nero himself took his impulse from my legs and seat and developed a forward urge that surprised those riders at the Cavalry School who had slaved to make him go forward. With this initial success and his increasing eagerness to learn, Nero made work a pleasure and achieved progress for which I had not dared to hope. It is one of the basic principles that all movements and especially the collected paces can be developed only from going briskly forward.

With no other horse have I obtained success so quickly as with Nero. Hardly eight months later, at the age of six, at the 1933 Concours de Dressage in Vienna, he was placed second behind Nora against international riders in a medium test and appeared with honours among the top half of the competitors in the difficult class. Nero attracted the attention of the experts and was no longer ridiculed. Nobody ever thought of calling him a "poor little sausage" any more.

Two years after his first appearance, Nero won the Grand Prix de Dressage in Budapest, which was organised by the FEI and in which the best riders of Europe participated. On that occasion the well-known German hippological expert Gustav Rau wrote about him: "The greatest surprise of the day was the victory of Nero, who belongs to the Austrian Federal Army and who was ridden by Captain Podhajsky. This Thoroughbred gelding had not yet revealed his future greatness at the Concours de Dressage in Thun last year. But here, in Budapest, he placed himself in front of the best dressage horses of Europe. . . . Nature and Art have joined to create a horse and a rider that give joy and pleasure to everyone. In these two the honourable old tradition of the Austrian cavalry has lived to see its rebirth!"

And this was the same Nero whom only one year before the critics used to call a "long-legged gelding without charm and personality." Correct work had made him more beautiful, his muscles had developed, and he moved cheerfully and powerfully in balance and harmony. He was, once again, like Nora, convincing proof that systematic and methodical work will result in the increasing beauty of the horse.

In another year, 1936, Nero and I won the bronze medal in the Grand Prix de Dressage at the Olympic medal won by Austria in the first and so far the only Olympic medal won by Austria in equestrian competitions. Nero's performance was of such harmony that the thousands of spectators who were packed into the stadium were spellbound. The Berlin paper *Sportwelt* wrote on August 14, 1936: "Right at the end we were fortunate to see a superb performance when Major Podhajsky (Austria) presented the German Thoroughbred Nero. Many experts expected to see him win the gold medal. Horse and rider lived up to the great reputation which preceded them. The rider impressed by his excellent seat and the lightness with which he guided his horse. All movements were perfect, there was a tremendous charm in this performance so that with many spectators Nero was the favourite for the gold medal. . . ."

If he did not win it, it was due to the German judge who marked him down as the most dangerous competitor to the German riders, who in Nazi Germany evidently had to win at all costs. When ten days later the majority of the participants of the games went to the Aachen show, Nero confirmed the excellent form he had displayed in Berlin and won all the dressage tests.

He also gave a touching proof of his obedience. From the beginning of our work, Nero's greatest problem was jumping. At the mere sight of an obstacle he stopped, trembling, and neither good words nor energetic aids were capable of drawing him nearer, let alone getting him to jump. It had cost infinite patience to persuade him to take the obedience jumps demanded in dressage tests. Again the motto "I have time" had proved the best counsel. Nero had to take a good look at each fence. If he knew it well from all sides and had seen another horse take it several times, he was convinced at last that nothing could happen to him and finally decided to jump. Moreover, his hooves were extremely brittle and broke easily and I was forced, therefore, to limit jumping to the minimum. But later, together with the progress in the rest of his training, he became more and more obedient. This obedience helped him to overcome his fear and take any obstacle I presented to him. He had confidence in me and knew now that I would not ask anything from him that could do him any harm. In order to spare his delicate hooves for the Olympic Games, I had not dared to jump him over a fence for a whole year. And now in Aachen I was supposed to make him jump as a proof of submission at the end of a dressage test of the difficult class. I am sure both our hearts throbbed not with joy but with anguish. But Nero followed my command willingly and with determination took the fence necessary for the victory.

It is interesting to note that when Nero was retired five years later, he cantered with me at the head of the Lipizzaner stallions through the Lainzer Park every morning and without hesitation was the first to jump ditches and fallen tree trunks. He had unlimited confidence in me; he knew that I would never ask anything he was not capable of.

In spite of his abilities and his excellent character, Nero was a little sissy and easily frightened by all sorts of things. Besides jumping fences the various pots of flowers used for decoration on a show ground were a rich source of his fear and so were the three white lines drawn along the center of the dressage arena for Olympic tests so that the judges could check the straightness of the horse. At first sight of them he stood still, shaking with fear, or he tried to jump over them, jeopardising his marks. I found out after a while that he did not pay any attention to these lines and crossed them willingly if he had had the chance to take a good look at them beforehand. Consequently I had similar lines drawn on the arena in which the horses were warmed up for the tests. Snorting and with his forelegs wide apart, he eyed them suspiciously and thoroughly but then, in the test, passed over them as if they did not exist. This preparation was successful only if the lines were drawn in exactly the same way and with the same material. If not, his complex became immediately apparent.

On one occasion, after a dressage competition, Nero bore testimony for my method of training and for my style of riding and settled a question in an excellent manner. Against my habit and conviction I allowed the Swedish Colonel Clas Cederstroem to ride him. I was not at all certain how this experiment would succeed since for years nobody besides me had ever ridden Nero. Besides I was informed by the Swedish riders that the colonel had not sat on a horse for many years. With my heart in my mouth I watched the colonel begin to ride the simple exercises. Lateral work followed and his face gradually turned purple when he increased the demands up to the airs of high school and performed piaffe and passage. But everything went well and when he finally dismounted he was satisfied and said with a big smile: "I was one of your judges in this competition. You have just won the free style test and with full justification. And yet I myself have been unjust to you when in the scoring I noted that Nero seemed at times to have too strong a contact with the bit. Now that I have ridden him myself I realise my mistake. Nero's contact is so steady that it may look as if it were too firm. However, he is ideally light in hand!"

Talking about judging at dressage tests I want to say a few words on the subject. It has always been and will always be difficult to judge dressage tests, as is true for all decisions when the performance cannot be measured with technical instruments and the verdict is left to the experience, honesty, and tact of the judge. This manner of judging should necessarily imply a much better understanding between riders and judges. Having participated in numerous horse shows throughout Europe and overseas, both as a rider and as a judge, I have been in a good position to gain experience in this matter.

As a rider, I have known the conflicts that may arise from an unjust or wavering verdict, especially if two scorings contain remarks of completely opposed meaning or if I discovered, for instance, that one of the judges was unable to decide at first sight on which side the horse was stiff. Apart from the fact that they create confusion in what should be clear and simple and comprehensible to all, such divergent opinions cannot give a line of conduct to the rider. For the judge should be an advisor who helps the rider in the execution of his work. In order to fulfil this task the judge should be able—or should have been able—to practise what he has to judge; in other words, he should himself be a rider at the same level. In former times this was taken as a matter of course because sufficient accomplished riders came from the cavalry schools and cavalry regiments to act as judges. Nowadays, however, it is a serious problem because there is a real lack of qualified persons.

As a judge I have on various occasions been confronted with the difficulties of this responsibility, and I have come to the conclusion that not every good rider is necessarily a good teacher or a good judge. However, it is impossible for a man to be a good judge if he has not been a good rider in the category which he has to judge. The attempt to ignore this fact has led to a sad state of affairs almost everywhere: today, judges no longer enjoy the same appreciation and authority they used to have and very often they themselves have brought about this loss of prestige by their superficial knowledge and incomprehensible verdicts. In most cases—with the exception of the winner—the riders are dissatisfied with their marks because they overrate their own abilities and do not bow to the authority of the judge. On the whole it is a very precarious development for a sport that for generations has been called the most noble of all.

Through the years 1934 to 1937 I was fortunate enough with Nora, Nero, and Otto to have three horses in the stables who were well confirmed in the standard of the Olympic tests and with whom I practically ruled over all the horse shows. Furthermore, Nero, who had seemed so insignificant in the beginning, developed into my greatest teacher.

It was he who taught me, above all, that where there is much sun there is shadow, too, and that life has both in store for us. He learned quickly and easily and made rapid progress, but his brittle hooves were our greatest impediment. They gave the greatest trouble every year from spring to fall—during the season of horse shows, of all times—and often compelled me to interrupt his training for several weeks. Fortunately Nero possessed great intelligence and an extremely good memory, which enabled him after these forced periods of rest to move as if he had not interrupted his work for a single day. In view of this experience, it seems to me that nobody who wants to be taken seriously should maintain that horses are stupid. Of course, there are more intelligent ones and less clever ones among them, but the same may be said about humans.

Nothing could cure Nero of his bad hooves, neither the best vets whom I consulted nor the application of every conceivable kind of remedy, all of which were recommended as dead sure. Each time I hoped that the vet had at last found the miracle treatment, but each time after the horse show season I knew better. We had had the same trouble again. The hooves became so brittle that shoes could hardly be fitted. When I competed in a foreign country for the first time in 1934, Nero's hooves had grown so bad that the blacksmith of the Swiss Cavalry School in Thun invented in despair a special shoe for the right forefoot which enveloped it on three sides and was fastened to the hoof with a single nail. This new shoe was heavier than the one on the left side and Nero went completely unlevel for a few steps. I went into the competitions worrying about how this would end. Nero, however, soon found out that all he had to do was to lift his right foot with a little more energy and he presented himself in perfect balance throughout the Grand Prix test. Nobody would have believed that this was his first ride since he had left the railroad car after the two days' trip from Vienna to Thun.

As no other horse did, Nero taught me to perform correct changes of speed, extending the pace like a shot out of a pistol and shortening the stride in a single smooth and elastic motion. This powerful crescendo and soft fading gave a brilliance to his performance and a charm that outweighed all physical shortcomings.

During the years of Nero's training he taught me another important piece of wisdom. I learned to organise our work systematically, which is of vital importance to a rider who wants to achieve the highest goal and at the same time avoid overworking his horse. It helped to keep Nero young and cheerful until his old age. In order to reach the goal he has set for himself and his horse, the rider must have a programme for the daily training as well as for the entire education. Work should be regular and well balanced, not too much on one day or not enough on the next. There is a rule that governs the entire time of training: in the forefront must be the cultivation of the basic paces—walk, trot, and canter. For these simple exercises, though they are not at all spectacular, are not easy to perform correctly. They develop the horse's muscles and prepare him physically and mentally for the more difficult airs of high school. If problems arise in the advanced stage of training, the rider will find the solution in riding briskly forward and in concentrating again for a while on the movements and exercises of the basic phase.

In each lesson for the accomplished horse or one that is advanced in training, the rider should pass again through all the phases of the entire training. He may spend only a few minutes on them and then devote his time to the new or difficult exercises. But while it

is vital to have a plan and not just ride along, the rider should be
warned against clinging to a rigid pattern set once and forever. The
plan must be flexible and adjusted to the requirements of the day.
How often I began my work with the intention of concentrating on
a certain exercise but then had to interrupt the schedule and shift to
an entirely different problem.

Once I wanted to practise pirouettes with Nero and after warm-
ing up—which is nothing else than the preparatory work I have
just described—I began to execute this exercise. But on that particular day the pirouettes, in which the horse should turn around
on his hindquarters at the canter without altering the rhythm,
would not succeed. As soon as I led Nero into the pirouette he
became slower and lost the rhythm and finally the canter died down
altogether. In another attempt I pushed Nero forward more energetically, with the result that he threw himself around in irregular
bounds, a fault just as bad as dying down.

I gave up my plan and rode Nero forward at a lively canter and
practised changes of speed and striking off from the walk and the
trot in order to induce the hind legs to jump energetically under
his body. When he no longer lost the rhythm as I changed from
the large circle to the straight line and vice versa, I practised voltes
of an ever smaller size until they, too, succeeded to perfection. After
this modest achievement I dismounted and sent Nero back into the
stables. As I've noted, he had an extremely good memory; which
is why I was always intent on bringing our work to an end with a
well-performed exercise so that he would recall an agreeable moment which had led to a well-deserved rest. Since it is a reward for
the horse if the rider dismounts, he must not do so after an unsuccessful exercise, let alone send the horse into the stables after a
display of naughtiness. The very next day the horse would remember and begin the naughtiness right away in order to obtain the un-
merited reward and be left in peace.

During the following days I practised these voltes until I was
able to make them smaller and smaller without Nero losing the
rhythm of the canter. From these gradually diminished voltes there
at last developed pirouettes which were well measured and rhythmic
and looked effortless.

If the rider plans his work with intelligence and tact he avoids
overworking his horse and making him listless and disinterested.

I remember a certain officer who attempted to teach the piaffe to his good-natured and talented mare. Every day there was the same scene. The mare would perform a few steps of piaffe correctly but instead of rewarding her with a period of walk before demanding this difficult air again, the lieutenant would prolong the exercise until the piaffe became hesitant and gradually died down. He would push the mare further on, she would become nervous, he would lose his cap and, at last, swearing, send her into the stables. Having looked on for a few days I asked him what, in his opinion, was the reason for this failure. "Oh, this blooming beast just does not want to!" was the angry answer. "No," I told him, "she is not able to. Look here, she performs the first few steps quite nicely but she is not yet strong enough to do more than these few steps. Give her time! Just think—if I were to ask you to do ten genuflexions, you would be able to execute them. But if I demand a hundred, you will say, 'This is too much.' But your mare cannot speak. All she can do is resist your unreasonable demands."

Nero was the living proof that sport, if intelligently practised, will never shorten the life of the athlete but, on the contrary, will prolong it in spite of the highest demands. He reached the age of twenty-eight in perfect health, and that is a very old age for a Thoroughbred.

Whenever Nero entered a competition in Austria or in foreign countries he was among the first, and usually he was the winner. His career came to an end at the international horse show in Insterburg in August 1939, with a victory that was memorable in more than one respect. This horse show was one of the last big competitions before the beginning of the Second World War. When I saw this formerly pleasant old town in the east of Germany seething with soldiers and resembling a military camp, it suddenly dawned upon me how far along the preparations for war had been pushed. And it was at this horse show that Nero gave me the greatest trouble we had in all the years of our work together.

Before going to Insterburg I had participated in competitions in Verden and Hannover (northern Germany) and in Munich in Bavaria, and Nero had travelled long distances in a railroad car and had worked hard in between in order to be up to the demands of the difficult tests and compete with a great number of entries. After the first working session in Insterburg I noticed to my dismay that Nero turned around very haltingly when he was put back into his box and swayed when I had him walked up and down in the stables. We called the vet immediately and his diagnosis corroborated my apprehension. It was the beginning of Azoturia. Commonly called "Monday-morning sickness," this is an illness which may appear with horses who have undergone very concentrated training when they begin to work again after a few days of rest. It is accompanied by a process that dissolves the fibers of the muscles in the back and hindquarters especially, which may poison the entire organism and lead to serious trouble in the hooves in particular. If the sickness is not discovered and treated at the outset, it is usually fatal.

The vet administered injections and bled Nero, and his immediate and energetic action prevented this dangerous illness from developing to its full extent. Of course it was very doubtful whether Nero would be able to enter the show. For the few days left I had him taken to the Angerapp River to stand in the running water in order to control and alleviate the inflammation of his hooves, which was particularly bad because they were so sensitive anyway. It was interesting to note that while Nero went the short distance to the river in the morning with great difficulty, he returned to the stables in the evening with much better strides. For this cold water treatment the groom tied Nero to one of the posts of the bridge and he himself remained on the bridge. Nero was a very good patient and willingly stood in the water, but only as long as he could see his "nurse" leaning on the railing of the bridge. If the man left his post even for five minutes, Nero became restless and began to neigh woefully. The contact with human beings was essential to him.

The cold water brought about an amelioration surprisingly quickly and we were able to participate at least in one test of the difficult class. It was due solely to Nero's absolute loyalty and reliability that I was able to win this competition in an outstanding manner in spite of his sickness and the fact that there had been no possibility for any training. Nero had gone into the test practically from the sickbed. For me this last ride to victory was extremely difficult. Nero's back had become so sensitive from massaging him with all sorts of embrocations that I had to muster all my skill not to disturb his balance by sitting firmly in the saddle. I felt literally as though I were sitting on raw eggs, but Nero went through the test in his habitual superior manner and this last victory of his career was much applauded.

Nero was a real character. Like most horses he loved sugar above all things and, cunning as he was, he knew how to get more than his share. Once after a competition I gave him a lump of sugar and noticed that he did not chew. I gave him another one and the same thing happened. Thinking that he had dropped it I looked down but saw nothing on the ground. Like a hamster Nero had gathered the sugar in his cheek and obviously wanted to get as much as possible and then in peace enjoy his beloved titbits. Later, when Nero had become a great star, he loved it when he was surrounded by the crowd and given delicacies from all sides. He paid not the slightest attention to me and tried to get as many titbits as possible from his admirers because he knew only too well that his master's reward would not fail him.

If, however, he refused to take any sweets from me I knew that the worst had happened, that I had done him wrong in the course of the training or had demanded too much from him. It was his manner of disapproving the philosophy of "sugar-bread and whip"! To me this behaviour was a serious warning that I had made a mistake and that I should be more moderate in my demands. So I should like to remind every rider to look to himself for the fault whenever he has any difficulties with his horse.

Nero accompanied me through twenty years of my life and our names became synonymous. Together we lived to see triumphs and were loyal to each other in times of disaster. When the American troops marched into Austria, Nero rendered perhaps the greatest service of his life to me. An American major discovered him in the stables of the small village where the Spanish Riding School had found refuge from the horrors of the war. The officer had been in Berlin in 1936 and remembered every detail of Nero's ride at the Olympic Games. This circumstance gave me the opportunity to contact the victorious troops and to induce General Patton to save the Lipizzaners from the chaos the Second World War had left behind.

Nero and I gave a last display before the American officers and then he was to retire and lead a quiet life on the stud farm. But the old gentleman became so excited at the sight of the white mares, and so tried to impress them by constantly performing the passage and flying changes, that I seriously feared for his heart. I decided to keep him near me with the Lipizzaner stallions at the Spanish Riding School and was fortunately able to render his last years calm and pleasant. When Nero closed his eyes in the autumn of 1953, I lost my most loyal friend and the worthiest companion of my equestrian career.

When going through my store of reminiscences, in which Nero figures so deeply, I also see the bay mare Judith before my mind's eye. Although I rode her for a short while only we became good friends very quickly. Judith was the charger of General Graser, a cavalry inspector to whom I am greatly indebted for, among many other things, assigning me to the Spanish Riding School in the years 1933 and 1934. One day the general asked me whether I wanted to take Judith and retrain her because she was quite spoiled. He did not have the time to ride her every day and had left her to another officer for a while but now she had become so crazy that he took no more pleasure in riding her. In fact, Judith was very difficult indeed. She wanted to rush off if the reins were applied, she jumped at the slightest noise, and upon the sight of anything unusual—sometimes it was just a speck of sunshine or a dark bush —she took to flight as if followed by furies. It was certainly no pleasure to ride her cross-country. So I began working her in the indoor school, established in her the basic principles of calmness, obedience, and going forward, and won her confidence, which to me was the most important thing.

If Judith was frightened by anything—and she was ingenious in finding a thousand opportunities—it was not out of naughtiness but out of nervousness and fear. It would have been absolutely wrong to punish her. If anything awakened her suspicion I led her carefully near with a long rein. My legs were firmly applied so that she knew that I was there to protect her and that nothing could happen to her. Talking to her softly, I allowed her ample time to take a good look at the object of her fear and even to sniff at it. If she remained calm, I patted her and rewarded her. If she continued to manifest fear, I had to repeat the whole procedure until she calmed down. Of course, this sometimes took quite a while but nevertheless it was not a waste of time for gradually Judith gained confidence in me and lost her spookiness. If I had administered punishment, she would have become worse and worse because to her nervousness would have been added the fear of punishment.

The next thing she had to learn was to move in regular rhythm and with steps of equal length, and to forget the nervous and hasty tripping into which she fell all too easily. At the same time I attempted to accustom her to a steady contact with the bit, for Judith threw her whole weight on the rein at one moment and at the next did not take any contact at all and went behind the bit. To make work easier for her I renounced any changes of speed and limited all transitions from one pace to the other to the absolute minimum.

Judith made progress more quickly than I had expected. After a while she was able to maintain a regular tempo with a long neck. She remained on the bit with her mouth closed and moist and she had a relaxed expression on her face. She regained her physical and mental balance and became calm and poised and was no longer disturbed by any insignificant detail. Having obtained this result it was not difficult to make her follow the slightest aids and to maintain this obedience in every situation. After a few weeks of training Judith was a completely different horse, behaving reasonably when we rode cross-country because she was entirely under my control. Building on this progress I began to lengthen her stride carefully and render it more lively, which was most effectively done at the rising trot. I was very careful, though, because I wanted to prevent her from relapsing into those hasty, irregular steps. This work resulted in making her go forward with more impulsion and now I realised what beautiful movements Judith was capable of showing. Of course, I had to be content with only a few steps to begin with, but gradually increasing demands developed these few steps into paces for which I had not dared to hope.

When General Graser rode Judith in the Prater Park after a while, he was full of enthusiasm and praise for the improvement of his horse and told me that he would be pleased if I would continue the training and bring the mare to the standard necessary for horse shows. I accepted with great zeal because I had begun to take much pleasure in working with her. Judith had completely forgotten her spookiness and nervousness because she had confidence in me and had learned to understand what I wanted from her. Since she had regained the regularity of her paces I was able to work her in a shortened tempo. In between I rode periods of medium speed in order to maintain her impulsion and to increase the liveliness of the stride or the bounds of canter. When I taught her various exercises she understood in a surprisingly short time what was expected from her because she was in complete physical and mental balance. I made plans to enter her in horse show dressage tests of medium class in the year 1934.

The general came to inspect her progress every now and then and approved of this plan, but one day he asked a question I was unable to answer right away with a clear conscience. He told me that he had an opportunity to sell Judith, who in the meantime had become his property, at a good price but that he would forego this chance if I could guarantee that Judith's training would be advanced enough within the next two years so that she could participate successfully at the Olympic Games in Berlin. At this moment I was well supplied with two horses who were ready for the games, Nero and Nora. They did not, it is true, look nearly as attractive as Judith but were superior to her as far as their abilities were concerned. Besides, I knew only too well about the numerous difficulties to be overcome before reaching so high an aim. And, one more point to be considered, the general was famous for his acid criticism. Having turned the matter over in my mind, I replied at last that at present I was in a position to promise to train Judith up to the standard of a dressage test of the difficult class but that it was beyond my judgement to tell whether I would be able to accomplish the training of piaffe and passage in time for the Olympic Games. Consequently the general decided to sell Judith to a horseman in Switzerland.

One year later when I came to the horse show in Thun, the new owner showed Judith to me. She stood apathetically in her box, not paying any attention to her surroundings. I called her by the pet name I had used with her. As long as I live I will never forget how she lifted her head and pricked her ears as if searching her memory for the owner of this voice. Slowly she turned around, came towards us, and greeted me with a soft neighing, rubbing her nose on my shoulder in a familiar gesture. Her owner watched with amazement and murmured: "How funny, never has this strange creature come towards me. I could have called as often as I wanted!"

This was the last encounter with Judith, who taught me to explore the mentality and the character of the other creature in order to establish a close contact and mutual understanding. To be the owner is certainly not enough!

In the late autumn of 1934 I was transferred as a riding instructor to the Cavalry School, which had been reestablished in Kaiserebersdorf near Vienna several years before. Among the young remounts I chose a four-year-old chestnut mare from the Austrian federal stud farm by the name of Rokoko and began to train her from scratch. Rokoko was young and had a somewhat long back and, remembering Otto, I took great care not to proceed too quickly. It happens only too frequently that a successful dressage rider is inclined to push the training of his young horse and demand more of the animal than he is able to give at his age and with the degree of his physical and mental development. This temptation is particularly great if this young horse is the only one the rider has at his disposal at the moment. Since with Nero and Otto I had two horses equal to the highest demands of dressage tests, I was able to take plenty of time with Rokoko and concentrate on laying the basis of correct training in calm and well-organised work.

The initial work with a young horse offers little distraction to an accomplished rider and, above all, no opportunity to impress any spectators with spectacular exercises. It is the stage of making straight and riding forward in which the rider tries to ride his horse briskly on, avoiding turns and, at the rising trot, making him used to carrying the rider's weight. If he employed the sitting trot at this stage, the horse would feel his weight uncomfortably and too heavily on his back, which is still weak, and this discomfort might be the origin of many difficulties that would arise later on. If a horse carries his head and neck too high, if he does not go sufficiently forward, or, finally, is inclined to resistance, it is in most cases the consequence of having neglected the basic training or having forced it too quickly. If, on the contrary, the rider knows how to initiate his horse slowly to his demands, if he plans his work methodically and with intelligence and takes the physical and mental development of the young animal into consideration, he lays a sound foundation for correct and successful training.

Rokoko was a horse without problems, and the result of this well-planned and systematic work became already obvious in the spring of 1936 when, at her first start barely fifteen months after the beginning of her training, we were able to win a dressage test of the medium class over the older dressage cracks who had certainly had more experience—a victory that was uncontested and drew much attention among the experts. It was an unwritten law for me and most of my comrades that a riding instructor of the Cavalry School was not supposed to enter in dressage tests of the beginners' classes, not even with a young horse. Preliminary and novice tests were reserved for the young generation of riders. This rule made the participation of instructors more difficult but was dictated by fairness because the young riders should be encouraged in their careers and not suppressed and disheartened by having to ride against more accomplished riders. In any case, it was a nobler attitude than chasing after ribbons at any cost. Likewise, a horse that had been entered in tests of the difficult class was not supposed to appear in preliminary classes, or a horse of Olympic standard in dressage tests of the medium class. Besides, there was a limit of age in each class: after a certain age, the horse had to enter in the next higher test or, if he was not up to the standard, disappear from the show grounds altogether. Today, when everybody strives for quick success, the limit of age is not directed upwards but, on the contrary, downwards. This practice is to protect the horse and avoid confronting him when too young with too high demands so that he used himself prematurely.

Our gentleman-like rule and the small number of horse shows in Austria in those days offered very limited possibilities to compete, so Rokoko had to wait another year before participating in a second competition and repeating her victory. In the same year, 1937, there was an opportunity to measure her against internationally renowned dressage horses at a horse show in Germany and she stood her ground well. Although Rokoko ranked among the best young horses of the Austrian Cavalry School, it became clear to me, to my great regret, that in quality and conformation she was very inferior to the international dressage horses.

In the autumn of 1937 Rokoko won for me the trophy I cherish most of all. It was one of the pictures of Ludwig Koch given by the famous painter with the dedication: "In memory of the Austro-

Hungarian cavalry schools." Several years previously I had visited Koch, who was a great friend of mine, in his study. He had shown me a painting he had just finished and which represented an officer of the hussars in a "prize-riding" of the Austro-Hungarian monarchy. Koch said: "Here is your prize. You must win it. It was you who gave me the idea to do this picture when you rode Nora for me on the curb only in the main test after her victory over Nero and all the other international dressage horses. In you the time-honoured Austrian equitation lives to see its renaissance and there is no one worthier than you to win this trophy." The condition of this particular test was that the horse should not yet be seven years of age and the rider should ride him twice in a difficult test of the medium class on the curb only. Emphasis was laid mainly on the performance of impulsive paces. This was to point out the tradition of the old Austro-Hungarian cavalry schools. "On the curb only" means that the rider guides his horse with the reins of the curb in the left hand while the reins of the snaffle are loose and do not enter into action. The right hand is either placed on the thigh or holds the whip upright. To ride on the curb demands an extremely light hand and much sensitiveness on the part of the rider. The horse must be very well trained and respond to the most delicate aids. I was overjoyed when Rokoko helped me to fulfill the wish of the great painter who, in the meantime, had passed away.

It was with Rokoko again that I won the difficult dressage class in my last competition in Vienna in May 1938, bringing my Vienna show career to a worthy end before I was transferred to a new post in northern Germany.

As I have mentioned before, I had at my disposal only horses that belonged to the Army, because officers were not permitted to have private horses. The administration of the Army, however, had only a small sum with which to buy horses. Consequently, all my dressage horses were of inferior quality because the better horses came into private hands. Moreover, the civilian riders were able to buy as many horses in foreign countries as they pleased, while the Army satisfied its needs mostly from Austrian stud farms. For years I rode in horse shows against these private horses. If I did succeed in beating these high quality horses with my army horses, it may be taken as the best proof that in dressage it is first of all the rider and the training that count and only second the quality of the horse. Fortunately, success cannot be achieved simply by buying a good horse. This fact cannot be underlined too often, especially nowadays when everything is expressed in terms of money. Have we not almost reached the point where many riders believe that by buying an expensive horse—if possible, in a foreign country—they have bought uncontested victory?

The charger with the best conformation was Teja, a handsome Hungarian horse with good paces who came from the Hungarian stud farm of Ludwig, Prince of Bavaria. Teja had been bought in 1937 because the Austrian stud farms were not able to fulfill the demands of the Army and the police. He was a bay gelding, a half-bred, and like most Hungarians he had an ardent temperament and a very difficult character. Much later I found an explanation for his shyness and unruly behaviour. I heard that when a military commission had come to buy horses in Budapest, Teja was to be tried as the charger for a general. Afraid of the unknown rider, Teja did not want to stand still when the rider tried to mount into the saddle and was refused by the commission for the time being. During the following days, the dealer had anybody he could get hold of come into the stables and mount Teja, and he thrashed the horse every time he made the slightest attempt to move. No wonder that Teja was so intimidated that he did not dare to make difficulties when the commission came again! He was bought for the general, but, having arrived in Vienna, he was even more difficult and the general was unable to mount. This is how I got Teja as a charger.

My experience with Otto had given me good training and came in very handy now. First of all, I avoided being influenced by anybody and declined all advice that might have diverted me from my line of conduct. And Teja offered every conceivable kind of difficulty against which those with Otto dwindled into insignificance. These problems began with the resistance with which he opposed himself to being saddled or shod up to the complexes he manifested when being ridden. For instance, he refused to pass any horse coming towards him. At sight of such, he whisked around and tried to run away, which was most disagreeable, especially in the beginning when he was not yet sufficiently under the control of the aids. Whenever this occurred—and it occurred maddeningly often —I made a point of not paying any attention to this naughtiness and continued my work as if nothing had happened. I turned around calmly and led him again in the direction in which we had been going.

Head rider Polak, who watched me at work and saw how Teja gave me the same trouble over and over again, asked me one day why I did not for once give him a good whacking—he certainly deserved it. But this time I paid no attention to my beloved teacher because I was convinced that patience was the better way to reach my goal. It took months until I had succeeded in making Teja forget his naughtiness, but on the other hand he forgot it for good. I was sure that it was fear that had provoked those difficulties and that they could be overcome by patience only.

This proved to be true when in 1939 we rode in the Deutschland-halle, which is the huge indoor stadium in Berlin. The first test was held in two arenas at the same time. They were next to each other and separated by a simple, low partition. When the rider in the other arena rode towards me for the first time, Teja stared at him as though mesmerized. I felt the imminent danger and expected that he would suddenly come to a halt. Lowering myself deeply into the saddle I made him feel the pressure of my legs until his confidence won over his fear, with the result that he was third behind the experienced horses of Colonel Buerkner and Mr. Loerke, which was a nice accomplishment for his first horse show. This first success was followed by numerous others, including those of high school, in which he was especially brilliant in the performance of piaffe, passage, pirouettes, and flying changes of lead. But to these equestrian triumphs I preferred by far the psychological victory I had won over Teja at the beginning of his training.

As already mentioned, Teja hated being shod, especially on the hind feet, and he defended himself with all his strength and intelligence. His aversion increased as time went on and the operation became more and more difficult. While this fight between horse and man left insignificant scratches at first, there were serious injuries later on and the blacksmith was forced to use more and more drastic measures to shoe Teja. He began to use a longe rein to lift Teja's hind legs and ended up with the "pipe," which is a particularly painful instrument to make a horse behave. With a rope and a gag the upper lip of the horse was twisted until he forgot everything else for the pain in his lip. This was also used by veterinarians to immobilize a horse during surgery until, a few years ago, the more effective means of narcotization became available.

In the end it became impossible to shoe Teja without drugging him first with an injection. He got morphia shots which dazed him for a while so that he endured the procedure without resistance. But I could feel the effect of the injection for several days when riding him, especially in his nervous reactions. Teja was even more hysterical and although it was impossible that he still felt the prick of the injection, I did not dare to touch his neck. After a while he did not allow the vet to come near him any more even though he did not wear his white jacket, and finally Teja even sensed the syringe hidden behind the vet's back and immediately presented his hindquarters ready to kick.

After this disastrous development I endeavoured to overcome the difficulty by way of psychological influence. Having finished my work, I dismounted in the arena and tried to lift Teja's hind legs one after the other. Immediately his suspicion was aroused and I was content that he allowed me to lift his feet for one or two seconds while I talked to him and caressed him. I gave him sugar and had him taken into the stables. On the following day he tolerated the procedure with less suspicion and was again sent into the stables as a reward. I repeated this little ritual daily and prolonged the time in which I lifted his hooves but gave up immediately when he became restless. A few weeks later I had reached the stage when, before, during, and after the lesson, Teja allowed his hind legs to be lifted for five minutes and more without any resistance. The next step was to achieve the same result in the stables, where I had to begin all over because at first he became excited and nervous again. Very obviously he remembered the efforts which had been made in the stables to shoe him. I chose the moment just before feeding time so that he would be able to enjoy his oats as a reward. The preparation I had practised in the arena began to bear fruit. In a much shorter time I succeeded in lifting his hind legs for as long a period as in the arena.

So far I had carried out these experiments alone but now, since Teja remained absolutely calm, I had the blacksmith come with me into the box. When I noticed that Teja became nervous, I limited the time of lifting his legs to a minimum and gradually increased it again on the following days. The next step was to have the blacksmith come into the box with his tools and later on manipulate Teja's hooves very carefully and for a short moment only; gradually he could handle them more strongly and for a longer period. At the end of six weeks we were able to shoe Teja without any difficulties and without any forceful methods but just with kind words. From now on I watched carefully to be sure that his hind legs were never lifted for more than five minutes at a time and that he had a chance to rest in between so that he would not have any pain. Very probably all his resistance had come from the fact that his feet were lifted too high and for too long a time, which happens so often and causes pain to the horse during shoeing. Since Teja was very intelligent he had remembered that there was discomfort every time the farrier had come near him. He was not willing to suffer and had defended himself as best he could.

Although this incident has nothing to do with riding itself, it demonstrates so clearly the two methods—and all their consequences—with which to obtain services from a horse. On one side there is the unconditional subjection by force and punishment with which the rider may reach his goal more quickly but only if he has a good-natured creature with no tendency to fight. This kind of education, however, will undermine the individual character of the animal and result in obedience out of fear. The brilliance of such a horse will be lost and he will be indifferent towards man or even hostile. If on the other hand the training of the horse is based on kindness, calmness, and ample reward as well as understanding for his personality, the result will be happy obedience on the part of the horse and pleasure in his work. It may take a little longer to obtain progress than with the other method but there will never be that ugly fight between man and animal. The charm and brilliance of the horse will be maintained, even enhanced, and preserved until his old age.

Thus Teja's problems lay less in the technically equestrian sphere than in the psychological field, but although, or more probably because he had been so difficult in the beginning, we became very close to each other. Contrary to Nero and Otto, he possessed a wonderful forward urge which rendered work with him easy and agreeable. He understood very quickly what was required of him and seemed to enjoy his own movements. His smooth canter was equal to that of a Thoroughbred and his trot was elastic and full of impulsion. Therefore, it was not too difficult to develop this beautiful regular trot into the passage. The passage is a proud and solemn movement in which the horse swings himself from one diagonal pair of legs to the other, hovering in the air for a moment without touching the ground. A horse at liberty who gets excited in his paddock or encounters other horses unexpectedly will show this wonderful pace, which resembles an elevated trot in slow motion.

To begin with I taught Teja to go forward energetically and with long strides upon the slightest aids of my legs and to shorten his steps immediately when I braced my back. The main thing was that his steps should not become slower but more elevated. Having stretched his legs to cover the ground at the ordinary trot and even more so at the extended trot, he had to lift them higher now to allow the stride to become shorter while the same rhythm was maintained. Gradually I decreased the interval between extension and collection. After four, then three, and later even less steps of going forward energetically, Teja was induced to shorten his stride by my braced back. Finally from this lively extension and instantaneous collection there developed a few elevated and floating steps which were the beginning of the passage.

This description should not convey the impression that I did not work on any other exercise and had obtained these steps of passage in a short time. On the contrary, it took about six to seven weeks until Teja performed the first floating strides I had made a habit of demanding only at the end of the daily lesson. Since this preparatory work is a great strain on the horse both mentally and physically, I made a point of practising them at the end of the training session so that I could send Teja home afterwards as a reward. Of course the rest of the exercises, like lateral work and the training at the canter, were not to be neglected. Slowly and gradually these few steps of passage were increased in number until Teja was able to execute them alongside the wall for half the length of the arena and finally for a full length. Half a year later this brilliant air of high school was so well established that Teja performed it on the center line just as powerfully and with as much impulsion as on the track alongside the wall which helps the horse to remain straight and keep the direction. At that point he was strong enough to circle the whole of the arena in proud passage.

I have already pointed out the difference between a round passage and a long one. The round passage is mostly to be found with the Lipizzaners while the long one is the domain of the half- and Thoroughbreds who do not have the high knee action of the Lipizzaners and therefore cannot perform such an elevated passage. However, they are capable of a wonderfully expressive extended trot. Although Teja's trot was full of impulsion and covered much ground to the front, in his passage he showed a high knee action and his hind legs stepped under his body with such energy that his passage allowed comparison to that of a Lipizzaner.

It was most unfortunate that Teja's promising career had to be interrupted for more than ten years by the war and its aftermath, and I could show him only in private. Still, I was able to bring both him and Nero through the war and keep them near me in those difficult times. In 1948 we participated in the Olympic Games in London. In these first games after the great war, attempts were made to render the tests easier for the dressage horses and the competition was based on a Grand Prix without piaffe and passage, which was an absolute disadvantage for Teja as he performed both exercises in an exemplary manner. Besides, there were a few other impediments which, however, had nothing to do with the art of riding. If the fact that I was not a German had been a disadvantage for me in Berlin, in London the fact that I had necessarily been a German during the Hitler regime was a similar disadvantage in the judgement of my performance.

Nevertheless, Teja impressed the public so favourably that in the following year we were invited by the British Horse Society to give a display at the great International Horse Show in London in July 1949. Because we had not won one of the medals at the Olympic Games of the previous year, this invitation was issued to us as a mark of distinction and as a protest against the verdict of the judges. With his performance of high school in the principles of the classical art of riding in London in 1949 and in Dublin in 1950, the Hungarian half-bred reached the peak of his career. He succeeded in rousing the public in the gigantic White City stadium to storms of enthusiasm and, what is even more, shook the preconceived ideas of many sceptics and antagonists of dressage in England.

Several days before the horse show began, the chairman of the

British Horse Society, Colonel V. D. S. Williams, had invited me to his beautiful home in East Burnham Park near Windsor to give me an opportunity to prepare Teja and the two Lipizzaner stallions Pluto Theodorosta and Neapolitano Africa for their tasks. I agreed to his suggestion that he invite all his friends who were interested in dressage as well as all opponents of this kind of riding to come and watch my work. This invitation was eagerly accepted and every day there were several dozen spectators, including quite a few who were watching for something negative. I had to summon all my abilities and experience to prepare my horses well for the display and at the same time to prove that dressage riding was by no means unnatural or even cruel as was the opinion of many horse-minded people in England at that time. Apparently this idea had its origin in the violent methods of the Duke of Newcastle, who lived in the seventeenth century and who had advocated a very forceful system.

Teja helped me initially because the critics were more interested in his work than in that of the Lipizzaners as he was closer to the type of the English horse. Talking to them I tried to find out about their doubts and then to show exactly what had aroused their distrust. Gradually convinced by the work that went on without any secrecy before their eyes, even the most suspicious adversaries turned into very interested spectators. For instance, one of the greatest opponents of dressage was Colonel Guy Cubitt, and he said in a press conference afterwards how much he had been impressed by the training of my horses, especially of the Thoroughbred (by which he meant Teja), because it should certainly be a pleasure to ride a horse that was so light in hand and in such ideal balance.

From the beginning of the horse show, every afternoon and evening I presented one of the Lipizzaner stallions first and then Teja. The spectators were to be introduced to the idea of the classical art of riding. They were to see for themselves that the art of high school was nothing else but the development to the highest degree of perfection of the natural movements every horse is able to perform at liberty and without a rider. They were to understand that the fundamental schooling on which this art of riding is based is exactly the same that should be given to every horse, whether it be a hunter, a jumper, or an ordinary riding horse.

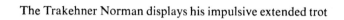
The Trakehner Norman displays his impulsive extended trot

Relaxation after concentrated work

An old friendship renewed: Conversano Nobila in a passage

Neapolitano Africa gains friends for dressage in England

Neapolitano Africa in the spotlights at White City

Maestoso Alea performs a piaffe in London in 1953

His majesty in exile: Neapolitano Africa in Wels

Pluto Theodorosta in a passage

Back in Vienna at last, with Maestoso Alea

A very rare exercise: Favory Monteaura in a capriole
between the pillars

Favory Brezia in a levade in hand

The "Flying Horse": Neapolitano Santuzza in a capriole in hand

Siglavy Brezovica in a courbette in hand

Like all horses, Norman loves to be caressed

Full of confidence, Teja comes to his master

Alone with Maestoso Mercurio

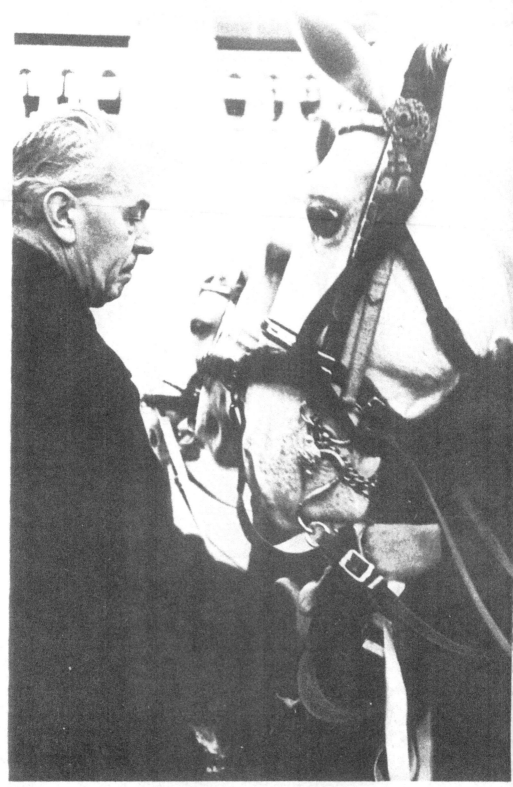

A sad farewell to my friends the Lipizzaners

Furthermore, it was proof that a horse of a type similar to the English horse, like Teja, was just as capable of performing the art of high school as the Lipizzaners were.

My first appearance was an overwhelming success. I had never dreamed that I would be able to conquer the English public at my first ride and as a single rider to arouse the enthusiasm of thousands of spectators. And the enthusiasm grew from day to day. When I crossed the street from the stables to the show ground with my horses, the children ran after me and called: "This is the dancing horse. . . ."

The entire press was full of reports about this great enthusiasm, which a single rider had seldom been able to stir up in the vast White City arena. A weekly magazine recorded in a long article: ". . . When Colonel Podhajsky had demonstrated the art of high school on one of the Lipizzaner stallions, he presented a similar programme on the English Thoroughbred Teja and with this ride gave the proof that it is above all the rider and only in second place the horse that counts. . . ."

As Colonel Williams assured me over and over again, Teja had made an essential contribution to arousing the interest of the English horse world in dressage, which up to that moment was almost entirely unknown in Great Britain or, as we have mentioned, even rejected as unnatural or cruel. In the following twenty years the classical style of riding was to spread widely in that country. Teja's success induced the Royal Dublin Society to invite me in an official letter to the Austrian government in 1950 to appear with my horses at the Spring Show—a great agricultural show in Dublin. For the first time, a dressage rider was given the opportunity to display the classical style of riding in the domain of the hunters and jumpers—in the lion's den, so to speak. I solved the problem in the same manner as I had in England and rode Pluto Theodorosta first and afterwards Teja. Both performances were rewarded by tremendous applause, which was unusual even for the temperamental Irish public. The daily paper, *Evening Herald*, remarked, among other things, that it had been very wise to present two different types of horses. Thus it was clearly demonstrated that it was not necessary to employ horses of a special breed for successful work in dressage. The Hungarian

Teja, equal in quality to a well-bred Irish horse, had underlined this fact better than any words.

By the way, Teja established my credit in Dublin as surely as today some high-priced automobile might. On our day of rest I went into town to do some shopping. When I had made my choice and received the bill, I realised that I did not have sufficient money in my wallet. I asked the owner of the shop to keep the parcel for me and I would come and pay the following day. But he pushed it into my hand saying that I should take it along and bring the money some other time. When I expressed surprise that he had that much trust in a complete stranger, he answered with a smile: "But everybody knows you, the whole of Dublin is talking about you and your dressage horses."

The displays in White City and Dublin ended Teja's public appearances in a manner worthy of his career and I was happy that friends in Switzerland took him into their care and allowed him to spend the rest of his days in peace and comfort on their farm. While enjoying the sunshine and the lush grass in his paddock, Teja saw the lady who so kindly took care of him and cantered towards her. Suddenly he rose on his hind legs and crashed to the ground. A stroke had brought his life to a close.

The last charger I had in the Austrian Federal Army was Bengali, a Thoroughbred who was also the last of all my Army horses. He had been successful on the racecourse in Vienna for two years and then his owner, Baron Nikolaus von Ditfurth, had sold him to the Federal Army on the condition that I should ride him. Bengali was a beautiful dark brown gelding and a very good mover. But in spite of his achievements on the race track he had little impulse to go forward when we rode alone. On the contrary, his reaction to any surprise was to run backwards as fast as lightning. I had hoped to correct this bad habit by riding cross-country in the company of other riders, but soon I realised that he had little ambition to jump either. One beautiful day in October I rode with a group of riders on a dam along the Danube and when we came to a fence, Bengali refused to jump. In order to make it easier for him, I asked two riders to ride on either side of me and together we approached the fence once more. In a brisk pace we rode towards the obstacle, the two other horses cleared it, and Bengali remained as though rivetted to the ground in spite of the brisk tempo and the good example of his comrades. Had he limited his naughtiness to stopping it would not have been too bad. But immediately he took to flight, running backwards as fast as he could. Never again in my life have I seen a horse run backwards as fast as Bengali. Thank God I also never again experienced the surprise Bengali had in store for me now. He came off the track and got his hind legs on the steep slope of the paved dam. He pawed frantically into the air with his front legs and together we fell over backwards into the ice-cold water of the Danube. When I had crawled up the steep side of the dam, I saw with horror that Bengali was drifting in the middle of the stream and being carried off by the fast current. This part of the Danube is very deep and rapid and at that moment I was sure I was seeing the last of my horse. Instinctively I called his name—it seemed a weak attempt to interfere with inevitable fate. But the familiar voice worked wonders. Bengali lifted his head, neighed hoarsely, and began to fight the current with all his strength in order to reach the bank where I stood. It was quite a task to drag him up the steep and slippery dam to safety.

This incident underlines again that with a Thoroughbred, too, the impulsion and the will to go forward should not be taken for granted, even if he has been racing. There is a great difference between whether a horse is made to go forward by the herding instinct or by his own impulse. Besides, this episode gave me another proof of the intelligence and the loyalty of the Thoroughbred as well as of his extremely keen hearing. How much he was attached to me Bengali proved on yet another occasion.

One day when we were going cross-country he unseated me by an unexpected buck-jump and, thrilled to be suddenly at liberty, he turned around and cantered in long strides in the direction of the stables. I sat on the grass and found myself in a rather unpleasant situation. I was without a companion and at a distance of several miles from the barracks. Apart from the prospect of being exposed to the malicious joy of my comrades, such a long walk was certainly not very tempting. As loud as I could I yelled "Bengali," but without much hope, for he was rapidly disappearing in the distance. When he heard my voice, however, he turned around and came toward me in a large circle and was calm and willing when I mounted into the saddle again.

I have said before that a horse's hearing is much better than his sight. Therefore the human voice is important to him and a horse is very well able to distinguish his master's from that of a stranger, and also to tell his mood. I remember an episode with Nero, whom I had taken with me to my new post near Berlin in 1939. I had come home from a trip in the evening and wanted to see him as I always did when I had been absent for some time. He had been taken to the stables for sick horses and I could not find him among some forty horses in these unfamiliar surroundings, especially since the light was dim. Disappointed and sad I was about to leave when as a last attempt I called him by his pet name, "Burschi". Immediately Nero answered by neighing softly from the far corner of the stables.

But back to Bengali, who learned gradually to accept the aids of my legs and go forward when I pushed him. I, too, had learned in the meantime that he might stop suddenly when he was frightened by anything and I was prepared to keep him from running backwards with my upper body angled behind the vertical. With this first progress his impulsion increased and I began to alternate work in the arena with taking him cross-country. When I noticed the slightest loss of impulsion I discontinued work in the arena immediately in order to avoid a relapse at all costs. The tendency to run backwards is also caused by a lack of impulsion and the reluctance to go forward.

Beside this reluctance to go forward there was yet another problem which weighed on my mind during the first period of my work with Bengali. He hung his tongue out of his mouth at the left side. In the beginning I was not worried about it too much because I knew from experience that most horses who come from the racecourse are inclined to have this bad habit. To begin with much can be done to obtain a quiet mouth by choosing the bit carefully and adjusting it correctly in the horse's mouth. It is also most effective to fasten the noseband underneath the snaffle in order to limit the activity of the jaws. Of course the noseband should not be fastened so tightly that the horse is unable to accept sugar or titbits. The size of the bit may also play a part when there are difficulties with the mouth. A very thin snaffle will have a more severe effect and a thick one will influence the horse in a smoother way. But none of these remedies were of any help with Bengali. His tongue continued to hang out of the left side of his mouth. The commission which bought the horses for the Army had noticed this bad habit, too, for I found a remark in his papers that he used to hang the tongue out of his mouth.

It is not at all easy to make a horse forget this bad habit. Apart from the fact that a horse with his tongue hanging out of his mouth is by no means a lovely sight, he does not take a steady contact with the bit either. Consequently the aids of the reins cannot have much effect. The horse stiffens against the hand of the rider and the actions of the reins have no influence on the activity of the hind legs as should be the case with a well-trained horse. A horse with an open mouth or with the tongue hanging out does not concentrate on his rider. On the contrary, he is in a state of opposition and there is no mental and therefore no physical balance. An open mouth or the tongue hanging out points to faults in the basic training and also in most cases to hard or clumsy hands of the rider. The final, desperate attempt to master this undignified situation is to employ a tongue strap, which is a thin strap of leather with which the tongue is fixed in the horse's mouth. It is a rather cruel means of education that ceases to be effective the moment the tongue strap is removed.

As I have been opposed to any kind of forceful method all my life, I tried to ride Bengali with the contact as light as possible. After a few days I was pleased to notice that if this was the case he did not hang his tongue out so continuously, especially when the left rein, the side on which he hung his tongue out, was hardly in contact at all. It also struck me that he kept his tongue in his mouth for a few short seconds when I gave a series of half-halts. A half-halt is a very short action of the rein, taking the rein and giving it immediately again so that there is no pulling action. When, several weeks later, he kept his tongue in his mouth for the full length of the arena while I applied these short half-halts, I dismounted on the spot, rewarded him, and had him taken into the stables. And to my surprise and pleasure this remedy worked wonders for I was able to repeat the whole course of actions on the following day with the same result, and gradually he kept his tongue in for lengthening periods until he finally forgot this bad habit altogether. The phrase that one of my riding instructors had used came into my mind. He had said that the rider should ride the horse's tongue into his mouth from the rear. This was a notion I had not quite understood at that time. But now it became clear to me what he had meant: together with the action of the rein to counteract this bad habit, I had to push Bengali energetically forward with both legs or he would have come to a halt upon the action of the rein or have shortened his speed. With both aids coordinating, the pushing aid of the legs put his tongue in order.

Of course this kind of correction is no miracle cure applicable to every horse who hangs his tongue out, for there are no miracle remedies at all in riding. Finding a particular solution to a particular problem is the faculty that makes the rider grow, which means that he knows how to employ his knowledge and abilities, his experience and intuition, and last but not least, his imagination to choose the appropriate method for every task and every difficulty for each of his horses, finding the suitable means with which to remedy any faults and achieve success.

To my great regret I had to content myself with this initial progress with Bengali because the beginning of the war interrupted our work and shortly afterwards I fell seriously ill. In 1940 Bengali became the victim of a pectoral infection that had broken out at the Spanish Riding School and which interrupted all work for many months.

During the following years I rode Lipizzaner stallions almost exclusively and I shall report about them in a separate chapter, but I had opportunities to watch and also to ride the dressage horses of my friends and gather many interesting observations. For years I had ridden only horses I had trained myself and it was a new experience to see horses in different stages of training and to ride, so to speak, "strange" horses.

In 1950 I encountered Pilgrim, an English Thoroughbred who belonged to Mrs. V. D. S. Williams. The wife of the chairman of the British Horse Society, she had been among the "victims" of my display in London in 1949. Riding to hounds with great enthusiasm all her life, she had maintained an indifferent attitude towards dressage. But after my two stays in England, during which she had had the opportunity to try my horses, she took so much interest in this kind of riding that she began to prepare Pilgrim for dressage competitions. During my visits to her country I was able to give her advice and help. In Pilgrim I found a very intelligent and willing horse but one who raised his head and neck too high for the degree of his training, a common fault. Consequently he had difficulty stepping under his body with his hind legs and finding the correct balance. Also his movements were hard and jolting and he failed in a number of exercises. As a correction I tried to make him go briskly forward and seek the contact with the bit with a long neck and a low head. The impulsion I gained in this way helped to maintain his balance when I shortened the tempo and collected his paces, and added to the improvement of his physical training. Soon he was able to execute with great ease all exercises with which he had had difficulties before and he became so smooth in all his movements that the rider sat on his back as though in an easy chair. Mrs. Williams was so much impressed by the difference in his movements that she continued Pilgrim's schooling with double zeal. She wrote to me for advice, which I was able to give because I knew the horse, and which she followed religiously with the result that she was able to enter Pilgrim in the Grand Prix de Dressage at the Olympic Games in 1956 and to win numerous competitions both in England and in foreign countries. She was one of the first English dressage riders who participated in horse shows on the Continent. She had learned so much from her work with Pilgrim that at the Olympic Games in Rome in 1960 her excellent performance on the grey Little Model attracted the attention of the public and later she won at many horse shows in competition against the best riders of her time. The most satisfactory aspect of her victories, however, was that she had trained Little Model all by herself, because I had returned with the Spanish Riding School to Vienna in the meantime and had no more time to help her except by giving advice in my letters.

To me the experience with Pilgrim was yet another proof of how important it is to give the horse a solid basic training which is nothing else than making him go forward in balance. There is a deep meaning in the saying of an old riding master: "First of all the horse must learn how to move correctly before we may demand that he perform any exercises." Is it not the same with a human being who must first learn how to walk before beginning to dance?

I remembered this doctrine many years later when I had retired from the Spanish Riding School and visited Colonel and Mrs. Williams again in East Burnham Park. They showed me a very attractive five-year-old chestnut gelding who in the beginning gave more trouble than pleasure. He had a tendency to shy and be disobedient and also presented a number of other difficulties. Forty Winks was to become one of my most interesting dressage horses. His training had been pushed a little too quickly and he had found out how he could oppose this work. Now he offered resistance at every occasion so that Mrs. Williams had begun to take a dislike to him. I saw myself how difficult he was in front of the stable when she had mounted. He was reluctant to leave the courtyard and reacted to her pushing aids by rearing. This was a fight with absolutely unequal means and was, moreover, a great risk for the rider because the courtyard was concrete. I suggested that for the moment she should mount Forty Winks in the field where the training took place. "But a horse must allow his rider to mount anywhere!" objected Mrs. Williams. I promised her that this should be achieved in a short time but I certainly did not want to start a fight on the concrete where defeat was certain. Usually I am not inclined to compromise so easily but I am equally not inclined to begin a fight when there is not the faintest chance of winning. Besides I maintain that if possible there should never be a fight with a horse because he should not be subjected by force but brought to submit by his own will, which is an entirely different thing.

When I rode Forty Winks for the first time I saw immediately that he was very reluctant to go forward. He refused to take a contact with the bit and raised his head and neck too much. He also went with an open mouth and was interested in everything except his work. I felt uncomfortable on this really rather difficult horse and decided to go back to the very basis of training and teach him to move correctly. I rode long straight lines at the rising trot in a large flat field which was very well suited for the purpose. First of all I wanted to get to know him. This was not at all easy in the beginning because he shied away from practically everything, even the most familiar objects, and everything was welcome to divert him. He took the opportunity to shy at a horse on the road or in the field next to ours just as much as to an automobile or a shrub that he had certainly seen a hundred times before. Sometimes it was just the red sweater of a spectator that made him dash off wildly. In spite of his unreasonable behaviour, I felt when I knew his mentality better that it was much less viciousness than fear and maybe also the incapability to execute certain exercises.

When I had reached this understanding it was clear to me that the first and most important thing was to gain his confidence. I had to be calm and not lose patience even though the same fault occurred irritatingly often. Again and again I led Forty Winks towards the objects of his fear, especially to the cars of the spectators which stood around in the field. I gave him time to look at them from all sides and repeated this procedure every single day because he noticed immediately when a car he had not seen before appeared. The second principle was that I would not begin practising any exercise before the foundation was well established. And this second principle demanded great self-control on my part because not only was Winky's owner waiting with impatience for progress but also eighty to a hundred spectators came every day from all over England expecting to see a little more than a young horse being taught to move correctly. To my satisfaction I realised that English people do indeed have much horse sense because while they are not yet really familiar with classical dressage, they were able just by watching to recognise the progress in balance that I felt. The progress in Winky's mental balance—the increase of his confidence—was much more obvious. The moments of shying became shorter and occurred less often until he forgot about it altogether after a few weeks. At the end of my two months' stay I was able to ride him towards the cars and pass between them at an extended trot without Winky altering the regularity of his steps or stiffening his body.

When his confidence was well established I knew that the moment had come to mount in the stables. It worked without difficulty. When he gave a start every time there was the slightest noise, however, it was clear to me that all his difficulties had been due solely to a fear complex. In the course of his later training he lost this completely, and as his confidence in me increased I was able to make higher demands on him. This was the moment to work more intensively at the sitting trot and to cultivate his suppleness by frequent changes of speed. The progress in this work also influenced the canter favourably—it had been particularly difficult as long as he had not gone forward correctly and with impulsion. Striking off frequently into the canter from the trot and smooth transitions from the canter back into the trot should not only increase the activity of his hind legs but also contribute to obtaining a brisk and energetic collected trot. Practising these exercises one day I had demanded very frequent strike-offs on the circle on the left rein because on this side the bounds of canter were less energetic. But suddenly Winky refused to strike off and for the first time after a long period of willingness he began to show resistance. Looking back on the day's work I realised that I had worked Winky very intensively and for a good measure of time and that it was very probably from fatigue that he refused to follow my commands. Relinquishing the strike-off into the canter I rode a round at a brisk ordinary trot and sent him into the stables. I was convinced that many of the spectators did not understand my reaction and took it for weakness. And yet it was the only possible thing to do. It was the moment when the rider should recognise his own fault and act accordingly. As a matter of fact, Forty Winks was working the next day as if there had never been a misunderstanding between the two of us and never again did he make the slightest difficulty when I demanded the strike-off. The conclusion I had drawn from his behaviour had been correct.

I had another occasion to make a similar observation. When Winky had learned lateral work at the trot and at the canter and made correct transitions from one pace to the other by increasing, as from the trot into the canter, and by reducing, as from the trot into the walk, he began to reveal a very brilliant extended trot. Of course I was pleased with it and made the mistake every rider easily commits and demanded too many and too long periods at the extended trot. But suddenly I felt Winky stiffen against the pushing aids of my legs, which was a sign of alarm to me. I contented myself with a few good steps and brought work to an end. Forty Winks' owner was of the opinion that I had given in to his naughtiness but she was mistaken. The fault was mine: I had demanded too much. The young horse had no other choice. He could not tell me: "Stop! I am at the end of my strength!"

Whenever difficulties appear the first thing the rider must do is ask himself: does the horse not want to execute my demands, does he not understand what I want, or is he physically unable to carry them out? The rider's conscience must find the answer. If there is any doubt it is much better to assume that the horse is unable to carry out the commands and leave it at that, which is much wiser than obtaining the exercise by force. An omission is never of such bad consequence as an injustice.

Forty Winks was a late maturing horse, as it were; he took a long time to understand each exercise, and although he was strong and work developed his muscles, it was necessary to take his physical and mental growth into consideration and allow him ample time. It is interesting to note that at the beginning of work he used to sweat profusely, especially on his neck and chest, which is a sign that he was excited and not yet strong enough. Later, when he had become stronger and the work had developed his stamina, his forehand remained absolutely dry. The sweat on his hindquarters was proof that his hind legs had worked correctly and with impulsion.

He was the first horse with whom I had trouble when I began to teach the rein-back. There had never been a problem with any other of my horses. Winky, however, threw his weight onto the rein, bulged his neck, and did not move a single foot. Having dismounted I tried to make him understand this exercise by standing in front of him and by a light pressure on both rings of the snaffle making him set his feet back step by step. The reason he refused to rein-back was that the action of the rein did not pass through his body as it should to influence his hind legs correctly. On the contrary, Winky stiffened against the action of the rein. He did not take a correct contact with the bit and his collection was not yet well established. Instead of continuing to concentrate on the rein-back, I began to practise the move-off. For some time I had noticed that Winky had acquired the habit of beginning the movement from the halt without the correct contact with the bit. At the first step he came off the rein for a moment and only adopted the correct position of the head a few seconds later. This short moment was sufficient, though, for Winky to stiffen and begin to show resistance. For days, besides the normal work at the trot and the canter, I tried to obtain the very first step in the correct contact with the bit. I moved off into a walk, rode for a few steps, came to a halt, moved off again, until he began the movement in a state of complete relaxation being very light on the rein, and came to a halt again in the same light contact with the bit. The next phase was to induce him at the moment of the move-off by light actions of the rein to set his feet back instead of forward. When he executed two steps to my satisfaction I dismounted on the spot and gave him sugar, for which he had a particular liking. Gradually I increased the number of steps of the rein-back and chose the end of our work for this exercise so that I was able to send him back to the stables if it was well executed.

The second problem was the canter, in which Winky's reluctance to go forward was particularly obvious. An intensive programme of work at the canter with many changes of tempo and frequent strike-offs was necessary to increase the activity of his hind legs and make them jump well under his body at each bound of canter. It was not easy for me to remain faithful to my motto of taking time while Winky's owners as well as the spectators were longing for the sensation of the first flying change at the canter. But there was no alternative than to wait and see, especially as Mrs. Williams intended to enter Forty Winks in several dressage tests of the novice and preliminary classes. If I had worked too intensively and forced the flying change I might have compromised his mental balance and risked his success at the horse shows. But the long period of patient preparatory work made the canter smooth, supple, and energetic, and was rewarded by the ease with which Winky performed his first change of leg after the horse shows were over. When I had left England, Mrs. Williams continued the work I had begun and had no trouble whatsoever during the course of training in obtaining changes of lead every four and three strides and, later, every other one.

Although I worked in a very concentrated way with Forty Winks I had gained his confidence and friendship, which he proved among other things by remaining calmly at a standstill when I had dismounted, even when I did not hold his rein. He remained just as calm when he had lain down, his legs comfortably tucked under him in the straw, and I came to see him in the stables in the afternoon. Since a horse is taller than all other creatures around him, he is not used to seeing something towering above him. If somebody enters his stall while he rests, he almost always gets up on his legs the very next moment. Therefore I valued it as a special proof of his confidence when Winky did not interrupt his siesta but allowed me to come near him and lifting his head up to me, accepted sugar from my hand. It goes without saying that I avoided any noise or sudden movement that might have scared him.

By this psychological programme of work and the unconditional cooperation of Mrs. Williams I was happy to achieve success in a relatively short time. That year Forty Winks won the novice championship and many other horse shows and what is even more, gave Mrs. Williams a comfortable ride at each of the competitions. Thus he fulfilled one of the requirements of a dressage horse: he should not only be brilliant in the various exercises but above all be an obedient riding horse who is smooth and supple in all his movements.

Simultaneously with Forty Winks for a few weeks I worked another interesting horse. Valentine was a twelve-year-old Thoroughbred and belonged to a colonel. It was astonishing how much his master had taught him, considering that he had begun to be interested in dressage rather late in his life, and how much he intended to teach him, as I gathered from his questions about piaffe, passage, and flying changes from stride to stride. But the realisation of keen projects demands a solid basic training which Valentine did not possess. He was a huge lanky grey, rather stiff and crooked, incredibly good-natured and willing, but without brilliance and, on the whole, a bore. His master presented a programme for me which contained a remarkable number of exercises but most of them executed as if he wanted to demonstrate how not to do them. Valentine went through his paces with his hindquarters away from the track, often with irregular steps and an open mouth, and without any trace of collection. I had never seen a Thoroughbred's canter so bumpy.

I admit that I did not attack this work with too much enthusiasm because I had only eight weeks in which to correct this multitude of faults. But then I became interested because I felt that there were treasures hidden in this good-natured fellow. Again I had to start at the very beginning and first of all teach Valentine to move correctly and in balance. His conformation was the first obstacle. He was much higher behind, that is, his hindquarters were higher than his withers, and it was much easier for him to go crooked instead of straight. In order to place his hind feet into the prints made by the forefeet and go straight he would have had to bend the joints of his hind legs, which, stiff as they were, demanded a special effort. I am sure that Valentine was often sore in all his bones and muscles in the early stages of our work together.

A few weeks later, though, there was a difference to be felt. The simple gymnastic exercises—making straight, changes of speed, large and small circles, and, later, shoulder-in—had made him more supple, he moved in balance and had a quiet closed mouth with foam from the correct flexion in his gullet. When his hind legs had become supple and stepped correctly under his body, his hindquarters became lower and he appeared to be higher in front. At this point it was possible to collect him. The suppleness of his hind legs made the canter smooth and elastic and one day—without any special preparation—he performed a correct and rhythmic pirouette.

The effect of the daily intensive training was not only to be felt in his movements but became obvious also in his exterior. Valentine's muscles developed and made him look more handsome. His face, too, had a much more alert and attentive expression. "Since you have been riding him he has grown five years younger," said the president of an Olympic committee who had come to see me ride during his short visit to England. The work with Valentine gave me much pleasure and satisfaction, for there is no better proof of the rider's method and programme than that his horse becomes more beautiful in the course of training.

When I left England Valentine was well on his way to maturing into an Olympic horse. Whether he will ever reach this standard is another question. Not because the horse lacks the necessary talent but because his rider changes direction too often and succumbs too readily to all sorts of influences. Riding is by no means a mystic science which may be explained with mathematic formulas. Besides a well-founded knowledge and ability, it is a matter of feeling, which cannot be taught by even the best teacher if it is not innate in the person. What a pity! I would have considered myself very privileged at any time of my life if I had always had such good horses for my work as Valentine.

The last in the long line of my dressage horses—so far—is

Norman, an eight-year-old chestnut gelding with a Trakehner sire. From the north of Germany he came to friends in Canada and travelled by air and on the railway for more than three days without any difficulty. When I began to ride him two months after his arrival he was completely acclimatized. This beautiful horse was a sensation in the western provinces of Canada, for while riding is much practised in these parts, there is little knowledge about the correct training of a horse. It even happened that our friend, who rides exclusively in a side saddle, was asked by passersby whether she had only one leg.

Norman had been taught quite a number of things by his breeder in Germany. He knew how to perform lateral work, flying changes, and even some sort of passage. This was quite a great deal but most of it was superficial and not as correct as the new owner wanted it to be. She herself had been trained by very good instructors of the old European school. Once again I met in Norman a horse without sufficient urge to go forward unless pushed and often he offered a passage without its being demanded. But his passage was not the artistic solemn movement but a tense sort of hovering trot which had its origin in his reluctance to go forward. It is a great temptation for the rider to accept an exercise that the horse offers but it would have a very negative effect on the rest of the training. The idea of dressage is to cultivate and improve the natural movements of the horse so that he executes them upon the slightest aids of the rider. If he anticipates these aids he proves that his obedience is not sufficiently well established. Besides, a horse will anticipate only to make work easier for himself and to execute the exercise incorrectly. Consequently the standard of work will decline. If this is the case the rider must interrupt his present work and go back again to the basic training until it is well consolidated. Obedience is of utmost importance.

It may sound strange, but we had the greatest trouble making Norman strike off into the canter from the trot. Either he tried to run away or he offered his "passage." He had been taught to strike off into the canter exclusively from the walk and became nervous and excited upon this unusual demand. However, it is a very important exercise which improves suppleness and helps achieve the correct activity of the hind legs in response to the actions of the reins. It also furthers the will to go forward and establishes obedience and is therefore a necessity in thorough gymnastic training. Besides, it is much more natural and easier for the horse to strike off into the canter from the trot. Nevertheless, it took quite a long while until Norman understood this unaccustomed exercise and I had to allow him this lapse of time because I did not want to confuse him or make him nervous. Once again I relied on my proven remedy—good for anything and everything, one might say—which is to teach the horse to move correctly and with suppleness and balance, to make him understand his rider and follow him without reserve. So I began to take Norman on the same course of training I had pursued with my young horses, with the exception that I spent less time on the various phases. That is, I passed on when I saw that he had understood and was able to execute my demands. Of course I observed him closely all the time and found out that I could establish his confidence much more quickly after a few rounds at the walk on a loose rein at the beginning of work and that he paid much less attention to his surroundings than if I had begun our daily session with the reins applied and especially firmly applied. Maybe he suspected that his rider wanted to prevent him from having a good look at the environment and that there might be all sorts of surprising things hidden away under the bushes!

In this way Norman had a chance to look around in the open-air arena and the adjacent paddocks, and when he was satisfied with what he had seen, he would concentrate entirely upon his work. The rider should always give his horse a chance to look around before beginning serious training. His horse will never become "fed up" with dressage if the rider respects his particularities and allows the freedom of mind necessary for concentrated work. Norman was never in a state of tension when we began to practise, which I felt comfortably in all his movements. However, even on a loose rein I demanded a good walk with long strides and moving well forward. Norman's walk was completely relaxed, his hind feet overreached the hoof prints of his forefeet by more than a hoof's breadth, and his foreleg moved well out from the shoulder—a tiger's walk, as my wife used to call it. A walk like this is a wonderful means of education.

The first work at the trot, too, was begun on a loose rein and with short lazy steps in order to loosen Norman's muscles and relax his mind. This exercise was somewhat similar to the relaxing exercises such as shaking arms and legs or running on the spot which athletes execute before proper training. In this way he forgot quickly his passage-like hovering steps which had given so much trouble to his owner in the beginning. The result of these relaxing movements became obvious in the fluent transitions from the canter into the trot and vice versa which came about with an enchanting suppleness and ease and made riding a true pleasure. This suppleness enabled Norman to perform his already very impulsive trot with even more brilliance and enormously active hindquarters, so that a young man when passing by called out to his mother: "Come and look at this horse! I didn't know that riding like this existed!"

With Norman I made a new experiment. His owner was planning a somewhat lengthy trip to Europe and there arose the question of how to exercise Norman during her absence. The problem of grooms is quite a serious one in Europe, but in this part of the "new" world it is truly a difficult matter. Jimmy, the groom, was a very willing boy indeed but he was not able to ride Norman nor would our friend have wanted him to mount into the saddle. When I had been absent from the Spanish Riding School my stallions had been longed by my faithful groom Flasar, and when he had retired, they had been walked for an hour every day, led on a leading rein by a groom. However, it is absolutely unthinkable to make such a demand upon a Canadian groom as willing as he may be. It was equally impossible to have Jimmy exercise Norman on the longe because he had no experience or knowledge whatsoever in this respect. Then I remembered that I had allowed Teja and also my Lipizzaner stallions to trot freely in the arena for a few minutes at the end of the daily work and when I had called they had come towards me.

On his day of rest I went about teaching Norman this new experience, which of course took place in the indoor school. First I wanted him to get accustomed to going quietly on the longe at the walk and at the trot, which he understood in a surprisingly short time. When I called him he came towards me to be rewarded with a lump of sugar. When after a few sessions of longeing I was sure that he would come towards me at the call "Come here," I allowed him to go at a walk freely without the longe but with side reins. At first he remained exactly on the circle around me that he had followed when on the longe, and when I pointed the tip of the long longeing whip towards his nose he walked leisurely along the wall. The result I tried to obtain was that he would not rush off and that he would come towards me the moment I called him. All this time I talked English to Norman out of regard for Jimmy, who would have to exercise him later on in this way and who was very interested and also quite skilful.

In this fashion it was possible to exercise Norman for half an hour and he reacted beautifully upon the commands of my voice. He walked when I called "walk" and trotted on the command "trot." We did not practise any canter because it might have excited him and he might have gotten out of control. Besides the canter is not so necessary for exercising. The point was never to take one's eyes off him and call him the very moment he had an idea of doing anything not desirable. At the walk it was necessary to be very careful, especially when he tried to stop in a corner of the arena. Pawing the ground with his forefoot was a sure sign that he wanted to lie down and roll which, of course, was not allowed. First of all, it would have been another occasion to go out of control, and secondly, if a horse rolls in an arena he will ruin the footing for riding.

When Norman's basic training was well established and he had completely forgotten his hovering steps, I began to demand the passage again and this time he performed this air of the high school as it should be, with very active hindquarters and with as much brilliance as is usually seen only with Lipizzaners. Even considering the fact that Norman had had some extensive previous training, this progress, which was obtained in less than two months, was all the more satisfactory in view of a special circumstance. Every day I worked him for half an hour and for the next half hour he went under his owner in the sidesaddle. Changing every day from one rider to another and one saddle to another without the slightest disturbance was proof of the excellent balance he had found. Furthermore, it underlined his steady character. A good character is a must if man or animal is to achieve any high aim. It is an old equestrian truth that faults in conformation are easier to correct than those of character. Riding is essentially a question of character and the educational value of this sport has been known and underlined throughout the centuries. But only when there is good character present in both to begin with can it be made nobler by the successful cooperation of horse and rider. You cannot turn brass into gold.

My Lipizzaner Stallions

If I assemble my experiences in training Lipizzaner stallions into a separate chapter it should not convey the false idea that the representatives of the oldest European breed were trained after a method different from that used for other dressage horses or for jumpers—at least as far as the basic schooling is concerned. By separating my activity as the Director of the Spanish Riding School from the rest of my life I want to give a chronological order to those twenty-six years in which I rode mainly Lipizzaner stallions and in the last few of which I rode them exclusively.

I hope I will be forgiven if I repeat once again that the course of training, which is based upon the experiences and teachings of many outstanding riding masters of the past centuries, is exactly the same for every type of horse. It is the emphasis of the training that will vary according to the strong and weak points of the different breeds of horses. Without the subtle variations and adaptations of the method to the individual, riding would remain a sport limited to the level of a handicraft without ever rising to the sphere of art.

Today in the competitions we see mostly half- and Thoroughbreds, whose canter, especially that of the Thoroughbreds, is much easier than that of the Lipizzaner. There is no difficulty in obtaining the extended trot and their movements are generally smooth and consequently easy to sit. The difficulty of these horses lies in collection, when the steps of the trot are supposed to remain just as lively in spite of the shortened stride, and therefore the teaching of piaffe and passage may represent serious problems. On the other hand, most of the half- and Thoroughbreds do not have the pronounced individuality of the Lipizzaner stallions and surrender more readily to their rider. They submit more philosophically to the rider's will and so are easier to ride and may be ridden in a more primitive way. If, however, one of these creatures rebels against unjust treatment, he is quickly labelled "outlaw" or "rogue" and given up to disappear in the mass of unhappy horses.

Nature has given to the Lipizzaner more liveliness at the trot, which, together with the high knee action, becomes a very brilliant movement. I have already mentioned his special talent for piaffe and passage. The extended trot, however, may be more difficult to obtain because the Lipizzaner with his lively temperament has a tendency to take faster steps instead of longer ones. His movements are very powerful in most cases and make it more difficult for the rider to sit. The Lipizzaner's canter is not his strongest point. This fact has helped to spread the opinion that he is more the type of a carriage horse than of a riding horse. His intelligence, together with his physical power, demand a thorough understanding of his mentality and an individual approach to his training. In other words, his education must not follow a rigidly set pattern.

As a conclusion to this comparison between breeds of horses it seems necessary to point out that at the Spanish Riding School stallions are used exclusively for training while mares and geldings compete in horse shows and it is only in recent years that stallions have made their appearance on the show grounds. When I was at the Cavalry School I had an opportunity to ride Lipizzaner mares and I am, therefore, in a position to compare them with the male representatives of their breed. In general, mares are easier to ride than stallions except for the fact that they are more inclined to be nervous and touchy. But the Lipizzaner mares in most cases will not stand up in comparison with mares of other breeds and even sworn friends of the Lipizzaner breed have to admit that they were of better use as carriage horses. As a matter of fact, all Lipizzaner mares sent from the stud farm in Lipizza to the imperial court in Vienna were put into carriages. The Emperor Franz Joseph had a special liking for them and used them for his daily trips from the imperial castle in Schoenbrunn to the palace in town.

After the Second World War I participated repeatedly with Lipizzaner stallions in dressage competitions at International Horse Shows both in Austria and in foreign countries, and on several occasions found the judges prejudiced against this breed. It is almost an aversion and has gone to such extremes that some time ago one of the judges said to a young lady competitor: "You with your Lipizzaner, when I see you come in I don't even want to look at you! You may be as good as you wish, from me you will never get more than six!" (which is a mediocre score, the best being ten). This attitude is morally wrong, unjust, and unworthy of the responsibility of a judge. During a dressage test the breed, the exterior and the beauty of the horse (or of his rider, especially when female) should be of no concern to the judge whatsoever. The decision must be governed exclusively by the correctness of the training and the performance of the horse, by his obedience and the purity of the paces.

Doubtless the Lipizzaner has some serious disadvantages that become obvious when he is seen with other horses. He is of small height, measuring between fourteen and fifteen hands, and he has the thick neck of a stallion, which may make him appear compressed in the neck. His body may seem too bulky and out of proportion to his height. These negative characteristics are less manifest when the Lipizzaners are among each other and there is no comparison. On the contrary, by the proud carriage of the head and their powerful and elastic movements they appear much bigger than they really are. On many occasions I have heard the comments of the spectators when they visited the stables after a performance and asked for the horses they had seen in the arena: "But they are so much smaller than when we have seen them going through their paces!" In the throng of a horse show this difference in height is much more striking, especially when a Lipizzaner happens to be next to a Thoroughbred or a Trakehner, let alone a Hannoverian of seventeen hands or more. Although I have competed with great success with my Lipizzaners, I had to make a double effort and be twice as good as the other competitors in order to win.

The name of the Spanish Riding School is derived from the Spanish horses that were used for the "tremendous leaps into the

air and the dainty airs of the classical art of riding" at the time
when the Spanish Riding School was founded about four hundred
years ago. These horses came from Andalusian mares bred to
Arab or Berber stallions and received the name Lipizzaner when
in 1580 the imperial stud farm in Lipizza near Trieste was founded
to continue breeding on the same principles. Only stallions of the
Lipizzaner breed are used at the Spanish Riding School. This
institute had been founded for the equestrian education of the
young noblemen and members of the court, since in those days
being able to master the airs of high school was regarded as part
of refined manners. For the same reason, officers of the Austro-
Hungarian Army and of foreign countries were ordered there
to perfect their training. After the fall of the old monarchy in 1918,
the Spanish Riding School was put under the control of the Department of Agriculture and the performances, which to that date
had been reserved for the Emperor and his guests, were opened to
the general public. Since the financial situation of the institute was
a very delicate one, private civilian students were given lessons for
a certain fee. In the year 1925 the situation became so difficult
that a plan to dissolve the Spanish Riding School altogether won
many votes. It was exclusively due to the energetic reaction of the
public, especially of foreign countries, that this plan was not carried out. As long as there were cavalry regiments, Austrian and
foreign officers continued to be assigned to the School.

Thanks to a lenient fate, the Spanish Riding School was placed
under the command of the German Army when Austria was an-
nexed by Germany in 1938 and thus was out of reach of any
influence of the Nazi political party. This was great luck for the
old School but at the same time also represented an obligation.
Most of the German superior officers had had years of equestrian experience and were not to be dazzled by the silver coats of the
Lipizzaners. On the contrary, frequently there were blunt questions about the importance of the Spanish Riding School to the
Army and what its role was to be in the education of officers.
There was General Fromm, for instance, who was an accomplished
rider himself and commander of the reserve army until he was
executed after being involved in the attempt on Hitler's life in
July 1944. He in particular was known to have a definite dislike
for the Spanish Riding School. In 1938 he had been to a perform-

ance and was very disappointed to see in the Lipizzaners so little of the forward urge he expected from any riding horse and especially from a horse of a School that was supposed to exert a beneficial influence on riding in general in Germany.

Such was the situation when I was appointed Director of the Spanish Riding School in 1939. The first Lipizzaner I rode was Pluto Presciana II, one of head rider Polak's horses, whose training had been forced a little. Polak had a tendency to work a little too quickly sometimes for two different reasons. One was the ambition to provide the School with a sufficient number of stallions for the performances and the other was to give constant evidence of his own abilities in order to counteract the jealousy of the other riders. When I was made Director and began to build up and enlarge the School—the number of trained stallions was to be raised from thirty to seventy—Polak went to work with all his strength and enthusiasm. But in his zeal to produce more trained stallions it could happen that he overshot his aim and did not pay sufficient attention to small and yet important details.

Pluto Presciana II was quite advanced in his training when I took him in my care. He gave the well-known good feeling that all of Polak's horses gave to their riders. He had a very light contact, went with much forward urge, displayed lively steps and an elastically swinging back. But in his extended trot he had a tendency to run and take hasty steps and his passage was no good at all. In this pace he threw his whole weight from one shoulder to the other and his forelegs crossed over each other. It was a very unlovely sight as well as being incorrect. So I eliminated the passage completely from his programme of training and tried to increase the activity of the hind legs and make him shift his weight onto his hindquarters. By increasing the speed for short periods I wanted to obtain longer steps, alternating the work in the collected trot with periods at the ordinary rising trot.

This work brought me into a bit of conflict with the three head riders, who had previously been my instructors, a fact that made my position somewhat delicate. They maintained that riding the stallions forward at the trot with increased impulsion would ruin the passage and make it lose brilliance. I have always, however, had a steadfast belief in riding forward, which had become my first and most important principle, and my successes had been due to this approach even with the inferior horses I had had at my disposal. This was my argument in long discussions with the three head riders. I also reminded them that every rider needs to be checked in his work and that during the several hundred years of the Spanish Riding School's existence, the equestrian standard had been constantly checked by the Imperial Master of Stables and often also by the Emperor himself, both of whom were expert, accomplished horsemen. In the first republic, after the First World War, when the Spanish Riding School became the responsibility of the Department of Agriculture, it was supervised by government officials who were neither experts in horsemanship nor riders themselves and therefore incapable of guiding or controlling the standard of the performance of horse and rider. I then mentioned the opinion of the German officers who were currently responsible for the School and who were certainly not lacking in understanding as they were all experienced horsemen. Finally I quoted the Field Marshall His Excellency von Holbein who had been in charge of the training at the Spanish Riding School for a number of years at the end of the past century and who had stated explicitly in his "Directions" published in 1889: "In principle a school horse should with the same degree of excellence he shows in the collected movements excel in the extended paces, that is, go freely forward. . . ." Pointing out this sentence of the venerable director of the School, I succeeded in appeasing the ultimate objection of the three head riders, namely, that my idea of riding forward contradicted the tradition of the School.

My endeavour to make the Lipizzaners go forward with more impulsion was largely helped when summer quarters were established for the horses in the wide park of Lainz on the outskirts of Vienna. In this lovely natural park with its wide fields and woods which had belonged to the Emperor, the school stallions were taken out cross-country twice a week, a completely new undertaking which was met with shrugs and frowns from the three head riders. The success, however, was a tremendous one and riding master Polak was the first to acknowledge it. Once, in the midst of the summer, we had to take the school stallions into town in horse vans and present them in a performance to a delegation of foreign cavalry officers without any possibility of previous preparation. The display passed without any incident; on the contrary, it was especially brilliant and lively. The passage, expressive of both charm and controlled power, was especially applauded. After this overwhelming proof even the head riders were unanimously convinced that riding the stallions briskly forward does not harm the rest of the training but actually improves it and particularly in the collected paces. Several weeks later there was a performance for General Fromm, who afterwards said to the riders that this time he had been most favourably impressed and specifically so by the impulsion with which the stallions went forward. He had at last realised that the role of the Spanish Riding School was of great value to the training of the cavalry for a method that results in obtaining such a forward urge from a horse is of great use for any military horse too. And so we succeeded in turning an adversary into a friend. The word "forward," which has been preached by all great riders throughout the centuries, was again proved of value.

This reminds me of an episode that had happened some time before the above. Shortly after the annexation of Austria in March 1938, the Austrian regiments were inspected by a group of very high German officers. The plan was to dissolve the Austrian Army and to reestablish it within the German regiments and with German officers. The Austrian officers were to be incorporated in regiments stationed somewhere in Germany. It was General von Perfall who inspected the cavalry regiments. Before he came to the unit which broke in and trained the young horses for the cavalry and which I commanded, he had been to see the Cavalry School and the regiments of the Dragoons. Rumours preceded him that he had been quite dissatisfied with the standard of equestrian training he had observed and I admit that I anticipated his visit with somewhat mixed feelings. My cavalry group, however, met with his approval.

Many months later, in the autumn, I took part in the great manoeuvres in Fuerstenwalde near Berlin and this same general talked to the officers who gathered around him during a period of rest. He mentioned those inspections and concluded with the comment that the only place where he had found horses that went forward with calmness and confidence and where he had been convinced of a correct method of training had been with the cavalry group for the training of young horses. Unfortunately, he said, the officer in charge had had such a difficult name that he could not remember it. General von Perfall was greatly astonished when he discovered me in the group of his officers and recognised in me the major with the difficult name.

Riding busily forward and in particular riding cross-country had the same beneficial influence on Pluto Presciana II as on the other stallions. Very carefully I began again with the passage. As a preparation I practised the piaffe with him. He had learned it in work in hand with riding master Polak and was able to perform it now under the rider with great liveliness and brilliance, a symbol of controlled power. But to his own disadvantage he became so excited when performing the piaffe that he would not bring the exercise to an end. He went on and on until it was too much for him and he leaped off with a tremendous bound. As it is much easier to decrease too much of the liveliness necessary for the piaffe than to produce it, I practised very short periods of piaffe at a time and soon calmed down Pluto Presciana's overeagerness.

The faulty passage, though, was not as easy to correct. When I rode him forward from the piaffe into the passage I noticed that he performed a few correct steps of passage—sometimes only two or three—before crossing his front legs again. Since the movement demands an enormous effort, it happened at the precise moment when he became longer in his body, when the collection slackened and his hind legs no longer stepped sufficiently under his body. Therefore I contented myself with just a few correct steps and brought the passage to an end at the first sign of his tendency to cross his forelegs by going forward at a brisk ordinary trot. Had I brought the passage to an end by a transition into the walk he would have accepted it as a reward, a misunderstanding which might have jeopardized the result we had achieved so far. After a few weeks of training I augmented the number of steps with great care until he finally was able to execute a faultless passage. This tendency to cross his forelegs remained, however, and when I had exchanged him for Neapolitano Africa it reappeared every time he was ridden by a somewhat weaker rider. Four years later the horse I rode in the school quadrille fell ill and I had to take Pluto Presciana II as a substitute. Unfortunately he was crossing his forelegs again very slightly. I worked with him in the same way

I had done before and two days later in the performance he produced a perfect passage.

Pluto Presciana II gave me two important rules for the training of his successors. First, never teach the passage before your horse is sufficiently collected and is able to step well under his body with his hind legs. The impulsion must be well established because it is the impulsion alone that brings about the long moment of suspension and renders the passage solemn and brilliant. Second, the very moment your horse shows the slightest tendency to cross his forelegs or sometimes even his hind legs, ride briskly forward and make the hind legs step well under the body by the increased pushing aids of the legs and even of the whip applied behind the girth.

Neapolitano Africa was the first of my great school stallions whom I had trained all by myself from the very beginning. It is of interest to note that when he had come from the stud farm to the Spanish Riding School as a four-year-old, both the director of the stud farm and my predecessor at the School, Count van der Straten, had agreed to sell him right away. I opposed this plan for two reasons. Every single Lipizzaner was needed to enlarge the Spanish Riding School and increase the number of stallions from thirty to seventy. Besides, long before I had been appointed Director of the School I had made the observation that very often the better stallions were to be found in private stables and the less good ones in front of the marble cribs of the Spanish Riding School, because the established custom was to sell the surplus stallions directly from the stud farm without trying them out under a rider. So I decided that all young stallions should come first to the Spanish Riding School and be trained for a year, after which it would be much easier to decide whether one or the other did not meet the required standard and so sell him to a private horse lover. Thus Neapolitano Africa came to the Spanish Riding School, which, as it became obvious later, was enriched by this stallion who grew into a great star.

I learned from this case to understand the late maturity of the Lipizzaner and to take it into consideration in future decisions. Compared with other breeds of horses the Lipizzaner's development is slower by one or two years. It is well known to every expert that there is nothing more difficult and uncertain than judging a young horse. Many an ugly duckling has later turned into a gorgeous swan. Another proof of this fact was given to me in 1943. The great hippologist Gustav Rau, under whose supreme control the entire Lipizzaner breeding program was placed when all stud farms had been transferred to Hostau in Czechoslovakia during the war, came to Vienna to visit the Spanish Riding School. He was particularly enthusiastic about the stallion Maestoso Batosta IX and marked him as "excellent" for his conformation and paces, whereas only two years previously he had suggested eliminating him and selling him as a three-year-old directly from the stud farm. This was the moment when even Rau had to acknowledge the late maturity of the Lipizzaner breed although so far he had denied it.

Neapolitano Africa was very good-natured and willing to learn but as touchy as a prima donna. Any small trifle was enough to excite him and make him nervous. If he happened to make a mistake he was beside himself so that I had to calm him by patting and caressing and to comfort him by giving him to understand that everybody makes mistakes now and then and that there is nothing tragic about them. I called him "my sensitive little soul" and treated him with even more care and tenderness than my other horses. In a relatively short time—within three years—Neapolitano Africa reached the standard of training demanded of a dressage horse at the Olympic Games.

Neapolitano Africa was to live through a decisive moment in the history of my country and become an important part of my equestrian career. His abilities were almost superior to those of Nero and this is saying much considering the successes that faithful Thoroughbred carried off against the elite of the world. The seventh of May 1945 was a memorable date for both of us. It was on this day, after the American troops had marched into Austria, that the historic performance for General Patton and the Secretary of War, Mr. Patterson, took place and decided the fate of the Spanish Riding School and the Lipizzaner stud farm, which was lost in Czechoslovakia at that time. Both guests of high rank had flown from Frankfurt on Main especially to attend a performance and it was of the utmost importance not to disappoint them or bore them but put them into a lenient mood so that they would willingly listen to my request. It was certainly an exciting moment for me and perhaps the most decisive one in the history of the old School. It might have been called: "Lipizzaners appeal for help for the Lipizzaners"!

After a pas de deux, the airs above the ground, and the School quadrille, I rode Neapolitano Africa in a solo performance on the curb only—and incidentally it was the first time he had appeared alone. Even in the most difficult exercises, such as lateral work, pirouettes, flying changes at the canter, and piaffe and passage, I led Neapolitano Africa with the reins of the curb alone in the left hand while the right hand held the whip upright according to the classical tradition. I noticed how General Patton, a horseman himself, followed the performance with growing interest, captivated by the movements of the horse. There was no doubt about his enthusiasm, which made it very much easier for me to carry out my plan. At the end of my display I rode in the passage towards the guests of honour, lowered my two-cornered hat after a piaffe, and in a short speech requested the protection of the American Army. I shall never forget that moment. In a small village in Upper Austria two men who had both competed for Olympic laurels for their countries stood eye to eye. One had been in Stockholm in 1912 and the other in Berlin in 1936. Although this day they met in very different positions, one being a general victorious in a war that had been waged with much ferocity and the other a member of the defeated nation. Yet there was a touch of Olympic spirit in this encounter. General Patton rose from his seat when I made my request for help and protection for the Spanish Riding School in that time of chaos. I also asked for help in finding the Lipizzaner stud farm and bringing it back to Austria. Both requests were to be fulfilled. The Spanish Riding School was saved. During my speech and that of General Patton, Neapolitano Africa stood motionless as if he were conscious of the fateful hour.

When the Spanish Riding School began to undertake trips, in the first years after the war, to give displays in foreign countries, Neapolitano Africa's solo remained the highlight of the performance. Although he was so easily excited and nervous when there was anything new to him I was certain that I could always rely on him. With pleasure I remember the enthusiasm his performances aroused in Austria, in Switzerland, Italy, and Germany, and during his appearances in London in the years 1948 and 1949.

I took Neapolitano Africa to the Olympic Games in London in 1948 as a reserve horse to Teja in order to be well supplied for all emergencies. The day after the Grand Prix in which I had presented Teja, I was asked by the British Horse Society to ride a display with Neapolitano Africa after the dressage test of the Three Day Event. Depressed by the result of the Grand Prix de Dressage, my first reaction was to decline, but then I was informed that this invitation was meant as an appreciation of my equestrian knowledge. When I accepted without much enthusiasm I was by no means aware of the triumph awaiting me.

The next day, after the last Three Day Event rider had finished his test, I rode into the huge stadium of Aldershot near London. It was filled to the last seat. I presented Neapolitano Africa in a particularly difficult programme demonstrating everything that may be demanded of a horse in the airs on the ground, including piaffe and passage which, as I have already mentioned, had not been part of the Grand Prix test at the Olympic Games of that year (levades, courbettes, and caprioles belong to the airs above the ground). The spectators followed the harmonious movements of the white stallion in silence and when I saluted, doffing my black top hat, they broke into such a storm of applause as had not been heard after any of the dressage tests in this stadium. The success was so overwhelming that I was asked to repeat the display after the show jumping of the Three Day Event two days later. General Decarpentry, who had been one of the judges at the Grand Prix de Dressage, declared that the performance of Neapolitano Africa had been of such perfection that this stallion would have been awarded the gold medal had I presented him instead of Teja in the Grand Prix. Although this was a great compliment, I did not share the opinion of the general because the fact that there was no piaffe and passage would have been an even greater disadvantage for the Lipizzaner than for the Hungarian half-bred. Besides, the judges would certainly have compared him unfavourably to the other competitors as an "unmodern" horse, a relic of the baroque period.

In the following year, 1949, I saw my greatest personal success in London together with Neapolitano Africa and my other two horses as I have already related in the chapter about Teja. This wonderful descendant of the medieval Spanish horses helped to win friends for the classical art of horsemanship and also gave a touching proof of confidence and reliability. One day I was asked to ride my programme in the spotlights. Although I had never tried anything like it and there was no possibility of rehearsing before the show, I agreed, trusting in my good Neapolitano Africa. The well-known British show jumper Colonel Llewellyn, out of loyal comradeship, warned me against this experiment because he himself had had bad experiences when doing his round of honour in the spotlights. His horse Foxhunter had been blinded by the dazzling light and had been afraid to go into the complete darkness in front of him. Also he had tried to jump over his own shadow when it appeared in the spotlight.

I admit that it was with some forebodings that I cantered into the pitch-dark stadium of White City surrounded and followed by a circle of four blinding spotlights which embraced horse and rider. I could see barely two yards to the front. When one of the flower pots that marked the arena appeared in the circle of light, I knew that this was the end of the line and I had to turn. Neapolitano Africa had to remain absolutely straight and not miss a single one of these marks, otherwise we would have lost our direction in the vast arena. I am sure this was the most severe test of going straight and in perfect balance. The slightest swaying in the lateral work or in the change of leg at the canter, or a pirouette not executed correctly would have meant not meeting the flower pot and getting lost. Moreover, this display was the greatest proof of Neapolitano Africa's obedience and confidence. He allowed me to take him at the extended trot or the canter into the black darkness in front of him without hesitating for a fraction of a second. The public was ravingly enthusiastic and for the following nights the repetition of the display in spotlights was urgently demanded. But the president of the horse show, Colonel Williams, declined with the explanation that the art that horse and rider had demonstrated was far too great to need underlining by spotlights.

In London I fell ill with severe hepatitis, which sent me into hospital for several months, and my faithful Neapolitano Africa caught a mortal sickness in the autumn of the same year during a display of the Spanish Riding School in Zurich. Since there were no horse vans for the stallions they had to be walked for an hour through the streets of Zurich in order to go back and forth between the stables and the stadium where the performances took place. Neapolitano Africa caught a very bad cold, which turned into a chronic lung disease, from which he never recovered despite the best and most loving care. With the unique success in London in 1949, the brilliant career of this wonderful stallion had reached its climax. Once again it was proof for me that mutual understanding and confidence may bridge many a difficulty and that the calmness of the rider may turn even the most nervous and excited horse into a willing partner submitting cheerfully to his master.

As often in nature, brightness precedes the imminent end, so it happened with Neapolitano Africa when he appeared once more in his solo performance in Toronto in 1950 towards the end of the first American tour of the Spanish Riding School. By that time he had gained a great reputation, which is also a great responsibility, for disappointment is certainly one of the most bitter experiences in life. But the stallion accomplished his task faithfully as ever; he went with perfect precision and such brilliance that he not only lived up to his reputation and earned storms of applause but was also praised by the entire Canadian press which usually gave very little space to reports of equestrian events. At that moment I did not know or did not want to know that this success would be the last of a long line of triumphs.

It is impossible to speak about Neapolitano Africa's art without mentioning his special feat, which was the pirouette in the piaffe. This is an exercise rarely seen—even at the Spanish Riding School —and hardly ever in the perfection with which it was presented by Neapolitano Africa. In an extremely brilliant piaffe with steps of perfect regularity he turned the forehand in a slow motion around the hind legs as they moved elastically on the spot in the energetic rhythm of the piaffe until he had completed a pirouette. I am lucky to own a film in which the harmonious motions of the stallion are preserved as evidence. It was very sad for me that this faithful friend was to leave me in his nineteenth year, which is young for a Lipizzaner. I had done my utmost to alleviate the years of his sickness.

Pluto Theodorosta was another Lipizzaner stallion who was to be my companion for nineteen years. Although nature had given him great physical beauty, his brilliant career was not to be foreseen in the beginning. When the young four-year-old stallions first come from the stud farm to the Spanish Riding School, they are longed for several weeks and then assigned to the various riders to be initiated gradually in the training. Pluto Theodorosta happened to be allotted to a rather passive rider, which seemed to condemn him to remain forever a remount. After five years of training his abilities had not been furthered beyond the demands made upon the horses in the first year, which are demonstrated in the performance by the "young stallions." This is the traditional beginning of the display and is limited to the three basic paces: walk, trot, and canter. In the group of young stallions, it is true, Pluto Theodorosta attracted the attention of the spectators by the beauty of his natural movements, which made him stand out among the rest of the Lipizzaners. I felt sorry to see this superb horse remain eternally in the same stage of training without any prospect of developing his probable abilities. Since at that time I was not allowed to ride because of my heart condition, I asked riding master Polak to take him into his care. The great master was horrified by the stiffness and the hard movements of the stallion, who had in the meantime become nine years old. He wanted to make up quickly for what had been so long neglected in Pluto Theodorosta's training and on several occasions there was a fight between the two of them. In 1942 riding master Polak had a heart attack and sank from the horse during a performance. When he died after having been in the hospital for several weeks, I decided to work Pluto Theodorosta myself as much as I was able to at that time. I worked him in hand, that is, I led him along the wall with a leading rein and with side reins attached to his saddle and to the rings of his snaffle. I demanded a few short trot-like steps, which should make him more supple. Once, though, he responded to the pushing aids of my whip with an elevation of the forehand and a leap forward, which suggested a certain talent for school jumps or airs above the ground. I took advantage of this talent and in the work in hand trained him for caprioles (a movement in which the horse leaps into the air and kicks out energetically with both hind legs). Although this work continued to be very promising I ceased it after a while because it did not correct his stiffness.

When at last I was allowed to ride again I knew that I had been right; my suspicion proved true by the feeling he gave me when I rode him. His movements were so stiff and so hard that I was unable in the beginning to ride the length of a long wall at the sitting trot. I was thrown up and down in the saddle by the violent action of his unyielding joints and muscles. Very slowly I attempted to reduce to a shorter tempo the impulsive ordinary trot his former riders had practised as almost the only exercise. In order to achieve this I did not employ the sitting trot as with my other horses but the rising trot. His violent action would have made it too difficult and too strenuous for me to maintain a quiet seat. If I had slipped about in the saddle it would not have helped to loosen his stiffness, but would, on the contrary, have produced the very opposite effect. At the same time, I took great care to make his contact with the bit gradually lighter and to make him carry himself and not lean on the bit. When after a few weeks of steady work he was no longer going on the forehand all the time, I carefully tried to sit a few steps at the trot and realised with pleasure that his movements had become noticeably smoother. Gradually I increased the periods at the sitting trot, interspersing voltes and transitions into the walk and the canter and enjoyed the softer action that made it much more comfortable for me to sit in the saddle. This was the result of his increasing suppleness, which I could feel in all his movements.

On the whole, Pluto Theodorosta's training progressed only slowly and establishing a sound foundation took a very long time. Once again I found confirmation of the fact that it is incomparably easier to begin the training of a young horse in the correct way than to retrain a spoiled one. When retraining, the rider not only works on eliminating a number of faults that have become habits but also has to take the horse's age into consideration. The proverb applies to the horse as well as to man: You can't teach an old dog new tricks.

However, Pluto Theodorosta gained more suppleness and flexibility both physically and mentally through consistent yet varied work. His progress continued in an ever increasing pace. In May 1945, I presented him for the first time leading the quadrille during the historic performance for General Patton. Only four years later he accompanied Teja and his Lipizzaner friend Neapolitano Africa to London and participated in the display at the International Horse Show in White City. He had become one of the star stallions of the

Spanish Riding School. Only an outstanding horse was up to the demands made upon him in a solo performance in front of thousands of spectators. Pluto Theodorosta, like the other two horses, was able to captivate their attention and arouse their enthusiasm. Many British horse experts preferred him even to Neapolitano Africa because his paces had a longer stride and resembled those of the English horse. In the following year, 1950, together with Teja he helped to spread interest in dressage at the Spring Show of the Royal Dublin Society. His performance won the same appreciation as that of Teja although the Irish observed a certain reserve towards the Lipizzaner breed because of the high knee action. But Pluto Theodorosta's paces, as I have said before, were equal to the trot and canter of any Thoroughbred, which is not the case with all Lipizzaners.

Pluto Theodorosta had a sparkling temperament, which enhanced his lively and impulsive paces and gave a special brilliance to his whole appearance. His obedience was exemplary and he had unlimited confidence in his rider, which prevented him from shying or giving trouble by sheer gayety. He revealed his lively temperament in a very spectacular way on his trip home from Dublin. Quite obviously he took the rather dilapidated state of the French Railway Company car as an insult and not in keeping with his rank. Maybe it was also the continuous rattling and jolting that disgusted him. For a while his groom, my faithful Flasar, succeeded in calming him, but then he had enough of it. With a tremendous leap he tore his halter and gave vent to his rage. The poor man who had been the horse's best friend had no choice but to take flight. He squeezed himself through a narrow opening in the sliding door, pushed it closed again, and hanging outside on the step of the carriage in the brisk air of spring, frantically tried to catch the attention of the personnel of the train. When at last they noticed him, the train was halted on the spot. Flasar bravely ventured into the carriage again and tried to put order into the mess which the horses had produced and to calm them down, because rebelling Pluto Theodorosta had excited Teja, too, and instigated a veritable riot. His rebellion had a positive result, however, for at the next station their defective carriage was exchanged for a better one.

During the first tour of the Spanish Riding School to North America in the autumn of 1950, Pluto Theodorosta had to substitute for my faithful Neapolitano Africa who, apparently recovered, had been taken on the trip but fallen ill again in Harrisburg. This meant a new task for the hot-tempered stallion. So far he was used to appearing in the quadrille with the other Lipizzaners. He had led them on but had been accustomed to being always in the company of other horses. But now the question was to enter alone into the completely dark hall encircled by the spotlights and I had not had an opportunity to make him familiar with these lights before. A horse clings to his habits and the herding instinct is one of his strongest impulses. Therefore, having to appear all by himself suddenly is quite a shock even without spotlights. Besides, appearing twice a day both in the solo performance and the quadrille meant a great strain for Pluto Theodorosta. He met his task beyond expectations, however, and performed his first solo brilliantly. Never have I been more conscious of his abilities as when alone in the vast arena and impassive to the unfamiliar surroundings, the dazzling light and blinding darkness, he gave himself up completely to me in absolute obedience and full harmony, executing the most difficult exercises on the curb only. Encouraged by the success of Pluto Theodorosta's performances in London's White City and at the Royal Dublin Society, I decided to enter him in dressage competitions. He was the first Lipizzaner I rode in dressage tests and soon it became clear to me that his performance had to be twice as good as that of the other horses if, as a Lipizzaner, he was to stand comparison with half- and Thoroughbreds. I have explained before the reasons for the severe judging of the Lipizzaner.

Pluto Theodorosta's first appearance in the role of a dressage horse in 1950 was a complete success. In Frankfurt on Main we were placed second to Germany's idol Otto Loerke in a medium class and won first place in the difficult test in the same show. Soon afterwards we were victorious in an Olympic dressage test in Hamburg. It was the first time that a Lipizzaner had won a Grand Prix. I had little opportunity to take Pluto Theodorosta to horse shows but whenever he appeared he won. He reached the climax of this part of his career at the great horse show in Stockholm in 1952. In the free style test we left behind us seven of the best participants, who had come from the Olympic Games in Helsinki. Among them was the winner of the gold medal in the

Olympic dressage test, the Swedish Major St. Cyr, and what is more, this occurred in his own country.

In a free-style test the rider may choose his own programme according to the abilities of his horse. He is given a proscribed time limit and a number of exercises that have to be built into his performance, but the order of the figures and the airs are left to the imagination of the rider. Besides the correctness of the exercises and the horse's paces, his obedience and impulsion, the judges give a mark for the artistic value of the programme. In that particular test Pluto Theodorosta for the first time performed three pirouettes one after the other with such perfection that, together with the rest of his flawless performance, there was no doubt about his victory. Having completed the last pirouette, he continued in complete balance on the same straight line he had been going on before the pirouette. To me he gave the wonderful feeling that I could have asked for many more pirouettes, that all I had to do was to think and he would execute my thoughts. He gave me the incomparable sensation of complete harmony.

In Stockholm we had another unique experience which became one of the summits of the life of this brave stallion. As a display during the horse show, the Spanish Riding School gave its performance in the vast stadium in which the 1912 Olympic Games had taken place. These were the games in which equestrian events had been included for the first time. When the first part of our programme came to an end with my solo performance on Pluto Theodorosta, the organisers of the show asked me to come into the arena alone with him, for I was to be specially honoured during the intermission. Had I known what kind of honours lay in store for me I would not have entered the arena so calmly.

At a collected canter I rode into the completely dark stadium and reached the place of our performance surrounded by a circle of four spotlights which had followed me. All alone in the dazzling light I waited for what was to come. Suddenly I heard the deafening noise of a helicopter circling above me and saw its brightly lit cockpit. Pluto Theodorosta, too, discovered the deafening and blinding object, which sank slowly to the ground. Terrified, he prepared to take a hasty retreat, which would certainly have been the most natural thing for him to do. I was aghast at the idea of having him race around in a panic in the vast space of the arena, accompanied by the roaring laughter of some twenty-two thousand spectators. I was about to face the greatest disgrace of my life, the sublime and the ridiculous being so close together.

In a desperate attempt to save my reputation, I applied the reins and took a firm contact with the mouth of the excited stallion. I pressed my legs with all my strength to his body to make him feel that I was with him and to remind him of the obedience I had built up in years of training. I was not at all sure of the effect of my aids. Would I be able to hold the powerful stallion? It was a terrible moment. But Pluto Theodorosta remained motionless on the spot. His obedience was stronger than his panic! He continued to stand motionless when the brightly lit monster approached more and more noisily and the wind of its blades whistled around our ears. This hot-tempered Lipizzaner stood like a monument, and only my legs pressed to his flanks felt him tremble. The helicopter touched the ground at a distance of about twenty yards and two small children in Swedish national costume left the cockpit. Pluto Theodorosta again obeyed when I ordered him to approach, in a passage, the two children who waited for me in front of the helicopter. The little girl handed me a huge bouquet of flowers and the boy presented one of those well-known Swedish horses which are said to bring good luck. It was of solid wood and the size of a full-grown poodle. Hardly had I recovered from astonishment at the weight of this present when I realised that everybody had withdrawn into the darkness and that I was alone again in the arena, my hands full with reins, whip, two-cornered hat, flowers, and Swedish horse. How would I manage a decent exit with all these burdens? In a collected canter I set Pluto Theodorosta in the direction of the gate, followed by the circle of the spotlights, and carried by the enthusiastic applause surging from the darkness surrounding me. My burdens, especially the "horse of luck," seemed to become heavier all the time and Pluto Theodorosta became faster and faster. We reached the saddling area at last by the sweat of our brow but without accident, and there my faithful Flasar delivered me of my various loads and cavalry officers and experts crowded in on me congratulating me on Pluto Theodorosta's obedience. They proclaimed him the "perfect dressage horse"!

He had an opportunity to prove worthy of this praise a year later in London. The Spanish Riding School had been invited to give a display at the CHIO in White City and after an evening performance a reception was given in its honour at Kensington Palace by the Duke of Beaufort. At this party I had the privilege to be introduced to Her Majesty Queen Elizabeth II and the Duke of Edinburgh and to have a long conversation with the Queen which will forever remain engraved in my memory as an unforgettable experience. I was deeply impressed by the Queen's great interest in and knowledge of horses, by her sympathy with the fate of the Spanish Riding School after the fall of the Austro-Hungarian Empire and during the Second World War. I was most surprised to hear how much Her Majesty knew about this old institution. Later, the Duke of Beaufort explained that he had lent the Queen my book about the Spanish Riding School, and she had studied it with great interest. Her keen observation struck me, too, when she talked with enthusiasm about Pluto Theodorosta and said: "I have been full of admiration of your stallion. Although led only with one hand on the curb, he performed the most difficult exercises with great harmony and regularity. I have been most impressed that he did not do a single unlevel step at the passage, although he splashed through the water. Most horses would try to avoid the puddles. . . ." There had been a torrential rain just before our performance.

The Queen went on demanding explanations of various details of the training and in this connection asked whether I thought that she, too, would be capable of riding Pluto Theodorosta. When I replied that this would be the greatest honour for me, the Queen hesitated for a moment and avoided a definite answer, although the Duke of Edinburgh was very encouraging about it: "Why don't you ride him if there is the opportunity!" Shortly afterwards the Queen left the party. The Duke of Beaufort, who had accompanied her to the car, came to see me immediately afterwards and said that the Queen had charged him to find out whether I had really meant that she could ride my horse or whether the offer had been mere politeness. Of course I answered that I had been absolutely serious about it, and the Duke said that he would inform Her Majesty accordingly.

Queen Elizabeth's intention of riding a Lipizzaner stallion roused greater excitement among the various personalities of the

Court than I could have imagined. The opponents of this equestrian experiment underlined their views with the argument that it would be irresponsible to expose Her Majesty to the risk of being harmed by a foreign horse trained by a foreign rider from a foreign country, . . . etc., etc. . . .

But they lost their cause. On July 25, 1953, Pluto Theodorosta was taken in a horse van to Buckingham Palace and the Queen rode him in the indoor arena. When Elizabeth II had mounted and taken up the reins she asked who rode the stallion besides me. Upon my answer that he was walked in hand during my absences, the Queen drew a deep breath: "And I of all people should be the first strange rider on his back!" I admit that I felt very nervous, too, because Pluto Theodorosta had been ridden exclusively by me during the past ten years. I remained as close as possible to him, ready to help if it should become necessary. But walk, trot, and canter succeeded excellently. The Queen reacted promptly to my correction and said in a little period of rest, "How smooth this horse is in all his movements. How willing he is to strike off into the canter on both reins. With my horse there is always some trouble when striking off. He doesn't like to canter on the left rein!" When the Queen had executed several movements of the basic paces I asked whether she would like to try piaffe and passage. She replied: "Oh, I should love to, but I don't know what to do!" I gave short instructions and helped a little with my whip. Pluto Theodorosta was obviously conscious that this was one of the greatest moments of his life and performed both paces with such impulsion, regularity, and harmony that I myself was thoroughly astonished. Never before had I seen him under another rider and I had not known what he looked like in these solemn paces. The Queen's cheeks flushed and when she came to a halt she exclaimed: "I am thrilled!" It flashed through my mind: Her Majesty in the saddle on a majestic horse!

I considered Queen Elizabeth's ride on Pluto Theodorosta as the coronation of my work and the ultimate proof of the correctness of my training. The meaning of dressage should be to train a horse in such a way that he gives a comfortable ride at any moment and to anybody without any special instructions or the revelation of any secrets. I felt royally rewarded in the true meaning of the word when the Queen praised the softness of Pluto Theodorosta's movements which, of all things, had been so unimaginably hard in the beginning.

For Pluto Theodorosta, too, it meant the climax of his career, for his fame spread throughout the world. After the Queen's ride the crowds thronged into the tents where the horses were stabled at White City. Everybody wanted to see the famous stallion who had been ridden by the young Queen. His name became so well known that many months later I received a letter addressed to "Mr. Pluto Theodorosta, Austria." The writer of this letter could not remember my name but had kept in mind that of the famous stallion.

How far Pluto Theodorosta's fame had spread became clear to me when eight years later the American President came to Vienna to meet Khrushchev. After the performance of the Spanish Riding School, Mrs. John F. Kennedy inquired about the Lipizzaner stallion that the Queen of England had ridden. With great interest she looked at Pluto Theodorosta, who in the meantime had reached the age of twenty-nine, and asked whether the Queen had ridden sidesaddle. Upon my reply that the Queen had ridden the stallion in my saddle she said immediately: "But the Queen did not ride him in the high school?" My explanation that the Queen had ridden him also in piaffe and passage increased her astonishment and she asked: "How could the Queen ride the horse in the high school?" I explained that Pluto Theodorosta had been taught by me to perform these movements and that I had helped the Queen when she executed the difficult exercises. Mrs. Kennedy then asked: "Would you help me, too, if I rode one of your Lipizzaners?" The Austrian Federal Chancellor who stood behind us was greatly worried about the protocol, which did not project any equestrian exercises on the part of our honoured guest, and he whispered nervously: "What shall we do if she wants to ride now?" It was easy to calm him with the explanation that Mrs. Kennedy was unable to ride this very moment because she was not in boots and breeches.

This short conversation, however, seemed to have left a lasting impression, because a short time afterwards I received a letter from the White House in which Mrs. Kennedy wrote that the visit to the Spanish Riding School had been the highlight of her whole trip to Europe. At the end of the letter she had added by hand: "Do not forget you promised me one day I can sit upon one of your

Lipizzaners! I will be very careful and very honoured! Until that happy day, thank you again. . . ."

His appearance in London in 1953 was the summit of my work with Pluto Theodorosta but not the end of his career. Although I did not take him to competitions any more after his victory in Stockholm and the Queen's ride, he continued to be a vital part of all the performances of the Spanish Riding School. When he grew older I decided to make work easier for him. Instead of presenting him in the solo I rode him in the quadrille, the exercises of the quadrille being less difficult than those of the solo ride. When he had attained the age of twenty-nine, I wanted to retire him and give him his well-deserved rest. But he did not seem to be of the same opinion. One day he took advantage of the fact that the door of his box was always open and trotted through the time-honoured courtyard and across the street to the indoor riding school. The groom who raced after him stood horror-struck when a bus rolled through the busy narrow street that the stallion was about to cross. But Pluto Theodorosta paused, waited until the traffic had passed, and crossed the street when he had convinced himself that there was no danger. Appreciating his zeal, I continued to ride him for another year in the beautiful riding hall, taking care not to demand too much and gradually making him accustomed to his retired life. The last year of his life I had him exercised at the walk without a rider and without a saddle. When he was thirty-one years old his gallant heart gradually grew tired until at last, on a hot summer day, it ceased to beat.

His advanced age was not only proof of the strength of the Lipizzaner breed but also and above all proof of the correctness of the training that had maintained his health and stamina until the very end in spite of the demands made upon him.

Maestoso Alea was the name of the third Lipizzaner who was to be my companion for more than fifteen years. This majestic stallion had great beauty and tremendous movements but he ranked among the most difficult horses of my life. Never before had I ridden a horse who was so unsteady in his performance and whose mentality I had such difficulty understanding. The work with him required strength and patience sufficient to have trained three horses in the same time. As the Director of the Spanish

Riding School my position was incomparably more difficult than that of any other member of the School. If one of the riders did not get along with his horse he might exchange horses with another rider without losing face. But if I had difficulties with my horse I could not possibly turn him over to one of the riders, for I had to set the example for everything. A rider who would have taken over a horse from me would have had the ready-made excuse for any problem he might encounter: "The boss himself was not able to ride him!" I would have jeopardized my authority and any observation or correction on my part would have been unconvincing. You can ask from your men only what you are able to do yourself. There was nothing left for me to do but clench my teeth and go on with the training, for it was equally unthinkable to sell this magnificent stallion into a private stable.

My task was rendered doubly difficult by the fact that Maestoso Alea was already eight years old when I began to ride him and had passed through the hands of several riders. All of them had tried to cope with him with all sorts of means and not always the most gentle ones, I am afraid, and none of them had been able to get along with him. As I have mentioned, it is much more difficult to correct a spoiled horse than to begin to train a young one from the start. In this case there was the additional difficulty of Maestoso Alea's unfathomable mentality, which tempted me to comparison with a human who is not always in his right mind. Of all my horses he demonstrated most vividly the old truth that faults committed in the beginning of the training may be eliminated later only with great effort and in most cases not at all.

Maestoso Alea was extremely sensitive to all changes in his surroundings. Anything new captivated his attention to such an extent that he forgot everything he had ever learned. With all his power and intelligence he opposed any attempt to make him submit and accept the aids. In such cases he refused to take any contact with the bit, threw his head up, and made it impossible for me to collect him. For himself, too, he made work extremely difficult. When he raised his head too high his balance was disturbed and he felt discomfort in his back. The discomfort made him all the more resistant. He worked himself into an ever increasing excitement and was not to be calmed by any means. I had to muster all my patience and try to ride him with a lowered head and neck to prevent him from raising his head and neck too high in moments of excitement. Whenever I thought I had obtained a result which would last, he convinced me of the contrary in the very next moment for no visible reason. Once he jerked his head up with so much violence that he struck my chin and caused a slight brain concussion. I had his teeth examined and his snaffle bit checked and exchanged for another one, but nothing was to be found that might have irritated him and justified his unreasonable behaviour.

After years of hard work, during which I sometimes despaired of obtaining any progress, I had completed his training but I was never able to rely on him as completely as I had relied on my other horses. I entered him in dressage tests and although we won competitions of the standard of the Olympic Games, he might have just as well let me down completely. At a horse show in Hamburg Maestoso Alea won a dressage test of the difficult class in a superior manner and immediately afterwards sent me to fourth place in a competition at Dortmund. He had begun the test of the Grand Prix in beautiful style and the victory seemed certain. But suddenly and without any apparent cause he threw his head up so violently that our chances were gone.

He was so variable and unsteady in his behaviour, so unreliable, that even experts did not recognise him at once. After the performance of the Spanish Riding School at that particular show in Dortmund, in which I had presented Maestoso Alea heading the school quadrille, a friend who was also a rider asked me: "Why didn't you ride this stallion yesterday instead of Maestoso Alea, who let you down in the test?" On both days it had been the same Lipizzaner. In spite of our successes our relationship was overcast by a number of these unfortunate incidents. On his "good" days Maestoso Alea was of a breath-taking beauty and captivated and charmed thousands of spectators by the brilliance of his movements. He was even mentioned in novels and poems, but he could also have a complete disaster in store for me. He succeeded in convincing the experts although the judges were twice as severe with him, first because they had heard about his difficulties or witnessed them, and second, because he was a Lipizzaner.

I did not learn much from this stallion because I was incapable of understanding his reactions and penetrating his mentality. He confirmed within me the necessity of mutual and unrestricted confidence between teacher and pupil. How impossible it was to understand Maestoso Alea will be illustrated by two of those incidents with which he spiced his life and mine. Once he stood in the stables saddled and bridled and ready to be taken into the riding school. He was waiting in front of a tall glass door which was framed in steel and ajar. Maybe something had frightened him, for he threw his head up and the cheekpiece of the snaffle got caught in the handle of the door. When he felt that he was trapped he worked himself into a nervous fit and reared hysterically, jerking the high door out of its hinges. It was necessary to summon five men to put the heavy door into place again. Of course there was no work to be done with Maestoso Alea on that day nor on the following ones. All I could do was to ride him forward quietly with a low head and a long neck and try to calm him down.

The second incident happened at the airport in Baltimore where the stallions were landed for the great American tour in 1964. I had feared difficulties during the flight, which was the first in the history of the Spanish Riding School and which lasted twenty-two hours, but again Maestoso Alea acted in an unforeseeable way. Without the slightest nervousness he walked up and down the steep gangway of the turbo-prop plane and during the flight remained much calmer than all the other stallions although neither he nor the others had been given any tranquillizers. Having arrived in Baltimore at last and before being taken into the horse vans that were waiting at the airport, the stallions were allowed a short walk of half an hour on the concrete of the airport. It had been necessary to obtain permission in very high places in Washington for this concession while we waited for the result of the blood test taken before they were even allowed to come off the plane. This meant a delay of several hours but was a favour to the Spanish Riding School, for usually there was a two-day quarantine. All the other horses had submitted to their fate and stood patiently in the narrow horse van instead of the boxes that had been built into the plane. I was about to leave the airport as there was nothing to do but wait for the permission to move on. Suddenly my attention was drawn to one of the huge horse vans, which housed nine horses and from which sounded a drumming noise. In the same moment my groom ran towards me shouting that Maestoso Alea was behaving like a madman, piaffing incessantly in his stall, and that the other stallions were beginning to get nervous too. I ran up to the horse box and there he was, in fact, executing an exemplary piaffe in beautiful regularity and cadence—in a competition he would have won the first prize. But now he was covered with lather, deaf and blind to his surroundings, and inaccessible to my attempts to calm him. His eyes stared fixedly in front of him and his hooves were drumming steadily on the wooden floor of the horse box. It seemed to me that the noise increased his ecstatic state of mind and I was afraid that the consequence might be a heart attack. With the help of the groom I took him out of the van. He left his stall without difficulty, still piaffing on the ramp which led down to solid ground. Here at last he came to reason and ceased to dance. He allowed me to walk him calmly up and down for about an hour, obviously enjoying the brisk March air. After his walk he returned serenely into his stall in the van acting as if nothing at all had happened. As had so often been true, I was unable to comprehend the cause of his behaviour. The groom shrugged his shoulders: "Just his usual craziness."

If I succeeded in spite of all these inexplicable difficulties in presenting Maestoso Alea, and even did so in the solo performance on the curb only in order to make work easier for Pluto Theodorosta, who was growing old, it proved that conscientious work may overcome many an impediment. But it cannot eliminate the feeling of insecurity a horse will transmit when he is unreliable in his reactions. Errors committed in young years will forever reappear. This is a fact as old as education. The errors in Maestoso Alea's early training were due to the incapability as well as the ignorance of those riders who first worked with him. I learned from the bitter experience with him that in the future I had better start the training with young and unspoiled horses.

Strangely enough, in spite of all the trouble he gave me and my depressions caused by his unpredictable reactions, it is with affection that I think of Maestoso Alea and also with gratitude, for he did give me some wonderful and successful rides. Often the children who cause the greatest worry and grief are the ones dearest to the hearts of their parents. Thus I feel very sorry that I was not able to secure for Maestoso Alea those last years of retired life in peace and quiet which I had endeavoured to arrange for my other horses. When I was retired from the Spanish Riding School, the majestic stallion was used as a longe horse and he who had never been sick became lame and had to be taken repeatedly to the veterinary clinic.

Warned by my experience with Maestoso Alea, I began to work the next Lipizzaner right after the "Kindergarden," that is, after having him accustomed to saddle and bridle and the first lessons on the longe and under the rider. For the first year the young stallions are worked with great care in order not to harm their physical and mental development. As a four-year-old, Maestoso Mercurio had a marked resemblance in his mentality to Neapolitano Africa. He, too, was tender and affectionate, one of those horses who prefer by far a caress from their master to a lump of sugar. He was very willing to learn, never given to moods, and of an absolutely upright character. However, he was easily excited and nervous and very shy. Anything new frightened him and made him completely forget to pay attention to me. As I wanted to lay a solid basis for his further training and also take the late maturity of the Lipizzaners into consideration, I made a point of progressing very slowly with his training. I admit that for a rider who is used to riding horses on a more advanced level of dressage it is not always easy to work with a young horse. Either one may get bored at times and tend to neglect some of the many little details that combine to make the foundation of the advanced work, or one may demand various exercises far too soon, especially when the horse in his eagerness to please appears to offer them. Aware of this, I had the young horses in the first year broken in by the young riders under the supervision of an experienced rider. First of all, a young rider is of lighter weight than an older one; secondly, his knowledge is modest and he is more easily pleased with his horse. If there are no major troubles he is content and is not tempted to demand more than the horse is able to do. Thirdly, the riders know that the horses will be assigned definitely only after the first year, so the young riders will not be tempted to give way to false ambition and try experiments that might harm the horses.

The most important thing was to build up Maestoso Mercurio's confidence in me. He should know that I would never expose him to any danger nor demand anything impossible. I allowed him to take a long look at all strange objects and sniff at them while I caressed and patted him. This was not so easy to begin with for he was forever ready to whisk round and take to flight. Very reluctantly, at my pushing aids, he approached the stumbling block with a very long neck and his eyes bulging out of his head. Having contemplated the object of his fear from all sides on one day, he performed the very same manoeuvres on the following day. His spookiness drove me to despair sometimes but there was nothing to be done. I had to be patient and repeat the experiment every day until he finally had full confidence in me. I noticed that the difficulties decreased in the same measure that his contact, the connection of his mouth to my hands, increased in steadiness. It is not without reason that the old riding masters wrote in their books that it is the horse who should seek the contact with the hand of the rider and not vice versa. By the correct contact a relationship to the rider is established similar to that between two human beings when the weaker seeks shelter and leans against the stronger one.

When Maestoso Mercurio's confidence was established and he had learned to go straight forward, it was not difficult to teach this intelligent and willing horse all the exercises that are required from a school horse and presented in the performance of the Spanish Riding School. No major problem arose during his training and he himself seemed to take great pleasure in our work. In a way, though, this work took place under difficult conditions. While a dressage rider has the possibility of entering his horse into competitions and of gradually taking him through the various degrees of difficulty from the beginners' classes to the medium and difficult levels, the Lipizzaner stallion appears first in a short programme among the "young stallions" and then appears no more before the public until he has mastered the art of high school completely. For the rider there is no possibility in the meantime of having his work checked step by step and of having the correctness of his method of training confirmed, as is the case in dressage tests. It is left to his own judgement to exercise a continuous check over himself. Of course, remembering General von Pongràcz, I summoned the help of my groom to check the correctness of Maestoso Mercurio's movements.

Maestoso Mercurio's progress grew on a solid basis and found its expression in the great precision of his movements. His paces were correct even though he did not have an extended trot as brilliant as that of his predecessors Maestoso Alea and Pluto Theodorosta, because he belonged to the type of Lipizzaner with high knee action. There was only one difficulty, which appeared in the advanced training. He had inherited from his father a slight inclination to cross his forelegs. At the trot this tendency was easy to eliminate by increasing the impulsion and making his hind legs step well under his body. In work in hand, as the preparation for the piaffe, however, it appeared in such a marked way that I had to give up after a short while and teach him the passage first, contrary to my usual concept of work.

Imagination is one of the most important things for an instructor to possess to help him make the work easier for the horse and to obtain progress and overcome difficulties. But imagination can be applied successfully only when it is supported by a profound theoretical knowledge and much tact and natural understanding. I remembered that the French riding masters of the seventeenth and eighteenth centuries had defined the piaffe as a passage on the spot and not as a trot on the spot as most of the other great teachers had done. This gave me the idea of teaching Maestoso Mercurio the piaffe from the passage. By short and very gentle actions of the reins, repeatedly giving and taking, I tried to make him gain less ground to the front while my legs remained applied to his flanks, pushing him forward, and my braced back made his hind legs step more and more actively under his body until he finally produced one or two steps on the spot. This method prevented him from crossing his forelegs as had been the case in work in hand. Very carefully I increased the number of steps in the piaffe, until the exercise was well established and the unsightly crossing of the legs did not appear even in longer periods of work. Maestoso Mercurio is the only horse to whom I have taught the piaffe under the rider instead of in work in hand. There are not only many ways to Rome; in the art of riding, too, there are different approaches. It is important for the rider to keep an eye on the goal he wants to reach, however, in order not to get lost in the maze of various possibilities.

In the four years of work together Maestoso Mercurio and I had found each other in full harmony. He was forever intent on pleasing me and I knew that I could always rely on him. When dismounting after the daily work I allowed him to run around me freely on a large circle. Although there were other stallions in the Riding School he never attempted to run away or play with them and when I called "Come here" he trotted up to me and gently took his lump of sugar from my palm. This little ceremony served a double purpose. Trotting around freely meant a reward for the horse after strenuous work and to me it offered the opportunity to observe the stallion in motion which I could not do when I rode him. I could study his rhythm and balance at liberty, a method that gave me many a valuable hint for my further work.

Maestoso Mercurio's confidence in me and mine in him were so well established that I dared to lead him with the left hand on the curb only when presenting him in his first solo performance. The public seemed not to exist for him; there were no more frightening objects; there was only one idea: to listen and obey the will of his rider. During his many years at the Spanish Riding School he had the honour of displaying his talents to crowned and uncrowned heads of state. He performed before King Gustav VI Adolf of Sweden, Queen Juliana of Holland and Prince Bernhard, the Shah of Iran, King Bhumipol and Queen Sirikit of Thailand, the German presidents Professor Dr. Theodor Heuss and Heinrich Luebke, and many other eminent people.

Maestoso Mercurio reached the summit of his abilities during the long tour of the Spanish Riding School to North America in 1964. For weeks he performed his solo every night in the cities of Philadelphia, Washington, Boston, Chicago, Detroit, New York, Toronto, and Montreal. In the completely dark arena he took his place between the pillars and remained motionless when my name was called out and four spotlights enveloped us. I lowered my hat and when the music set in after my salute, he began to perform "All paces and exercises of the high school" in the dazzling spotlights, and led in one hand on the curb only. His obedience and his confidence were miraculous. Unimpressed by the change of surroundings in the different arenas, undisturbed by the enthusiastic crowds and the noise and the applause, he followed my commands and like a shot out of a pistol stormed into the complete darkness in an extended trot or canter. There was a particular brilliance in his pirouettes. He performed several of them one after the other on the center line, which required the utmost precision because after this exercise we had to pass through the pillars which materialised out of the darkness at the very last moment. Maestoso Mercurio was so straight and so exact in all his movements that on one occasion after a sevenfold pirouette—the greatest number of pirouettes I have ever performed in a row—he did not lose his direction and cantered on precisely through the two pillars in the center of the arena. In all these pirouettes he did not for a moment lose, either, the exact rhythm of the canter, and he performed them with so much elasticity that he surpassed even Pluto Theodorosta, who had been a master of this difficult air.

His confidence and obedience were submitted to a hard proof during a performance in New York. As always at the end of my solo, with the two-cornered hat in my lowered right hand, I rode in a passage towards the red and white striped curtain that closed the exit. Something seemed to be very wrong because Maestoso Mercurio had almost reached the exit before the curtain opened at last. In the very next instant the heavy curtain dropped again so that for a second I remained inside the arena while Maestoso Mercurio was half outside. I no longer saw the horse's head in front of me but only folds of striped material. A moment later the curtain opened again and gave way to the two of us. The man whose job it was to operate the curtain had chatted with someone and then in his hurry had instantly dropped it again after pulling it up. Maestoso Mercurio did not lose his poise for a moment, however, and left the arena as if nothing had happened. Next morning I found a white orchid in my dressing room with a note saying: "To Mercurio—for performing heroically beyond duty and beyond that d . . . d red curtain."

During both tours of the Spanish Riding School to North America, in 1950 and 1964, I observed the educational effect that the representatives of an ancient culture, such as the performing Lipizzaners, may exercise on the public. The huge arenas were packed full and the public remained in attentive silence; there was not a sound to be heard until the crowd expressed its delight in applause and not in whistling as is the custom in some places on that continent. And since the Spanish Riding School brought about half a million spectators together in those thirty-eight performances, this attitude surely signified reverence towards the old School and the art it presented.

At the height of his career I had to take leave of my brave Maestoso Mercurio. Shortly after the triumphant tour to America I was retired because I had reached the age limit. It was a sad farewell because Maestoso Mercurio was my best friend and had become a part of myself.

When I retired I left behind at the School, besides the two Maestosos, Alea and Mercurio, two more school stallions whom I had trained completely to the highest standard, Conversano Soja and Maestoso Flora. Conversano Soja was one of the few sons that Conversano Bonavista, the favourite stallion of head rider Lindenbauer, had produced. He had inherited his father's beauty but also a certain weakness in his hocks and a tendency to be nervous. I took Conversano Soja immediately after his first training on the longe, which I continued for some time. His natural balance and his beautiful paces were improved by several more weeks on the longe so that he developed a very brilliant extended trot with smooth transitions into the collected paces and an elastic and well-cadenced canter. Working him on the longe gave me the opportunity to study his temperament, his character, and his talents before beginning work under the rider. I realised that he was a very sensitive stallion and greatly attracted by his brothers whom he greeted with loud neighing when they entered the riding school or came near him. This, too, came from his father, who had also been one of those four-legged singers.

In later years this predilection sometimes grew into a violent outburst of temperament, especially when he saw one of the other stallions directly in front of him. In such moments his temperament won over his obedience and, neighing wildly, he tried to plunge upon the other horse, which was certainly not a very comfortable situation for either of the riders. This behaviour was not viciousness, but the overpowering impulse of a stallion. Nature was sometimes stronger than education. Fundamentally, Conversano Soja was a good horse, forever intent on fulfilling my demands. And he tried very hard not to give way to his temperament.

During my work on the longe he revealed talents for certain exercises in keeping with his temperament, for instance, the flying change at the canter, and gave me valuable hints for his future training. Under the rider he continued to progress at an astonishing rate. He performed the exercises required with the precision that is a must at the Spanish Riding School. His paces were capable of impulsive extensions in which his stretched legs covered much ground to the front. In short, he promised to develop into an extraordinary school horse. This supposition seemed to be corroborated by the intelligence he displayed when I began to teach him the piaffe in work in hand.

On still another occasion my method of training was confirmed when Princess Irene of Holland, who was spending some days in Vienna, expressed a wish to ride one of the Spanish Riding School horses. I put Conversano Soja at her disposal. He was not yet ready to be presented in a performance but had reached the standard of a dressage test of the difficult class. I had him brought into the riding hall with a snaffle and began to give a lesson to the princess. I was amazed to see how well Conversano Soja went under a strange rider for the first time and how beautifully he maintained the position of his head and neck. He performed voltes and large circles correctly and showed smooth and energetic transitions of speed. The princess rode lateral work and flying changes with much enthusiasm and in a very good position and was thrilled about Conversano Soja's soft movements in trot and canter which allowed her to sit both comfortably and beautifully in the saddle. I was very pleased with the result of this lesson and proud that Conversano Soja behaved so well. However, pride goeth before a fall.

Encouraged by her obvious pleasure, I gave the princess my "star," Maestoso Mercurio, to ride as a sort of reward. This was not a very successful enterprise. She did not feel very at ease on his back because he reacted to all aids with much more sensitiveness than Conversano Soja. He would have required a much lighter contact and when she applied the reins too firmly he began to run away. The result was tolerable at the trot but at the canter the situation was rather hopeless. At the slightest change in the seat of his rider Maestoso Mercurio executed a flying change. When because of this movement the princess slipped to the other side of the saddle, he promptly changed again. He went completely irregular and ended up in utter confusion performing changes from stride to stride for the whole length of the arena. In the end all three of us looked rather unhappy and the highlight with which I had intended to conclude this lesson did not come about. It became clear to me on that occasion that the abilities of the rider are of much greater importance with a school horse than with a less advanced horse or a jumper.

To my consternation the steady and satisfactory progress of Conversano Soja was interrupted one day when he showed a severe lameness. The diagnosis of the vet revealed a spavin on both hind legs. Spavin is an ailment of the hocks whereby the small bones of this joint grow together and gradually render it stiff. Would my work of three years be annihilated so shortly before reaching perfection? Would this magnificent young stallion remain an invalid for the rest of his life? My friend at the veterinary university, Professor Ueberreiter, agreed to operate on the spavin. In many cases he had operated successfully and had cured the disease completely, but Conversano Soja was the first school horse to be operated on. The difference between operating on a school horse and his previous patients with the same affliction was due to the fact that with a school horse the hocks are exposed to a greater strain because he must bend his hind legs much more than an ordinary riding horse, especially when performing piaffe, passage, and pirouettes.

The operation was a great success and Conversano Soja, after remaining in the clinic for six weeks, returned to the stables of the Spanish Riding School. He was confined to his box for another few weeks before being allowed to be taken for a walk, without a rider of course, and for only a few rounds to begin with. Conscientiously I followed the orders of the professor and waited several months before very carefully beginning to ride Conversano Soja. It was not more than exercising the stallion at first and then slowly increasing the period of work from five minutes to a longer span of time. Conversano Soja became visibly stronger every week and one year after the operation I was able to go on from where I had left off and continue his training, finishing with the airs of high school. Another six months and he entered the riding hall at the head of the quadrille in a performance for the first time and won the public's heart with the beauty and the harmony of his movements. His coat was partly dark and his mane still black, testifying that he was the youngest member of the group.

Although Conversano Soja had grown into a perfect school horse and his operated hocks stood the strain of the training beautifully, there was one bad habit I was unable to drive out of him. He would not forget his custom of greeting his colleagues with a loud neigh. A very famous German riding master had advised me to hit him over the head at the first slightest neighing and to repeat this until he no longer uttered a sound. Although this master was successful with his method, every fibre within me revolted against using it on Conversano Soja—or on any other horse for that matter. I preferred to put up with Conversano Soja's singing, which was not always of the same intensity and which he even stopped altogether at times so that I hoped that when I increased collection he would concentrate more on me and forget his untimely neighing.

It was particularly loud and piercing if he saw horses of a different colour, as, for instance, the young Lipizzaner stallions who still have dark coats. Once he gave me the surprise of my life when he grew excited about human beings of a different colour. It happened during a state visit of the President of one of the newly established African states. Conversano Soja had entered the riding hall at the head of the quadrille and came down the center line towards the presidential box. Suddenly he stared as though mesmerized at the guest of honour and I had trouble making him advance, which was quite unusual for him. And then his neighing echoed from the white stucco ceiling of the riding hall and he repeated this resounding music every time he caught sight of the dark-faced African visitor. Maybe it was his idea of greeting the representative of the continent from which the male ancestors of the Lipizzaner breed had come hundreds of years ago. Who knows?

The delight he took in neighing created some inconvenience when Walt Disney's company made the movie *The Miracle of the White Stallions* in Vienna. The film deals with the fate of the Spanish Riding School during the last days of the Second World War and the rescue of the Lipizzaner stud farm by the American troops. The American movie actor Robert Taylor portrayed me as the Director of the Spanish Riding School, though I doubled for him on horseback, playing myself, as it were, in the equestrian parts of the film. Mr. Hiller, the director, needed several close shots of Robert Taylor on horseback at the halt and at the walk. Robert

Taylor, who had often appeared in Western movies, mounted into the saddle but dismounted the very next moment because Conversano Soja became restless and began to neigh. All my protests that the stallion would not do anything and would cease to neigh in a short while were of no avail. The actor was not to be persuaded to mount this temperamental stallion again. I had to find another stallion to replace Conversano Soja, which was not easy because of his black mane. Mr. Hiller, however, did not object to the substitute having a white mane. He said that he would cut the film accordingly. The substitute was an old and placid longe horse who was completely white and not to be disturbed by anything. From the thousands of yards of film taken every day the cutting was so clever that I was taken in myself when I saw it for the first time. I wondered about an air at the trot that I saw Robert Taylor perform, knowing for sure that he had never trotted in the quadrille. When I saw the black mane of the stallion I realized that it was not Robert Taylor who sat in the saddle but myself.

Conversano Soja also appeared in the short performance that was broadcast over the new Telstar in 1962. He then interrupted his activity at the Spanish Riding School in order to return to Piber, the stud farm in the mountains of southern Austria, and pass on his talents to the future Conversano line. Experience has revealed that the Lipizzaner stallions readjust very easily and after a short period of training are ready to resume their roles at the Spanish Riding School, even after a prolonged stay at the stud farm where some remain for several years. The activity at the stud farm is certainly no impediment to a further career as a school stallion at the Spanish Riding School.

The last Lipizzaner I trained at the Spanish Riding School was Maestoso Flora. He was a very sturdy stallion, and unlike Conversano Soja, had very strong hocks. He was a beautiful mover and one of those horses who appreciate being caressed and patted but prefer by far a lump of sugar. After a relatively short initial training he appeared for a year in the performance with the group of young stallions. But then it seemed that this was all that could be obtained from him and that this would be the end of his career. He did not get beyond this very modest beginning. In the performance he attracted the attention of the public with his brilliant trot but also with all sorts of disturbances he caused by his shyness and jumpiness. When after the first training during the winter months the young stallions are presented to the public for the first time in a performance, it usually happens that they get startled by the applause and caper to the right or to the left before leaving the hall. But after a few performances they grow accustomed to the clapping and even seem to enjoy it. Not Maestoso Flora, though. On the contrary, he appeared to be looking for an occasion to get his rider into trouble by all sorts of starts and bounds.

As the time wore on and the various riders did not get anywhere with Maestoso Flora, I decided at last to take him into my care. It is true that this was against my resolution never again to re-train wrongly ridden and spoiled horses, but I felt sorry to see this beautiful stallion remain in the elementary stage and never have the chance to develop the talents he undoubtedly possessed. So again I went back to the very beginning and started by longeing him, for I wanted to cultivate the regularity of his paces and also to obtain a steady contact with the bit. It seemed to me that the reason riders did not succeed in overcoming his spookiness was the fact that his contact was forever changing. Sometimes he went slightly above the bit and on other occasions he leaned on the rein with all his weight. As I also had to ride three or four other school stallions and work two or three horses in hand every day, I entrusted him to my old groom Flasar, who longed him on alternate days and who, following my instructions, accomplished his task extremely well.

After several months of work on the longe I began to ride Maestoso Flora and was pleased to note that now he took a steady but light contact on the bit and went forward with much impulsion. However, he was still looking for any opportunity to be diverted from his work and loved to give vent to his gayety with a capriole. I was intent on maintaining and confirming his good contact with the bit and his impulsion while I tried not to pay too much attention to his jumpiness. With infinite patience I continued to lead him up to places that seemed to scare him and did not take any notice of his caprioles. It was my endeavour to remain in the saddle and to continue work as if nothing had happened. I did not want to punish his youthful gayety and spookiness. And I was right, for a few weeks later Maestoso Flora gave up his nonsense and at last concentrated upon me and our work. Now the serious training could begin. I built it up with all the seemingly insignificant exercises, with changes of tempo and paces, and later with lateral work, starting with shoulder-in as the best basis for the others, such as half- and full passes. In the same measure in which his training progressed his tendency to shy disappeared. His confidence in me had increased and he remained motionless at a halt when I cut through the air with my whip, swishing it right or left past his ears. He knew that I would allow no harm to be done to him. His confidence was exposed to a hard test one day when an umbrella fell from the gallery where the spectators watched the morning training and brushed against his shoulder. Maestoso Flora continued on his path as if nothing had happened.

When I taught him the half-pass, in which the horse moves forward and sideways, his body parallel to the wall from which he moves away, I noticed that he began the movement in a correct position and regular rhythm but after a few meters gave up his position and no longer looked in the direction in which he was moving. His steps became irregular and hasty. It was effective to bring the half-pass to an end the very moment he showed the first sign of this bad habit and to ride forward on a straight line parallel to the wall. On a single track his hind legs were forced to step into the hoof prints of the forelegs, which is not the case on the two-track, where they step at the side of the front prints. This was the first attempt at correction but soon I found a much more effective remedy. When Maestoso Flora executed a half-pass to the left, for instance, I immediately had him perform one to the right if there was the slightest sign of his fault. Soon his steps remained regular in the two-track movements and it was no longer necessary to concentrate on this exercise. Once again I realised that it is essential to the thinking rider to find means and methods to render work as easy as possible for his horse. It is true that perfection can never be reached. The question is how near we may come to it. The idea of perfection, however, must be the magic pole towards which the rider is drawn.

As Maestoso Flora's training proceeded and he was able to move in a collected canter full of spring and energy, I prepared him for the flying changes by frequent strike-offs into the canter on both reins from the trot and the walk. This preparation, in fact, enabled him to perform the flying change to the right at the first attempt. It took a little longer to obtain it to the left side because, like humans, horses are usually stronger or more adept on one side than on the other. When the change of lead to the left side finally succeeded, I made the mistake of not having it checked immediately by my faithful Flaser. A few days later I noticed that Maestoso Flora did not jump with the hind legs under his body as completely when changing to the left as when changing to the right. His movements were so smooth, however, that I was unable to feel the fault. Once more I remembered the advice of the old General von Pongràcz that the rider's work needs to be controlled constantly. It took a much longer time to correct this fault than to teach the exercise originally because I had to begin all over again with all the preparatory work of cultivating the collected canter and rendering it full of energy, in order to achieve a proper flying change to the left.

When I began with the work in hand I was pleased to see that Maestoso Flora went forward with so much impulsion that he had no difficulty in gradually decreasing the length of his steps at the trot until at last he performed a few steps on the spot, his first piaffe. I am sure that the pleasure we both took in this work best guaranteed the progress he made in learning this difficult air of high school. Later I used these ten minutes of piaffe in hand as an introduction to my daily work as a morning gymnastic, as it were, because it made Maestoso Flora relax much more quickly. His hind legs grew very strong and his suppleness increased remarkably. As a comparison I thought of an athlete strengthening the muscles of his legs by deep genuflexions. Teaching the piaffe under the rider and the passage were the last bricks I added to the building of his education. I had deliberately allowed him the necessary time to develop his strength, to understand what I required from him, and to obey willingly and with pleasure. The brilliance with which he performed all movements and exercises testified to the correctness of this method.

In May 1962, Maestoso Flora had the opportunity to give special proof of his abilities when Queen Juliana of the Netherlands came for a state visit to Austria. During one of the preparatory conferences the Dutch ambassador transmitted the wish of the two princesses, Beatrix and Irene, to ride in the Lainzer Park on the outskirts of Vienna. It was natural to ask the Spanish Riding School to arrange this excursion as it is the only governmental institution in Vienna that has horses. In the years 1941 to 1944 the Spanish Riding School had been transferred every year to the Lainzer Park for a holiday during the summer months, and I was familiar with its fields and woods. But my stallions were not. Having spent their youth in freedom in the pastures of the stud farm, they come into their marble stables in the heart of Vienna and hardly ever leave the city again. Therefore it was obviously necessary to take the stallions chosen for this excursion out into the country for at least a week.

Because of the numerous official performances at that time it was among the young stallions that I had to make my choice. Every morning they were to be taken in horse vans from the stables to the Lainzer Park and ridden cross-country. Unfortunately the weather thwarted my plan. It rained persistently that week and there were only two days left for preparing the horses. With Maestoso Flora I led five of the stallions aged from about five to six. We rode up and down the hilly country, we jumped small ditches and waded through a pond, and I was surprised and pleased by the reasonable behaviour of the horses. Of course they had been excited at first. They found themselves in a completely strange place, which to a horse is very disturbing, habit-inclined as he is. Besides it had been years since they had seen a landscape and been in the open air. Maestoso Flora especially seemed to remember his long-forgotten jumpiness and excitement; there were numerous opportunities tempting him to skip and buck and he did not intend to miss a single one of them. But after the first quarter of an hour the obedience the stallions had learned in the Riding School won over excitement and curiosity and the two days of training in the countryside proved quite sufficient. During those summer holidays of the Spanish Riding School in the Lainzer Park the Lipizzaners had already proved that they are excellent cross-country horses. Moreover, the white stallions cantering quietly through the grass, not rushing but allowing their riders to lead them with a light contact, were a lovely sight.

Once during the war a cavalry officer who was responsible for the affairs of the Spanish Riding School under the administration of the German Army had taken part in such a ride, having chosen the young stallion himself out of a group of twenty five-year-olds.

He was most impressed by the wonderful feeling his horse gave him on this ride and no longer negated the suitability of the Lipizzaner as an all-purpose horse.

Princess Irene came alone to the riding excursion in that spring of 1962, for her sister, Princess Beatrix, had been taken ill. I had planned about an hour's ride across the fields and woods with simple natural obstacles such as ditches, little brooks, and fallen trees. But upon the wish of the princess it was prolonged to almost two hours. When the princess dismounted she said that she had thoroughly enjoyed her ride through the lovely countryside on a stallion who was so easy to lead and light on the rein, quite in contrast to an experience she had had some time ago in Mexico in which the horse lay on the rein so that she had had great difficulty holding him and her arms had ached for hours afterwards. The ride with the Lipizzaners, however, she would remember in a very pleasant way.

I had spent so much time on Maestoso Flora's basic training, on the simple and modest exercises, that rumours began to spread that I would never bring the training of this stallion to an end. But when I had established and consolidated this broad and sound foundation there was little trouble in teaching him the difficult airs of the high school in a remarkably short time. When Conversano Soja had to go to the stud farm, Maestoso Flora was ready to replace him in the quadrille. At the age of ten he was the youngest stallion ever to lead the great school quadrille. He performed his task brilliantly, not only in Vienna but also on the ten-week tour to the United States in 1964, although the performances took place in eight different cities and there were constant changes in surroundings and conditions of work.

It will be easy to understand that I was sad at parting with Maestoso Flora when I retired from the Spanish Riding School. I had given several years of my life to the work with him and now that the time had come when it would bear fruit I would not be there to enjoy it. But we had to take leave of each other.

As I have repeatedly mentioned, my outstanding instructor at the Spanish Riding School had been riding master Polak, who, among other things, made me familiar with work in hand. He was a genius in this respect. What I learned from him was not only of great value in the training of my dressage horses but also of utmost importance in the education of the Lipizzaner stallions in the airs above the ground. These are the levades, caprioles, and courbettes, exercises in which the horse raises his forehand or both fore- and hindquarters off the ground. In the seventeenth and eighteenth centuries, when the art of riding was at its summit, these school jumps belonged to the general training of a school horse and of every rider. The Spanish Riding School is the only institution where these airs are still preserved and today they are executed only by Lipizzaner stallions. When I was appointed Director of the School, it was left to me, after the death of riding master Polak, to continue his work in this sphere.

He had taught me the first notions of work in hand when he helped me to teach the piaffe to my good Nora. The first thing I learned was that the ordinary conception of work in hand is completely erroneous. Many people think that you put side reins on your horse and take him alongside the wall. Standing next to him you would hold him with the leading rein and with the whip make him lift his hind legs. This is not at all true. In reality work in hand is a very painstaking activity, in particular for the trainer, for it means a lot of exercise for him. First of all the side reins must be adjusted in such a way that the horse is able to adopt the position of head and neck he has already learned under the rider. He should remain alongside the wall and go straight. In order to put the horse in motion the trainer will have to run with him, which in the deep sand of the arena is quite hard work. The leading rein is attached to the cavesson and in light contact. It regulates the length of the steps and the ground gained to the front, and in weeks of patient work the stride of the horse is shortened gradually, while the whip, applied to the girth, substitutes for the pushing aids of the legs and makes the horse go forward with lively and energetic steps. The coordination of these aids with opposite effects—pushing and holding—will induce the horse after a while to perform a few lively steps that gain little ground to the front; in short, a dancing movement. This was the way on which I began to teach Nora the piaffe. In the beginning it is very strenuous for the rider as well as the horse, and I limited it to ten minutes daily. Riding master Polak advised me, corrected me if necessary, and also found words of appreciation when I had done well. It did not take too long before Nora was able to execute a few piaffe-like steps. Only when the horse has mastered this exercise in work in hand and has become sufficiently strong may the rider proceed to teach the piaffe under saddle. He has to begin all over again to shorten the collected trot increasingly until the horse performs a few steps on the spot.

These lessons in work in hand took place mostly on the Ameisenwiese, a riding field in the Prater Park where there was a fenced-in dressage arena. Often they were watched by other cavalry officers who then tried to do the same and practised work in hand with their horses in the barracks with varying success. Polak tried to help one of these officers with the training of his dressage horse Infant but gave it up after a while because he did not think too much of the horse. He said to me, "This horse is like a centipede, he has a thousand legs! I don't think it is possible to turn his irregular steps into a rhythmic pace." In spite of this crushing opinion I obliged my comrade and helped him with Infant. Much sweat went into this work because for the first two weeks there was nothing else to do but run up and down with him every day during the ten minutes of work in hand until at last he forgot his hasty way of tripping and found the correct rhythm at the trot. Then I was able to shorten his strides gradually and very carefully and obtained great progress after a few weeks. In this way Infant learned the piaffe at last and his rider was chosen to go to Berlin in 1936 and take part with him in the Grand Prix de Dressage at the Olympic Games. These accomplishments with Nora and Infant were my first with work in hand. Later came those with Nero and Otto.

I gained valuable experience in this work and enriched my knowledge considerably. For instance, Otto proved clearly that the capriole is a jump natural to a horse. In a capriole the horse leaps off the ground with all four legs and kicks out energetically with both hind legs at the moment when his body hovers horizontally in the air. He is supposed to land with all fours on the same spot from which he has taken off. Colts in their youthful play very often perform a sort of capriole when out at grass. Once when working Otto in hand I made him step more actively under his body with his hind legs because I wanted him to bend his legs more and at the same time with the leading rein I prevented him from rushing off. With his impetuous temperament he flung himself into the air with all four legs and kicked out with his hind legs, making the sand fly around my ears. It was a perfect capriole, which I had never taught him nor wanted him to learn.

With Rokoko, too, I made a similar observation in later years. When during work in hand I demanded with the aids I have described that she should step more under her body, she tried seriously to follow my command. She put her hind feet so far under her center of gravity that her weight shifted to her hind legs, relieving the forehand for a regular levade. She was much calmer of temperament than Otto and her reaction was not as rebellious as his—in accordance with his lively temper he had tried to evade any further effort with this school jump.

On several occasions I had witnessed such improvised school jumps which were certainly not very much appreciated by the riders. For instance, at the European championship in Copenhagen in 1963 there was the most horrible weather. The rain poured on the dressage arena and turned it into a regular mud bath. I was glad not to be taking part in the horse show as a rider and relieved to be a judge of the intermediate and free style tests. It was indeed no pleasure to ride but at least the conditions were the same for all competitors. In the Grand Prix, which I did not judge, it happened that the horse of the Swiss rider slipped in the mud and out of fear and anger produced a regular capriole instead of the halt he was supposed to perform on this particular spot. That the Swiss rider won this test in spite of the obvious disobedience of his horse is another of those inexplicable verdicts of dressage judges nowadays. Years before this incident, in 1933, a sergeant of the Austrian Federal Army who had taught his horse some sort of levade out of sheer vanity, had been judged more severely. When in a dressage test his horse produced this undemanded levade instead of a halt, he was immediately eliminated.

A dressage test is certainly no place for levades and caprioles, but at the Spanish Riding School they are taught and cultivated as the classical school jumps. Not every stallion possesses the power and the talent necessary for these difficult exercises, however. When riding master Polak died in 1942 he had numerous horses in training. Among them was Siglavy Brezowica, an eleven-year-old stallion who was a brilliant school horse in the performance and who had been chosen for training in courbettes. He was to be the first courbetteur at the Spanish Riding School in a great number of years. In this exercise the stallion rises on his hind legs and leaps forward with both. He is supposed to perform several jumps without touching the ground with his forelegs. Polak had succeeded in obtaining one single jump from Siglavy Brezowica and the beginning was promising. I took the horse under my special care, checked the work of his new rider very carefully, and continued the work in hand that Polak had begun. By and by it was possible to make the stallion increase the number of jumps on the hindquarters without the forelegs touching the ground, until he matured into the best courbetteur that the Spanish Riding School had had for many years and probably will ever have. Not only did he perform the exercise with much precision and regularity, jumping off with elasticity and landing on exactly the same spot, but also in the prime of his career he produced an incredible number of jumps, as many as ten consecutive ones. The inspector of riding and driving in the administration of the German Army, General Weingart, who often came to Vienna to inspect the Spanish Riding School—he called it a visit—once witnessed such a courbette and advised me strongly to have a film taken. There might be a time, he said, when nobody would believe that this was possible for a horse to perform. Unfortunately in those war times I was unable to obtain the necessary film.

From 1943 on, Siglavy Brezowica performed the courbette under the rider with the same perfection but with a smaller number of jumps. Although the weight of the rider is an enormous hindrance he was able to execute four to six jumps, which is an extraordinary performance. In 1944 there was suddenly a setback, the courbettes lost in accuracy and sometimes did not succeed at all. Work in hand did not help to straighten out the difficulty either and I decided to ride Siglavy Brezowica myself. I found out that the stallion was very stiff on his left side and tried to loosen him by riding voltes, large circles, and changes of the circle, which are very simple exercises. When he had relaxed and become more supple he accepted the bit steadily on both sides again and no longer braced himself against the action of the rein. His regular rider tried the courbette again and succeeded beautifully at the very first attempt. The relation between the basic training and the airs above the ground, as well as of the high school, cannot be demonstrated more emphatically. For a while I helped the rider by exercising the stallion in the loosening movements until he achieved them himself and no longer failed in the airs above the ground.

The wonderful stallion Siglavy Brezowica participated in the performances of the Spanish Riding School for eighteen years and for sixteen of them executed the courbette with and without a rider. He also spent frequent times at the stud farm fulfilling his responsibility to the Lipizzaner breed. Although he had years of hard work at the School, he reached the age of thirty-one.

In 1943 I began to train in work in hand two Lipizzaner stallions of Yugoslavian origin that had been given by Prince Paul of Yugoslavia as a present to von Ribbentrop, then foreign minister of Germany. Ribbentrop had them trained for a while in a riding school in Berlin and later gave them for training to the Spanish Riding School because ever since he and Italian foreign minister Count Ciano had visited it in April 1941 he had been a great admirer of this old institution. He had to pay for the upkeep of the horses and I was glad to have two more Lipizzaner stallions at the School. I was very anxious about the future, especially since the stud farm had been transferred to Czechoslovakia against my will six months before, and in this uncertain situation I seized every opportunity to increase the number of my stallions.

As school horses these two stallions were of no particular importance, but in work in hand I soon discovered a talent for caprioles in Favory Monteaura and began to work on it systematically. After a surprisingly short time he performed the caprioles energetically and perfectly but also with such tranquility that I decided to put him between the pillars. The pillars are two sturdy wooden poles firmly embedded in the center of the arena. The horse is fastened to them and between them may execute certain airs on the spot, such as the piaffe, levade, or capriole. The French riding master Pluvinel, who was active around 1600, had a great predilection for the training between the pillars, but at the Spanish Riding School it has been less and less practised in the last century because it demands great understanding and patience on the part of the rider and much confidence on the part of the horse. If these qualities are not present, work between the pillars may do much more harm than good.

So I was very pleased when at the first attempt Favory

Monteaura offered a capriole, parting from the piaffe I had wanted to make more energetic by the aid of the whip. It was towards the end of the last century that a capriole in the pillars had last been performed at the Spanish Riding School. It is depicted in the painting by Julius von Blaas that portrays the morning training. Favory Monteaura made such rapid progress in the work in hand that after two years he demonstrated his caprioles in public. He performed them in hand, between the pillars, and under the rider. It was very important that he be able to replace the four now aging caprioleurs who had been trained by Polak. After the war Favory Monteaura took part in all the foreign tours of the Spanish Riding School and was an essential member of the performances until July 1957. When, after twelve years of constant work, he had difficulty in performing the caprioles, he was used as a longe horse for the young students and served faithfully until a quick death at the age of twenty-one.

His half brother, Favory Brezia was of a much calmer temperament. He had a talent for levades, which at first I taught him also in work in hand. Pleased by his good progress I tried to make him execute the exercise in the pillars and succeeded very well. Gradually he became a substitute for Conversano Savona, head rider Zrust's wonderful levadeur on whom I had learned to perform the levade. Favory Brezia taught me to demand the levade slowly by way of a pesade. The pesade is an exercise that had been known in ancient Greece. The army commander would perform a pesade in front of his troops to demonstrate his abilities and his authority and it has been taken as a model for many equestrian statues and monuments. With well-bent hind legs the horse raises his forehand in such a way that his body forms an angle of forty-five degrees with the ground. Rearing of the horse should not be mistaken for a pesade because in rearing the hind legs are not bent at all and the horse's body is at a much wider angle to the ground. In the levade, an exercise developed only in the second half of the last century, and definitely a more difficult one than the pesade, the forelegs do not rise as high and the hind legs are more deeply bent at the hocks. I taught Favory Brezia the pesade first and then, eventually, the levade. When he had mastered the levade he was able to perform it in the pillars as well as under his rider and from 1947 on he took part in every performance. Until

1957 he was a member of all foreign tours, which meant as many as twenty-nine trips to Western Europe and the United States of America and Canada. One month after having performed for the last time in Vienna, on July 7, 1957, he died at the age of twenty years. He took leave of the Spanish Riding School at the zenith of his capabilities, his beautiful levades preserved for posterity in numerous photographs and movies.

While the Lipizzaners spent their summer holidays in the lovely park of Lainz I began to school another stallion for caprioles in hand, to the dismay of his regular rider who would have preferred some less spectacular but calmer movement. Pluto Presciana I had been trained with success as a school horse and already participated in the performances. He was always gay and ready for fun and had an obvious talent for caprioles. Taking pleasure in work is an essential ingredient for success, and so, I decided to take advantage of his gayety and teach him caprioles, in hand at first. He understood quickly and jumped very high, kicking with so much energy with both hind legs that it looked as if he were trying to tear himself apart. Thanks to his well-founded general training he made progress so quickly that two years later by appearing in a pas de deux and also by performing his caprioles in hand in the performance for General Patton, he helped to interest the victorious army commander in this kind of riding and make him willing to rescue the Lipizzaner stud farm.

Pluto Presciana I's role for the Lipizzaner breed was of even greater importance. The Pluto line of the Lipizzaners had become weak and Pluto Presciana I had to interrupt his work at the School on several occasions and do his duty at the stud farm. Finally he stayed there all the time. Thus his activity in the performances was limited to five years. During this period, though, he was kept very busy. He performed in the pas de deux, in the quadrille, and in the schools above the ground. When the Spanish Riding School went to America for the first time in 1950, he had to be taken out of the stud farm and he performed after a short period of training as if he had never left the School for a day. After the tour he returned to stud, produced very beautiful foals, and left the caprioles to the others—except now and then, when he thought it too tedious to be taken for walks by a groom and gave vent to his temperament with one of his special caprioles. Planting his front legs firmly on the ground, he kicked out playfully with his hind legs.

A somewhat marred career was reserved for Pluto Basowizza, who had been transferred to the German Cavalry School in Krampnitz near Potsdam as a nine-year-old and returned to the Spanish Riding School in 1942. In the meantime he had become twelve and his training was very incomplete and retarded by these changes of schools and riders. But he revealed a gift for courbettes that I decided to bring along in work in hand. The beginning was rather promising and in a surprisingly short time he achieved three to four leaps on his hind legs. Unfortunately, when he had reached this stage he was called to the stud farm, which had then been transferred to Hostau, Czechoslovakia, to help build up a strong Pluto line. When he returned to Vienna in the summer of 1944, the general situation had become very critical and insecure. There was no doubt about the end towards which the war was heading and the future was more than uncertain for everybody. It was my foremost thought to take the School out of Vienna before the final chaos broke in on us, an undertaking that seemed doomed from the beginning because of the adamant attitude of the responsible persons. After the unsuccessful attempt ın Hitler's life, all superior officers under whose command the Spanish Riding School was placed had been exchanged for fanatic Nazis. No wonder that under these circumstances I had no time or concentration to work with Pluto Basowizza, who for months was not more than exercised by his rider.

It was only after the successful flight and the fortunate rescue of the white stallions in the spring of 1945 that I was able to begin to work again with Pluto Basowizza—or to do so as much as the upkeep of the Riding School and the Lipizzaner stud farm allowed. Without any support from the Austrian government and with the help of the American military government alone I had to provide food, bedding, and grooming for over two hundred and thirty horses.

With Pluto Basowizza, who in the meantime had become fifteen years of age, I had to begin right from the start. He seemed to have forgotten everything he had ever learned. This was due to the fact that he never received a well-founded basic training. When I had just brought him along so that he was able to perform a few jumps in the courbette he was due at the stud farm again for a season. In the following year the work began all over again and at last he was able to perform up to five jumps in hand but with a rider on his back he was incapable of achieving the courbette. Not having learned it when he was young, Pluto Basowizza did not master this difficult exercise at his advanced age. This instance also gives an idea of the sacrifices demanded from the School in the interests of breeding, for very often talented stallions badly needed at the School have to be surrendered to the stud farm, as was the case with Pluto Basowizza. On the other hand, it is evidently in the interest of the Spanish Riding School to use for breeding stallions who possess talent as well as beautiful conformation. Unfortunately, Pluto Basowizza died at the age of twenty without having attained any heights of performance at the School. Neither was he very successful at the stud farm because none of his offspring rose above the average.

An unwritten tradition at the Spanish Riding School proclaims that there should be a bay stallion among the white sons of Lipizza. In the eighteenth and nineteenth centuries all sorts of colours were to be found among the Lipizzaner breed, even pie-balds and palominos, but as the years went on the white colour became dominant in breeding because greys were preferred at the imperial court of Vienna. Today we find white Lipizzaners almost exclusively. Although they are all born dark brown or dark grey, their coats turn silver-white between their third and tenth year. Only very occasionally one of the horses maintains his dark colour as a reminder of some long forgotten ancestor. Such a "black sheep" is, however, a pure-bred Lipizzaner and by no means the product of a *mésalliance,* as the wife of a French secretary of state assumed when she visited the stable with her husband after a performance in Vienna. A dark Lipizzaner's life is far more difficult than that of an ordinary one because he should stand out from his brothers not only in colour but also by some special ability. He cannot be used in a pas de deux or pas de trois or in the quadrille. He is expected to produce levades or caprioles. Siglavy Ancona was one of these bay Lipizzaners who had to learn some specialty. He had been trained by head rider Zrust for levades and he presented them in the performances under head rider Neumayer from 1941 on. When Neumayer enlisted in military service the bay continued to appear under several different riders. In November 1947 he apparently fell victim to a sort of mental disorder that might have been due to the scarcity of food, in particular of hay. I had ordered the walls of the boxes to be painted with carbolic acid (phenolum liquefactum) in order to prevent the horses from constantly chewing the wood. Unguarded for a moment, Siglavy Ancona precipitated himself out of his box onto the bucket full of carbolic acid that stood in the corridor and greedily drank the deadly liquid. Although he was treated immediately by the veterinarian, he died from poisoning. He was only sixteen years old. His behaviour remained an inexplicable enigma to all experts, for when tests were made with the other horses, they withdrew into the remotest corners of their boxes at the mere smell of the carbolic acid. They were not to be persuaded even to sniff at the bucket.

This unfortunate accident had broken the unwritten law, and for years there was no dark stallion to be seen in the performances. Not until 1950, almost twenty years after Siglavy Ancona's arrival, did another bay stallion come to the School at last. Four-year-old Neapolitano Ancona had no idea that he had a special mission waiting for him. First of all he concentrated on throwing his rider, in which exercise he became quite an expert. Maybe he wanted to show off in front of his white brothers. His gambolling gave me the idea of trying to teach him caprioles in hand, for we needed him desperately to fill the vacancy in the performance left by the death of the bay. This attempt ended in a complete disaster. Although under his rider he had been full of high spirits and fiery temperament, in work in hand it was hopeless to induce him to any expression of youthful gayety. When after this fiasco I observed his behaviour more closely, I realised that it was with sudden leaps to the side that he was causing trouble to his rider. Therefore, I tried pesades in hand with him and was luckier than with my first attempt. He rose very willingly on his hind legs and remained quietly in this position for a long time. Of course in the beginning he was straight in his body and in his hind legs. In his first attempts he looked much more as if he had reared. While as a rule the stallion is taught the exercises above the ground only when he has finished the complete training of a school horse, Neapolitano Ancona's work had to be pushed ahead somewhat quickly for the reason I have explained. Therefore he did not possess the necessary suppleness in the beginning. On the other hand, nature had endowed him with a wonderful gift of balance and in work in hand I succeeded by and by in turning his rearing into a pesade. When I pushed him ahead by the aid of the whip, his hind legs stepped better under the center of gravity of his body and were also made to bend in an increasing measure. The counter-effect of the leading rein limited the elevation of the front legs until his body remained at an angle of forty-five degrees to the ground. Neapolitano Ancona revealed so much intelligence and talent and understood so quickly that only a year later, in the spring of 1951, he made his debut in a performance as a five-year-old and appeared in the group "work in hand." He was capable of remaining remarkably long in the position of the levade and then put his front feet to the ground so daintily that it seemed as though the exercise had meant no strain to him at all.

When I tried to put a rider on his back he again performed a perfect levade, which I rewarded amply. There is a great difference between whether the stallion is asked to balance only his own weight on his hind legs or whether he has to carry a rider, too, who by his attitude may easily disturb the horse's balance. It took two more years to bring Neapolitano Ancona along so that he executed levades under the rider and when he appeared for the first time in the spring of 1953 he was by far the youngest Lipizzaner stallion ever to be shown in a performance. This should by no means suggest that the Lipizzaners may be presented in performances more quickly than other dressage horses. On the contrary, they mature much later than, for instance, Thoroughbreds. Neapolitano Ancona's career is an exception. This bay had an extraordinary constitution besides his obvious talent, and the circumstances required making use of it. This fact also had a negative effect, as was revealed in the course of his further training in dressage. When he was not of the same opinion as his rider he defended himself simply with an unexpected levade, which was not very pleasant for his rider. As Neapolitano Ancona was able to remain in this position for a very long time, his rider was completely helpless.

Neapolitano Ancona was a worthy member of the group of great four-legged acrobats, as we call those stallions who have mastered the airs above the ground. He had become such an expert that I took him on the tour to North America in 1964 although this was against my conviction. So far I had always avoided taking a bay stallion on a trip to foreign countries in order not to take away the illusion that the Lipizzaner is the very idea of a white horse.

In recent years one of the most brilliant caprioleurs at the Spanish Riding School was Neapolitano Santuzza. By appearing in the performances and having pictures taken of his tremendous leaps, his fame certainly spread farther into the world than that of most of the other stallions of the School. It seems worthwhile, therefore, to take a look at the career of this four-legged artist.

He was born in 1936 at the Lipizzaner stud farm in Piber in the green mountains of Styria and came to the school in Vienna together with nine young stallions of the same age in the autumn of 1940. Here he experienced the first disappointment of his life. While his brothers were admired by all riders for their beauty and their good paces and were flattered accordingly, nobody even paid any attention to Neapolitano Santuzza. On the contrary, suggestions were heard that he should not be kept at the School because he was obviously not worth any serious work. I am sure he felt like the ugly duckling. It was true that he was rather small and his head was just a trifle too big for his conformation. Nor did his eyes express the ardent temperament expected from a Lipizzaner. His paces were mediocre but his character was of an indescribable good-naturedness and docility.

I do not intend to boast of any personal intuition and maintain that I had immediately detected Neapolitano Santuzza's value and therefore kept him at the School. The truth is that the situation was such during the first years of my activity as the Director that no stallion was sold at all if he was sound. This was in the interest of the expansion of the School, which was planned when I took over. Besides, I admit, I felt sorry for the little chap who looked at everybody with such gentle eyes and of whose presence nobody took any notice. What had been mere pity at first slowly developed into a deep affection, which made me protect him. There was no question of my riding him because at that time I was not allowed to ride and besides he would have been too small for me. The others rode him with reluctance, as he was no horse with which to show off. Finally I assigned him to a rider of very modest ambitions who demanded very little from his horses and consequently would not do any harm to him. In this respect he led a quiet life but also progressed so slowly in his training that as a twelve-year-old he was still not advanced enough to appear in a performance. Again it was suggested we get rid of him and sell him to some private stable. But he had become so dear to my heart that I was reluctant to make any decision and wanted to give him one more chance. On several occasions I had noticed that he had jumped away when his rider attempted to teach him the piaffe in hand and in 1949 I decided to work him personally in hand. Taking advantage of his urge to jump away from his instructor I tried to teach him caprioles and was very pleased with his reaction to my aids. Although he was of a very calm disposition he possessed an extraordinary gift for this spectacular school jump. It was surprising to everybody who had followed his training to see how quickly he understood what I wanted, which was yet another proof of the importance of sympathy and mutual understanding for any successful cooperation. It was equally astonishing to all experts and non-experts to see how high he was able to project himself off the ground—he hovered at the height of my shoulder, which enabled him to kick out with his hind legs very effectively and forcefully. A year later, in 1950, Neapolitano Santuzza appeared in public for the first time in the programme "work in hand" in the performance at the Autumn Fair in Wels. The Spanish Riding School had lived in exile in this small town in Upper Austria in the years from 1949 to 1955, for it was not advisable to return to Vienna as long as the Russian troops occupied the city. Neapolitano Santuzza's debut was a great success and the beginning of a brilliant career. From 1951 on there was no performance in which he did not take part. He received the name "the flying horse" and pictures of his capriole in hand circulated throughout the world. Our relationship became closer all the time; he never let me down and it seemed in all those years as if nature had endowed him with everlasting youth. He never declined in his abilities and his performance remained unaltered in beauty and exactness.

To me he was attached with an almost pathetic loyalty. When in 1960 Shah Reza Pahlavi of Iran visited the stables after a gala performance given in his honour, Neapolitano Santuzza neighed in his friendly way when we approached his box. "This salute is not meant for me, it is for you, isn't it?" our esteemed guest presumed.

When in 1964 the Spanish Riding School undertook its second tour to the United States and Canada, the Lipizzaner stallions were to be transported in airplanes for the first time in the history of their ancient breed. For the first time in his career, too, the "flying horse" was left at home, for in spite of his everlasting youth I was afraid of the strain that the tour and the adventure of the flight would mean for Neapolitano Santuzza, who in the meantime had reached the age of twenty-eight. In the last performance in Vienna before our departure in March he aroused the enthusiasm of the public by his brilliant and unequalled caprioles, but when I returned from America in June, to my dismay I found an old man. Abruptly taken out of his regular training he had aged years within those two and a half months and was incapable of performing any more. It was with him just as it is with a man who is retired from intense activity and doomed to doing nothing.

Within a few months Neapolitano Santuzza declined more and more; he lost weight, became thin and worn, and had difficulties with his food. At last he was taken to the clinic of the veterinary university. In December the professor called me and said that the time of my friend was up and that he suggested putting him to sleep. I asked him to wait another day because I wanted to come and see him once more. My groom warned me because when he last saw him, Neapolitano Santuzza had not recognised him any more. Sad and depressed, I entered the stables of the clinic and saw my dear and loyal companion of over fourteen years as he stood in a corner of his box, thin and indifferent to his surroundings, his coat dull. I was prepared to have the same experience as my groom some days before. But when I called him softly he lifted his head, turned slowly around and came towards me, lifting his right foreleg as was his habit when he begged for sugar, although I had never taught him to do so. He took the sweets I presented to him on the palm of my hand, accepted my tender caresses, and turned slowly back to the wall as if he wanted to avoid prolonging the grief of saying good-bye.

Neapolitano Santuzza left the place of our mutual work two weeks before I had to retire from the Spanish Riding School to which we were both attached with every fibre of our being.

Of Horse and Man

On first acquaintance it may sometimes be possible to take the horse for a stupid animal because he is very good-natured and therefore tolerates far too many things. But a person who observes him at close range, studying him, as it were, as we do people to whom we wish to be closer, will never agree with this opinion. On the contrary, he will discover many a personality among these four-legged companions and be confronted with a vast diversity of characters. There are the serious ones, pupils eager to learn and forever intent on obeying unconditionally, on satisfying their master. Work with these animals is a pleasure and leads to quick success but needs much intelligence and tact because thoughtless treatment will discourage even the most willing creature and blunt his eagerness. Then there are horses who behave just like naughty little boys, always seeking an opportunity to spook and not taking work seriously. Others have only one aim, which is to make work as easy as possible for themselves. They know how to make life difficult for their riders either by definite laziness or, even worse, because they have found out in what situation the rider is helpless. Laziness may be cured by riding briskly forward. But if there are repeated difficulties the rider may easily be led to the conclusion that his horse is vicious. This need not be the case at all as we have seen, for there is a considerable distance from naughtiness to viciousness and the fault for both may be mainly sought in the rider.

Among horses there are tenderhearted creatures who are very sensitive also as well as those with a rather materialistic attitude towards life who do not pay too much attention to a caress but take a much greater interest in the titbits presented to them. Intelligence, too, is present in different degrees in different horses just as it is in other living creatures, a fact which cannot be overlooked by the rider. Intelligent horses will promise better and quicker success—just as intelligent children do—but they need to be treated with greater consideration for their individuality than less intelligent ones. With the Lipizzaner the intelligence quota is especially high, thanks to the principle observed in breeding. Only the stallion who has proved himself at the Spanish Riding School will return to the stud farm and pass on his talents and abilities to his descendants, continuing his bloodline in the ancient breed. In order to succeed at the School the stallions, besides good conformation, need great intelligence and good character, which in turn are reflected in exterior appearance.

When Field Marshall von Brauchitsch, an enthusiastic rider himself, visited the Spanish Riding School for the first time, I went with him through the stables and introduced him to the oldest inhabitant at that time. Lost in thought he contemplated the thirty-three-year-old Maestoso Borina for a while and then said to me: "Look at that head with the shining eyes. What a contrast to his emaciated body. Is it not the same as with a highly intellectual person whose eyes have preserved their liveliness, reflecting his brilliant mind, although his body declines in strength?" I have met with this phenomenon again and again in my life and have often remembered Field Marshall von Brauchitsch's words. Neapolitano Santuzza's head, too, had maintained his noble expression while his body had grown quite lean and frail. Pluto Theodorosta, on the other hand, had reached his very old age in full command of his mental and physical abilities. He had never looked like an old horse and preserved his beauty to his very last day.

Like a person, a horse may lose his memory when mental agility and receptiveness slacken. I even met with a definitely senile horse on one occasion. Not only did he eat his own droppings instead of his hay but also he no longer recognised his own master. All his life this horse had been particularly shy of everyone except his own rider, to whom he was deeply devoted, and his groom, whom he suffered to come near him. Whether he happened to be in the stable, in the arena, or in the pasture, as soon as his rider appeared he would come up to him and with the same steadiness of character he avoided any other person who tried to approach him. When he grew old, however, and was retired from active sport, he took to following anybody around without discrimination, not because his eyesight declined—he never missed a lump of sugar or a piece of bread that had been dropped—but obviously because he had lost the intellectual faculty to distinguish between the various individual humans.

Repeatedly I have mentioned the oldest stallion of the Spanish Riding School, Maestoso Borina, and I want to tell another story about him. As the senior of the Lipizzaners he had lived in the same box for many years and watched attentively all goings-on in the stables during the last years of his life. Although the door was not locked he never left his box in which he felt safe and at home. It was utterly incomprehensible to him when he was transferred to another part of the stables one day because he had to be separated from a number of horses who had fallen ill. He did not resign and keep quiet in his new box but went on fretting until he had succeeded in opening the door, although it had been closed with a latch, and returned to his old box. Who would have the heart to contradict the will of the deserving old veteran?

There was another Lipizzaner who did not appreciate being separated from his friends in spite of being promoted to a high position with all sorts of advantages. Some thirty years ago the Maharaja of Mysore bought a stallion named Neapolitano Africa, who had been trained to go on the long rein by head rider Polak. He took part in the solemn processions in India as a sacred horse draped in superb silks. As befitted his holiness, he lived in two beautifully furnished boxes, one for the day and the other for the night. He was offered the most exquisite food and all sorts of comforts, was treated with the utmost respect, and spoiled in every conceivable way. But he had been used to regular and hard work and luxury and holiness did not agree at all with our honest Lipizzaner. After a short while he departed from this far too extravagant earthly life.

When Walt Disney made the film *The Miracle of the White Stallions* in Vienna the Lipizzaners excelled once more as movie stars. They had been filmed repeatedly and were not disturbed by the huge cameras, the blinding spotlights, and the whole busy bustle of a team of film people. American producers, in particular, indulge in the habit of rehearsing each scene at least ten times and afterwards take about the same number of shots of film. This method procures an incredible amount of film material, which will be cut down to the final version. The stoical behaviour of the stallions turned out to be of a negative effect on several occasions. In one scene they were shown during an air raid as they were taken from the stables into the riding hall while the mortar crumbled from the walls and ceiling. Dust was blown into the air and firecrackers exploded to make the scene as realistic as possible and the stallions reacted accordingly by neighing, rearing, and trembling. But after the scene had been shot for the third time they understood that there was nothing terrible about all this noise and bustle. They shook the dust out of their ears and obviously took the whole thing for a new sort of game. It was the extras (those persons who constitute the crowds in films and are not real actors but mostly students) who acted most realistically of all. They had to run across the dimly lit courtyard leading the Lipizzaners while the firecrackers exploded on all sides—and they were scared to death of the powerful stallions.

During the real air raids the Lipizzaner stallions behaved with great courage. When Vienna was bombed it was usually during the morning hours, and all the riders were at work in the School. They ran across the street to the stables opposite the School at the first sound of the siren and lent a hand to the grooms to bring the stallions into the air raid shelter that was provided for them. Thus at the moment of noise and excitement brought about by an alarm, the stallions were surrounded by people who were familiar to them and took care of them. We have heard about the role that confidence plays in the relationship of horse and man. Willingly the stallions followed these men into the horse corridor situated alongside the riding arena. With walls that were almost two metres thick, it offered the greatest security. When the air raids increased in frequency and intensity, the stallions soon knew the routine. At the first howling of the sirens they would stand at the doors of their boxes and wait until somebody put their halters on. When the bombs fell all around the imperial palace and the Riding School, they remained absolutely sedate although they trembled with fear. When the earth rocked, they crouched low and slowly lifted their heads when the worst seemed to be over. There was never a panic caused by a stallion when the bombs fell on Vienna.

I have met many clever horses in my life and some were even cunning. Often I had heard older comrades tell stories about horses who simulated lameness, but I was not ready to believe such things until I had a strange experience myself in this respect with my Nero. As I've described, all his life he had trouble with his brittle hooves, which caused pains in his feet and finally led to lameness. On one occasion this lameness was of particularly long duration although the examination by the vet revealed no reason for it. When I repeatedly tried to trot Nero in hand in the courtyard of the stables he went as lame as ever, limping along pitifully. In despair I decided to make one more attempt although it seemed very cruel. I had the groom trot him up and down for a longer period and all of a sudden I saw that Nero was trotting along quite happily, absolutely level and putting all four feet equally firmly on the ground. I am not sure whether he tried to simulate because he knew that he would be immediately taken back into the stables or whether he remembered the pains so vividly that he did not dare to put his foot down even long after they were cured. In any case I am sure that there was an idea in his mind. In the interests of our horses, however, I want to stress that this experience must not be taken as a rule. If a horse goes lame and the cause cannot be detected, the rider should give him the benefit of the doubt and take him back into the stables rather than call him a pretender and decide upon more drastic measures to make him move. In all those years of work with horses I have had this experience only once.

This little incident should not cast any shadow on the reputation of my good Nero but, on the contrary, underline his intelligence. Besides, his character was as good as gold. One day when I rode along on a loose rein, my mind wandering, he unseated me by a sudden jump. Horrified by his own deed he stood immobilized on the spot of his misbehaviour and stared down with embarrassment at his rider in the dust as if he wanted to say: "I am sorry, I certainly did not mean to!" Nero also had extraordinarily good hearing, which he demonstrated one morning when I came into the dimly lit stables after a short absence. None of the grooms who worked in the stalls noticed me, but Nero, who was being groomed in the corridor, discovered me immediately, recognising the sound of my steps, and left his groom to come towards me. Of all present he was the first to notice me.

Observing closely the relationship of horses we will discover that they, too, may have sympathies or unfriendly feelings towards each other. Some will become such close friends that they grow restless if the partner has been taken away and will greet him with expressions of pleasure when he returns. My brave Neapolitano Africa was used to having his box next to that of Teja and especially on our trips to London and St. Gallen, Switzerland, the two horses were inseparable comrades. In the vast stables of White City in London, some hundred horses were housed in boxes and stalls but Neapolitano Africa did not pay the slightest attention even to the mares around him. While Teja was away performing or being trained he waited impatiently for him and grew quiet only when his friend was again safely in the neighbouring box.

It is not rare at all to find among horses this feeling that they belong together. The old head riders had told me that on the occasion of the trips to Germany that the Spanish Riding School had undertaken in 1925 the Lipizzaners had displayed great dignity and an obvious pride in their breed. In the midst of the other horses at the show they paid attention only to their brothers and did not miss an opportunity to watch them at work. Later I had occasion to obtain proof that these old masters had not told me any fantastic stories but that this was really true. I myself have seen that when the Lipizzaner stallions gave a display within a horse show they did not pay the slightest attention to any of the other horses around them or to the bustle of the show but stared intently in the direction where their comrades performed. It made me think of a theatre when some actors remain hidden in the wings to watch the stars of the group. It struck me especially on these tours of the Spanish Riding School that even stallions who had been to the stud farm for several terms never deigned to look at other horses although there were mares among them. Not even the different colour of the mares aroused any interest although on other occasions the white stallions had manifested a preference for horses of different colouring.

To what problems this predilection might lead was demonstrated by the stallion Siglavy Neapolitano—for some time it was not the name of the dam that was used in these double names but that of her sire. Siglavy Neapolitano was not at all inclined to favour the white Lipizzaner mares. He was simply not interested in them while he was strongly attracted by the brown Nonius mares that were used on the same farm for a half-breed strain. The director of the stud farm tried every conceivable method to put the stallion into a kind disposition because it was very important to produce foals of the Siglavy line, which was represented by only a few horses at that time. The white Lipizzaner mare was even dyed with calcium permanganicum, a method by which grey horses in the Army were made less visible from a distance during the First World War. But it did not help either, for the clever stallion was not to be taken in by a swindle and his aversion to the Lipizzaner mares manifested itself even more strongly. There was no use playing tricks on him. The director of the stud farm was in despair until he had yet another idea. He chose a young and lovely Nonius mare in season and had her walk up and down in front of the reluctant Lipizzaner stallion. Immediately he expressed the greatest interest and because she remained forever inaccessible his desire grew to such an extent that in the end he resigned and put up with the ersatz of his Lipizzaner bride who had originally been chosen for him. What a strange role for the poor Nonius mare to earn her oats as a "come-on"!

During the war I had to take a trip to Holland and visit the former Cavalry School of Amersfort. In a field I saw several thousand horses of a French Spahi brigade, all Berber stallions from North Africa and most of them white. They moved about in the large paddocks and pastures always in pairs. The weaker of the stallions walked in front while the stronger one remained in the rear ready to protect him. If the weaker horse was attacked his guardian precipitated himself from behind against the flank of the aggressor, diverting his attention from his victim and helping his friend to escape. The whole thing ended up in a tangle of fighting horses. And these Berber stallions had a tremendous capacity for fighting. A Berber stallion that had come to the Spanish Riding School for a short time to be tested once attacked the Lipizzaner Conversano Bonavista, whose rider had the greatest difficulty in protecting his horse. The Berber had not seen the other stallion before and hurled himself towards him although the Lipizzaner was much taller than he. He began to work at him with teeth and hooves until the other riders were able to approach at last and liberate a deadly pale head rider Lindenbauer from his more than uncomfortable situation.

Sultan was the name we had given to this little devil. He was small and dainty like a miniature Lipizzaner, reminding us of the fact that the ancestors of the Lipizzaners were Arab and Berber stallions bred to Andalusian mares in the fourteenth and fifteenth centuries. At that time the breed was named Spanish for only those horses received the name Lipizzaner that were born in Lipizza near Trieste, where the stud farm was founded in 1580. The Andalusian mares gave to the breed the size and powerful conformation while the Berber contributed intelligence and grace. The Berber stallions resembled the Lipizzaners to such a degree that riding master Polak, who had accompanied me to Amersfort, completely agreed with me when I pointed out the likeness of a Berber stallion to one of the horses in Vienna and both of us at the same moment pronounced the name of the Lipizzaner stallion of whom one of the Berbers reminded us.

This little Sultan gave proof of the great intelligence of the Berber breed although he had gone through an entirely different training than our Lipizzaners. Walk and canter were the main paces of the Berbers. They were not at all accustomed to the trot under the rider. Neither did our little Sultan have any knowledge of the aids with which every dressage horse is familiar and especially the Lipizzaners as the oldest representatives of the classical art of riding. He had no idea of the correct position of the head as he was used to having his head raised with both reins when he was supposed to canter and he remained in this pace until his head was taken down again. His teeth showed that he was approximately twelve years old. I had never thought it possible that a stallion of this age could change so quickly. After four weeks of work on the longe he was a different horse. Under the rider he remained in contact with the bit, broke into a trot or struck off into the canter without giving up the correct position of his head, and finally differed from the Lipizzaners only by his smaller size.

What a wonderful breed of horses these Berbers were was proved in the later course of the war when they were used as draught horses on the Russian front. These horses who had grown up under the searing sun of Africa weathered the cold and the unspeakable hardships of the unfortunate Russian war better than the descendants of most other European breeds.

It is impossible to speak about the proud Berber stallions without mentioning their unrestricted confidence in their riders. During the inspection in Amersfort this close relationship between horse and man was clearly demonstrated. There was very little food to be had and for each of the stallions there was not more than the scanty ration of one pound of oats while the meagre pastures which were burned by the sun were supposed to substitute for the hay which was simply not to be procured. The horses were hungry, hungry all day long, which may partly explain their constant readiness to fight. Feeding at noon, when they got their pound of oats, took place in a wild fight every day. Kicking and biting, every stallion tried to push his neighbour away from the crib in the center of the stables where the oats were spread. And yet these wildly kicking animals allowed themselves to be led calmly away from the feed by a man and to be inspected in the corridor or outside knowing that when they returned there would be not a single grain left in the crib. What a proof of confidence in man! More than that, it was real friendship with their riders and excellent testimony for the North African horsemen.

This chapter about friendship between horses and between horse and rider will close on an experience with my brave Nora. The poor mare had to submit to a long and very painful treatment after her accident in a hunt, which I mentioned earlier. She had stepped into a rabbit hole and sprained her fetlock very severely. She was fired and blistered, a treatment which may tempt the horse to stamp his foot and to tear away the poultice, especially during the very first days. Nora was very nervous and restless and was only to be calmed when the groom or myself came to her in the box and comforted her by whispering into her ears and caressing her. Certain of our sincere sympathy, she remained quiet but did not want us to go away. We alternated keeping her company and thus helped her over the first very painful days. We were like two good Samaritans who alternated in watching over our horse, the three of us growing together in an insoluble friendship.

Friendship to one person, however, may very easily provoke the jealousy of another and jealousy is not only ugly and unpleasant but may also be of severe consequence. Maestoso Alea could not stand it when I caressed Maestoso Mercurio or, even worse, gave him sugar. Since Maestoso Alea's box was situated opposite that of Maestoso Mercurio, he watched attentively everything that went on around his rival and when he felt neglected he began at once to knock against the door of this box. In the beginning he knocked softly in order to attract attention. But when success was not immediate he continued in a crescendo to pound on the iron plates of the door. Such behaviour might easily have led to all sorts of injuries or prolonged lameness. When we covered the inside of his door with upholstery he tore it down angrily for he wanted the noise to attract attention. In the end I had leather shoes made for him to wear during the day in his box. These "slippers" were a complete success because hearing no more noise when he pounded against the wall he soon realised that all his efforts were useless and gave up. Had he had his box right next to that of Maestoso Mercurio he would not have been content with knocking alone and would certainly have come to more serious fights. Jealousy is only the beginning of the path to hostility.

To what results animosity between two animals may lead I have had the opportunity to experience when I was at the Cavalry School in Schlosshof. It is certainly most uncomfortable to sit on a stallion who is attacked and even more so on one who attacks another. Schlosshof was a lovely castle of the seventeenth century near the Czechoslovakian border. It had been a property of Prince Eugene of Savoy, who defeated the Turks in 1683 and drove them out of Austria. Unfortunately it had been almost completely destroyed by the Russians after the Second World War. The variety of the landscape along the river March was excellent for cross-country rides. Once there were in my group two stallions of the Furioso line who were such ferocious enemies that it was impossible to ride them side by side. They had to be separated by at least the width of the road. At this respectful distance I rode along with a comrade one day and we became so deeply engrossed in conversation that neither of us noticed that both stallions slowly edged towards the middle of the road. The moment they came close to each other my stallion reared on his hind legs and precipitated himself upon his adversary. It was impossible to bring him to reason by any aids or by punishments. Neighing wildly he kicked me off, threw my friend out of the saddle with his forelegs and belaboured his enemy with teeth and hooves, tearing his saddle and bridle to pieces. The other stallion defended himself violently with all his might and it took quite a while until both my comrade and I were able to separate the two horses who had gone completely berserk. All cut up like a pair of brigands, with saddles and bridles in rags, and carefully keeping distance from each other, we reached the castle after a good walk on foot. While the stallions, deeply satisfied, concentrated on their oats, my friend and I had to weather the thunderstorm of our colonel, which broke over our contrite and aching heads.

Many years later I had a similar experience at the Spanish Riding School. Two stallions who had lived in peace with each other in adjoining stalls and had appeared to be the best friends had an altercation one night which the stable guard was barely able to straighten out. Next morning the loser bore visible traces of the nocturnal fight. The two enemies were stabled in new stalls at the greatest possible distance from each other in order to prevent another battle and to give them time to forget their hostilities. This solution seemed to be successful and several weeks passed without the slightest disturbance. But this was only the calm before the storm. One night the defeated stallion succeeded in getting loose. The young stallions are stabled in stalls instead of boxes for reasons of lack of space and it is unbelievable how skilful a horse may be if he wants to get out of his stall. He rushed to the other end of the stables and took thorough revenge upon his former friend, who had become a bitter enemy now. The other stallion was tied to the wall with a halter and a chain and was of course unable to defend himself successfully against the aggressor. Until the stable guard could rush to his help he was just as beaten up as his adversary had been several weeks ago. This animosity had become so deeply rooted that I had to house them in different parts of the stables in order to prevent them from repeating their nocturnal battles. Sometimes the stallions came to the School as sworn enemies from some bitter experience in the stud farm and had to be stabled as far from each other as the place permitted.

Thus we discover some rather human behaviour with our horses occasionally. But they lack the meanness of man. They are artless and declare war openly. They do not approach each other with a friendly face and the dagger hidden in the cloak. They do not conceal their hostility but announce their attack by their behaviour. With flattened ears the brood mares turned against my dachshund Lumpi, defending their foals because he was jealous when I caressed them and had begun to bark. The mares tried to encircle him and to hit him with their forelegs. However, as soon as I had picked him up and he stopped yelping, they approached very peacefully and took a close look at the little dog who knew that nothing would happen to him now that he was in my arms but who still eyed the mares with misgivings.

There may be a friendship even between different domestic animals. In the stables of the Wilhelms barracks there was a cat whom the horses allowed in their boxes and even let crawl on their backs, and they suffered all sorts of tricks that it played on them.

On numerous occasions I have been confronted with the intelligence of horses in the course of their training. They rewarded the patience with which I tried to understand their characters by giving their best, just as they manifested their unwillingness when I demanded too much or had been unjust or too fast in their training. These are the moments of truth when the rider has to pause and reconsider his line of conduct. Whenever there are disagreements it is best to seek the fault in oneself. It is entirely due to their intelligence and their excellent character that the Lipizzaner stallions with their great vitality and physical power submit so willingly to the demands of their riders and try to understand what is required from them. They are ready to acknowledge man as their friend as long as they are not disappointed, which may be seen from the behaviour of my Conversano Soja when he was four years old. Playing and fooling around with his neighbour he had torn his tongue so badly that a large piece hung away and had to be cut off. The vet did not fuss for a moment and nipped it off with a pair of special scissors. In spite of this certainly painful procedure, Conversano Soja remained full of confidence and allowed the vet in the white jacket to pat his head immediately afterwards. Another less intelligent horse would have become shy for a long time after such an experience and would never have behaved so sensibly.

My little dachshund Strolchi, however, did not seem to care much for the doctor in white. Apparently he had not forgotten any bad experience or he wanted to protect me, knowing that the surgeon would cause me pain when changing the bandages and treating my wounds. In any case he barked furiously at the doctor every time he came into my room at the hospital in which I lay with a bad infection on my hand. Since the little chap was only very exceptionally tolerated in the hospital and nobody was supposed to find out about him, his behaviour was not very diplomatic to say the least.

A special gift for adapting to all circumstances in life was demonstrated by the sixteen stallions of the Spanish Riding School when, after the triumphant tour to the United States and Canada in December 1950, they got into a heavy storm on the Atlantic Ocean that lasted for several days. The *American Importer* was a freighter of medium size. In a large square room under deck two rows of boxes were built in such a way that the horses were able to see each other across a narrow passage in the middle where luggage and food were piled. They were walked for exercise up and down this passage by their grooms. The boxes were large enough so that the stallions could lie down but of course not of the size of their boxes at home in Vienna in which they may turn and roll to their hearts' content. It was on purpose that these boxes on board the ship were of a smaller size, and they served that purpose well when the storm broke loose. At first the stallions were one after the other thrown off their feet but were not rolled about in the violent movements of the ship as much as they would have been in larger boxes. After a short while, however, the stallions had learned the trick. With their legs wide apart like any old salt they leaned against one of the walls of their boxes in order to stand more securely. Instinctively they developed a special technique to preserve balance in the rolling ship. When the box went up on the side where they could look out they made their necks long and stretched their heads out into the corridor in order to take the weight off their hindquarters, which stood much lower now. When the ship swung to the other side so that the hindquarters went up and head and neck became low they stiffened their forelegs under the increased weight and withdrew heads and necks as far as possible into the box. Coming down to this part of the ship the traveller was confronted with a strange sight. In the rhythm of the billowing sea the white necks stretched to the maximum into the corridor and disappeared again behind the wooden partitions of the boxes while a row of other white necks appeared from the boxes on the opposite side.

Except for one resistant man, the entire team of the Spanish Riding School, riders and grooms, lay seasick in their cabins. This last courageous one tried to take care of the stallions as best he could. But at the sight of the white bodies swinging back and forth, up and down, he, too, felt odd. Everything around him seemed in dizzy motion. He fled from the stuffy stables and groaned: "My God, I cannot bear to look at them, I am getting seasick, too!" This was the end of his resistance and the Lipizzaners remained the only members of the Spanish Riding School who weathered the storm safe and sound.

The second trip to America, in 1964, was at least as unusual. It did not take two weeks this time but barely twenty-four hours. It was a very daring enterprise. For the first time in their centuries-old history the Lipizzaners took off into the air. Every conceivable precaution had been taken. Twenty-one stallions were to be transported safely from Vienna to Baltimore in two KLM turbo-props with four engines each. The great question remained about how the four-legged artists would endure the whole procedure. Together with the professor of the veterinary clinic I decided not to administer any tranquilizers. According to this expert's opinion it would not have been advisable without first testing the stallions as to their individual reactions, which was not possible because the performances went on right to our departure. For the last three days before the flight the stallions were given less and less food. There was no more training and they were also exercised less every day. In the plane they stood in very narrow boxes, looking in the direction of the flight and standing close to each other. There were twelve stallions in one plane and the accompanying personnel. In the second plane there were nine horses plus the entire equipment, saddles, bridles, blankets, and uniforms and the private luggage of the riders. In spite of this well-planned organisation I felt not very much assured when on one dark evening of the last days of March 1964 on the airfield of Vienna the white Lipizzaners were led up into the plane one after the other over a very steep ramp that was planked in on both sides by high wooden boards. The calmest and most courageous stallions were taken up first and were supposed to give a good example to the others who waited for their turn to be shipped. The precise sequence was laid down beforehand so that the horses who were friends were side by side and the "chums" could see each other; they might even calm and comfort each other. Once in the plane it would be impossible to change places.

Contrary to all expectations, loading the stallions went on without the slightest incident. The wooden planks of the boxes were built around each horse and screwed together before the following horse entered the plane. The stallions who came into the plane later were greeted noisily by those already fastened into their boxes. They were all in good humour, greedily attacking the hay which had been withheld from them up to this moment. They had not had any food all day long, just water and now the hay was to play the same role as the chewing gum or the peppermint given to human passengers in order to compensate for the pressure or the cracking in our ears when the plane takes off and gains height. For the entire flight the stallions remained calm except for some nervousness during the start. At the takeoff as well as the landing each horse was held at the halter by the rider or groom who was familiar to him and was calmed successfully by caresses and kind words. When the plane landed in Amsterdam for refuelling, the Lipizzaners were a little restless but when it took off for the second start of their life they were completely at ease and remained calm during the landing in Baltimore as if they had been travelling by plane every day of their lives. The first words the captain said to me after the planes were safe and sound on American soil were: "What extraordinary horses! With these animals I would not mind flying around the whole world!"

Whoever had the opportunity to watch the stallions ten weeks later when they were loaded for the return flight at the airport in Montreal would not have believed his eyes. Patiently they walked on a large circle for hours and did not even look when jets started with ear-piercing noise at the rate of a plane every thirty seconds.

When they were loaded in turns they did not hesitate for a moment but climbed eagerly up the steep ramp as if they wanted to say: "At last, boarding time!"

From all these episodes and experiences within a space of time longer than half a century I learned to understand and appreciate the horse. I have come to value his qualities and to tolerate or to pass with indulgence over his weaknesses, which are so insignificant compared with his honesty and affection, his good will, loyalty, and undeniable share of intelligence. My horses not only taught me riding but they also made me understand many a wisdom of life besides.

There is a long line of horses in my life, beginning with the treasured rocking horse of the three-year-old and the good-natured Olga, to the jumpers who achieved my first successes in horse shows, on to Nora and Nero, with whom I won triumphs in international competitions. There was Forty Winks to whom an interested lady spectator pointed, saying: "Tell me, why do the horses look so gay and happy when you ride them—and so sour and miserable when we sit on them?" And there were the Lipizzaners, "the white steeds of Hispania," who helped me to express our gratitude to the American nation to which my country is so deeply indebted.

With all these horses who were also my teachers fate has lavished upon me an inestimable treasure of loyalty and friendship and as in the poem I loved when I was a boy I will be able to say on leaving this world: ". . . that I will have the honour of a devoted charger waiting for me when I come to join the eternal army. . . ."

CPSIA information can be obtained
at www.ICGtesting.com
Printed in the USA
JSHW012216070620
5967JS00001B/5

9 781570 760914